RINGTON,

VINCENT

ELLA

FFINGTON

ramatic Entertainment, call'd

EURYDICE

in Grotesque Characters.

L.'D

es of HARLEQUIN

llery 2 s. Upper Gallery 1 s.

nents of the MACHINERY w

the ENTERTAINMENT, it is hoped

g refused Admittance behind the Scen

EGGAR's OPERA

THE FIRST ACTRESSES

NELL GWYN TO SARAH SIDDONS

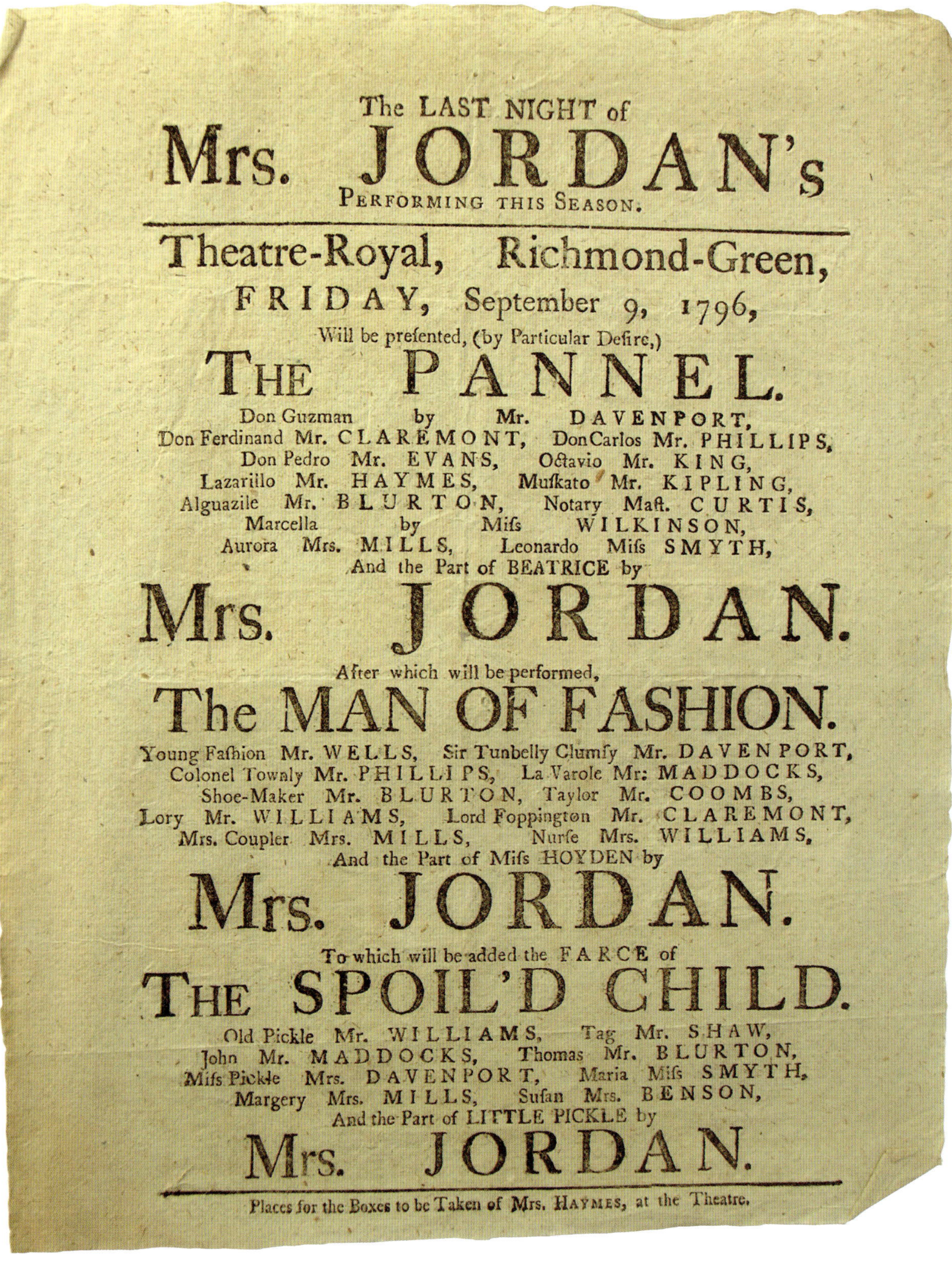

The LAST NIGHT of

Mrs. JORDAN's

PERFORMING THIS SEASON.

Theatre-Royal, Richmond-Green,

FRIDAY, September 9, 1796,

Will be presented, (by Particular Desire,)

THE PANNEL.

Don Guzman by Mr. DAVENPORT,
Don Ferdinand Mr. CLAREMONT, DonCarlos Mr. PHILLIPS,
Don Pedro Mr. EVANS, Octavio Mr. KING,
Lazarillo Mr. HAYMES, Muskato Mr. KIPLING,
Alguazile Mr. BLURTON, Notary Mast. CURTIS,
Marcella by Miss WILKINSON,
Aurora Mrs. MILLS, Leonardo Miss SMYTH,
And the Part of BEATRICE by

Mrs. JORDAN.

After which will be performed,

The MAN OF FASHION.

Young Fashion Mr. WELLS, Sir Tunbelly Clumsy Mr. DAVENPORT,
Colonel Townly Mr. PHILLIPS, La Varole Mr: MADDOCKS,
Shoe-Maker Mr. BLURTON, Taylor Mr. COOMBS,
Lory Mr. WILLIAMS, Lord Foppington Mr. CLAREMONT,
Mrs. Coupler Mrs. MILLS, Nurse Mrs. WILLIAMS,
And the Part of Miss HOYDEN by

Mrs. JORDAN.

To which will be added the FARCE of

THE SPOIL'D CHILD.

Old Pickle Mr. WILLIAMS, Tag Mr. SHAW,
John Mr. MADDOCKS, Thomas Mr. BLURTON,
Miss Pickle Mrs. DAVENPORT, Maria Miss SMYTH,
Margery Mrs. MILLS, Susan Mrs. BENSON,
And the Part of LITTLE PICKLE by

Mrs. JORDAN.

Places for the Boxes to be Taken of Mrs. HAYMES, at the Theatre.

THE FIRST ACTRESSES

NELL GWYN TO SARAH SIDDONS

Gill Perry
with Joseph Roach
and Shearer West

National Portrait Gallery, London

CONTENTS

FOREWORD

When women first appeared on the stage – released from the strictures of Cromwell's puritanical government – they were changing both artistic and social expectations. And what emerged were outstanding practitioners prepared to brave the barbed comments of gossips and columnists, knowing full well that the category of 'actress' might overlap with that of mistress to a gentleman, while talented stage dancers could be confused with women on the streets in Covent Garden, already emerging as London's dominant theatre zone and prime red-light district.

That actresses were often the subjects of portraits is no surprise, as their fame, and notoriety, made them the focus of acute public interest. The brilliance of the earliest performers, such as Nell Gwyn, was matched by those who followed, including Sarah Siddons. And they were portrayed in various media: in paintings, drawings and sculptures, and in prints for wider circulation. Then, these actresses redefined boundaries on stage, while off stage they became celebrated figures of the age. Now, they form the subjects for an outstanding exhibition.

I am very grateful both to Gill Perry, who first approached the Gallery with the idea of the exhibition and has taken the concept forward so creatively, undertaking further research and selecting the works, and to Lucy Peltz, the Gallery's Curator of Eighteenth-Century Portraits, with whom she has collaborated. Work on the exhibition has brought new images to public attention and will encourage a new understanding of the portrayal of women in this period. I am also grateful to Joseph Roach and Shearer West for sharing their extensive knowledge in the catalogue essays. I would like to thank Rosie Wilson, Exhibitions Manager, who has led the Gallery team in the organisation of the exhibition, and also Sarah Tinsley, Head of Exhibitions, Pim Baxter, Deputy Director and Director of Communications, Jacob Simon, Chief Curator, and other National Portrait Gallery staff including Nick Budden, Juliet Chippindale, Naomi Conway, Robert Davies, Andrea Easey, Denise Ellitson, Neil Evans, Ian Gardner, Amanda Gubbins, Richard Hallas, Celia Joicey, Sarah Moulden, Martin Oldham, Doris Pearce, Jude Simmons, Liz Smith, Christopher Tinker, Ulrike Wachsmann, Helen Whiteoak and Karl Lydon and his team.

In addition, a number of individuals are due thanks from Gill Perry, whose acknowledgements appear on page 140.

There are many generous lenders, private and public, who have made the exhibition possible, and I hugely appreciate their help and enthusiasm. I should particularly like to thank Brian Allen, Marcus Risdell and the members of the Garrick Club, and Gillian Dow, Robert Holden, Alex Kidson, Sheila O'Connell, Pam Schafler and Desmond Shawe-Taylor.

I should also like to give special thanks to those distinguished actresses who have been happy to act as ambassadors for the exhibition, helping us to draw attention to the history and significance of their work.

Sandy Nairne
Director,
National Portrait Gallery, London

INTRODUCTION

PAINTING ACTRESSES' LIVES

by Gill Perry

INTRODUCTION
PAINTING ACTRESSES' LIVES

ACTOR
1. He that acts or performs any thing.
2. He that personates a character; a stage-player.

ACTRESS
1. She that performs any thing.
2. A woman, that plays on the stage.
(Samuel Johnson, *A Dictionary of the English Language*, 1755)

A trawl through recent obituaries of female performers suggests that 'actor' is now used as often as 'actress' to describe the profession of famous women of stage and screen.[1] The term 'actor' can indicate an equality of gender and professional status. It can also help to deflect attention from the prurient sexual associations that have plagued perceptions of the actress since women first appeared on the legitimate public stage in England following the Restoration of Charles II in 1660. Before the Restoration the nation's theatre was famously transvestite, with men and boys playing female parts. This tradition was continued (in reverse) with the popularity of so-called 'breeches parts' for women players in late seventeenth- and eighteenth-century theatre, although such cross-dressed roles generated heated debate about the sexual availability and 'brazenness' of women players, who were widely seen to belong to the social sphere of the prostitute or courtesan (fig.1). The first actresses were thought to inhabit the same public spaces, and in the eighteenth century London's Covent Garden theatre district was as renowned for its sexual geography as its famous theatres. Local streets and landmarks were often defined by their associations with prostitution (figs 2, 3, 4). Although this book and the exhibition it accompanies examine these historical and cultural associations, especially in London's thriving theatre land, we also focus on women's remarkable and unprecedented entrance onto the stage, and the visual representation of their magnetic appeal, social status and acting abilities. Breeches and travesty roles for women were clearly designed to display the female body – especially the legs and thighs – and enthral the audience (both male and female). While breeches roles involved cross-dressing within the play (such as Viola in *Twelfth Night*), travesty parts involved women playing male roles throughout the play. Such roles were popular among actresses, enabling them to demonstrate their skills and show that they could play characters of either sex as well as, if not better than, men. Thus, after seeing *The Maiden Queen* at the King's House in 1667, Samuel Pepys noted in his diary on the acting abilities of Nell Gwyn: 'there is a comical part done by Nell, which is Florimell, that I never can hope to see the like done again, by man or woman.'[2]

The idea of the actress has a complicated visual and cultural history. Scholars are generally uncertain as to exactly when the term became common currency in the English language, but it was in popular usage by the beginning of the eighteenth century. Johnson's eighteenth-century definitions (quoted left), first published in his influential *Dictionary of the English Language* in 1755, appear deceptively similar. But his understanding of 'actor' includes the activities of acting and 'personating a character', which are missing in his interpretation of the 'actress', who merely 'plays on the stage'. Can we presume from this definition that the eighteenth-century woman performer was seen to be more likely to be playing herself, to be less actively involved in interpreting a role than her male counterpart? As this book shows, there are no easy answers to this question, and the identities and status of the earliest British actresses were the focus of endless moral and aesthetic debate. Her public 'femininity', often defined in terms of her sexuality, her social standing, physical appearance or ability to indulge

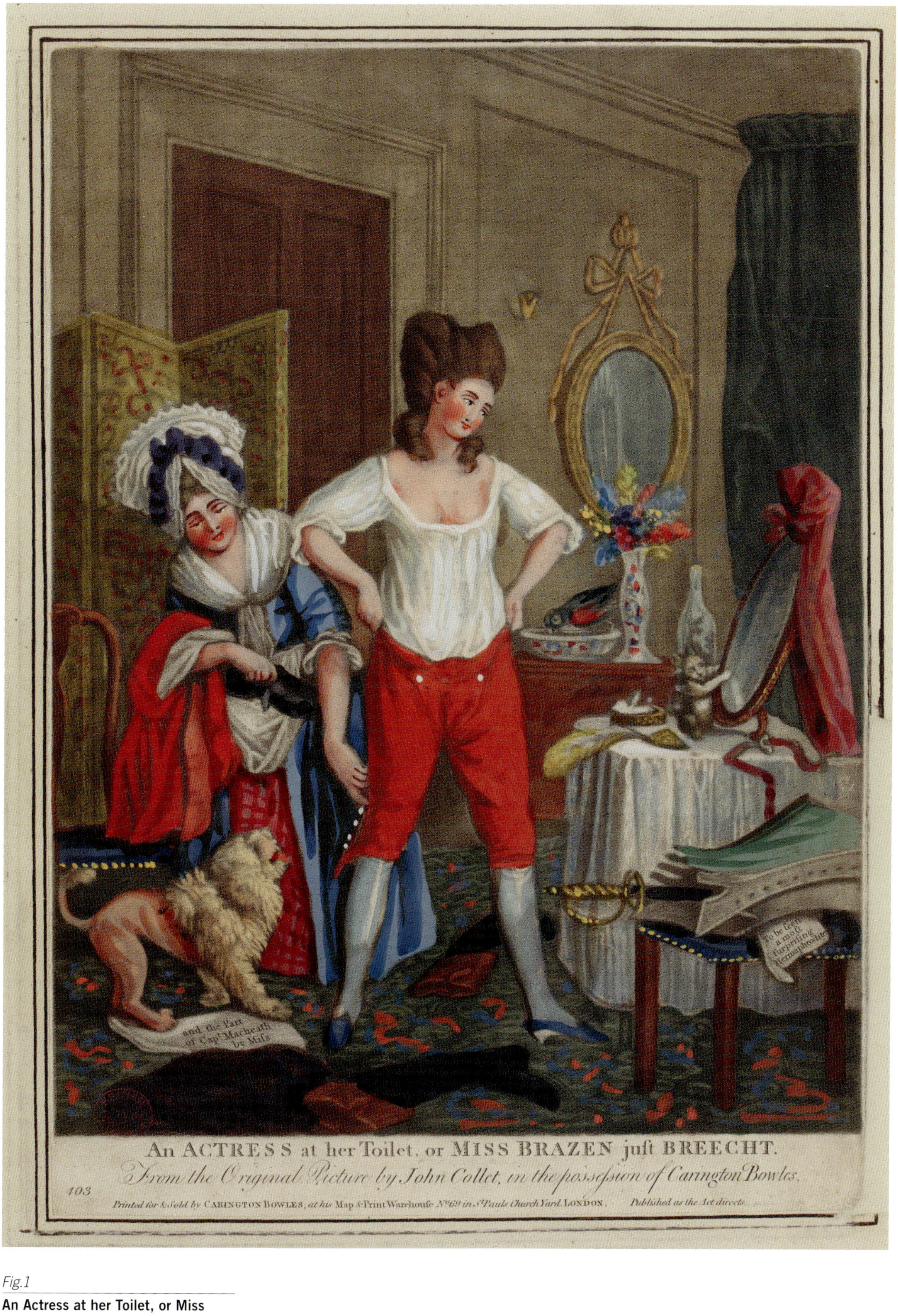

Fig.1

An Actress at her Toilet, or Miss Brazen just Breecht

Unknown artist, after John Collet, 1779

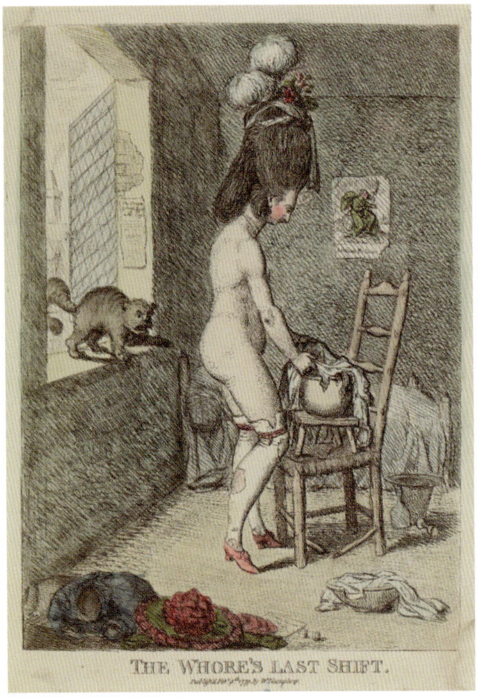

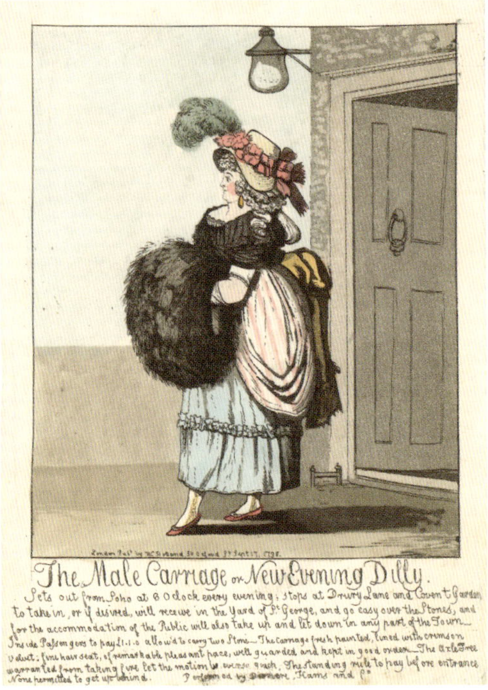

Fig.2 (above left)
The Whore's Last Shift
James Gillray, 1779

Fig.3 (above right)
The Male Carriage or New Evening Dilly
Richard Newton, 1798

Fig.4 (opposite page)
Harris's List of Covent-Garden Ladies or Man of Pleasure's Kalender for the Year 1793
John Harris, 1793

in masquerade, was as interesting to artists, critics and dramatists as her ability to interpret a specific role.

Yet women were becoming increasingly visible in public spaces of entertainment by the mid-eighteenth century. While they were excluded from political office, suffrage, property rights, universities and most coffee houses, they played a major part in an expanding cultural market for exhibitions, theatres, operas, dances and musical concerts. As seating capacities and conditions improved with renovations to the metropolitan patent theatres (notably Covent Garden and Drury Lane),[3] women – especially middle-class women – made up an expanding section of the theatre-going public.[4] And increasing numbers of women playwrights were active during the eighteenth century, contributing to a developing repertoire of plays and performances that sometimes featured spectacular female roles.[5] Many actresses, such as Susanna Centlivre, Charlotte Charke, Kitty Clive, Eliza Haywood, Elizabeth Inchbald, Susanna Rowson, Sarah Siddons and Mary Robinson, extended their creative ambitions and became playwrights and writers (sometimes after they had retired from the stage).

Moreover, women's appetite for pioneering roles and experimental styles often helped to give actresses a greater visibility and popularity than their male colleagues.[6] Women's tastes as important consumers *and* popular subjects of dramatic and painted portraits helped to define eighteenth-century cultural life. They had a powerful presence in the theatre and there is little doubt that the playhouse could not function without them.[7] As the literary scholar Felicity Nussbaum has observed: 'the theatre offered one of the few public places in which both sexes could freely congregate, where women's distinctive voices could be heard, and where women's critical opinions could be honed.'[8]

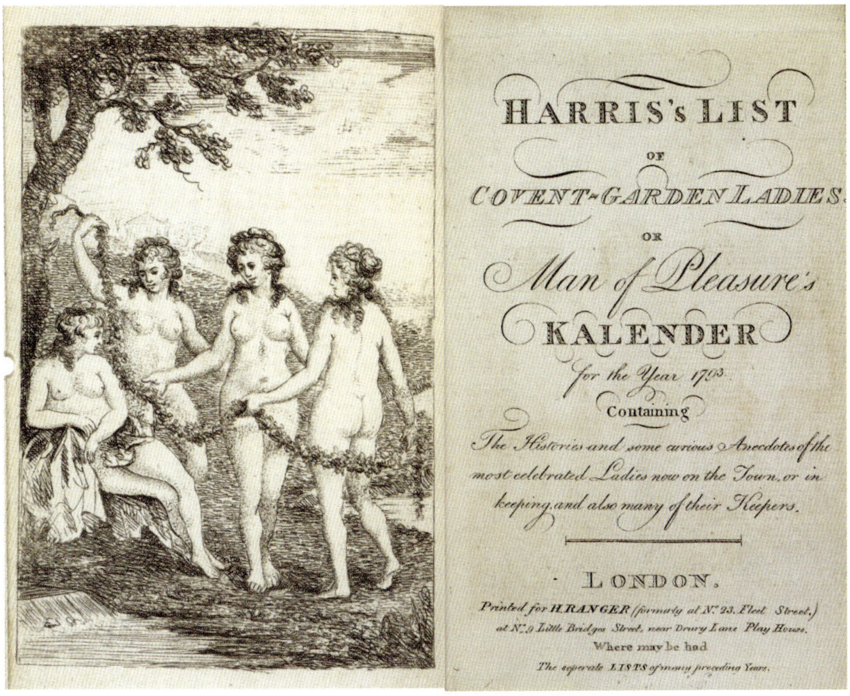

HARRIS's LIST
OF
COVENT-GARDEN LADIES.
OR
Man of Pleasure's
KALENDER
for the Year 1793.
Containing
The Histories and some curious Anecdotes of the most celebrated Ladies now on the Town, or in keeping, and also many of their Keepers.

LONDON.
Printed for H. RANGER (formerly at N.º 23, Fleet Street,) at N.º 9 Little Bridges Street, near Drury Lane Play House.
Where may be had
The separate LISTS of many preceding Years.

This book explores the remarkable visibility of the first women who performed on stage during the late seventeenth and eighteenth centuries. Popular exhibitions, an expanding print culture, increasing theatrical and art reviews and puffs (eulogistic accounts, sometimes commissioned or even written by the performer), and a growing biographical literature, contributed to the public appetite for images of and information about these female 'stars'. The eighteenth century saw a growth in a culture of consumerism and is now widely identified as marking the birth of modern celebrity culture.[9] As we show in this book, the growing circulation of printed images and personal histories could be seen to anticipate some aspects of a modern 'star system'. The sociologist Chris Rojek has argued that a key factor in the construction of celebrities is mass-media representation, a development that can be traced back to the dramatic growth of the periodical press and engraved reproductions in the eighteenth century.[10] With the decline in some aspects of organised religion (especially Catholicism) and court society in the late seventeenth and early eighteenth centuries, the idolatry usually conferred on kings and saints was progressively transferred to secular subjects, especially those who acted out popular roles on the public stage. We focus here on the ways in which visual and written portraits helped to shape the identities of our women protagonists as 'goddesses', tragic and comic heroines, models of feminine virtue, objects of erotic fantasy, shrewd self-publicists and even agents of transgression.

In acknowledgement of this visibility and the historical and metaphorical ambiguities that have surrounded uses of the term 'actress', we have reclaimed the feminine noun. As the theatre historians Maggie B. Stokes and John Gale have suggested, 'as the female performer came to represent the dangerous, destabilising intoxication of the theatre itself, might not the feminine noun be, in some respects, more appropriate than the masculine?'[11]

Portraits: The Actress as a Work of Art

In Act IV of Richard Brinsley Sheridan's successful play *The School for Scandal*, first performed, to full houses, in 1777 (fig.6), the extravagant Sir Charles Surface sells off his entire collection of family portraits to raise money and demonstrate his 'plain dealing' in business affairs. This mock auction serves as a comic interlude and is full of *double entendres*, but is also rich in literal and symbolic references to the value of portraiture and its role as social capital and evidence of 'character'. Surface defends his family collection as paintings that are not like 'the works of your modern Raphael, who gives you the strongest resemblance, yet contrives to make your own portrait independent of you'.[12] This may be a veiled reference to the 'grand manner' portraits of Sir Joshua Reynolds, who was using allegorical disguise, mannered poses and pseudo-classical costumes to dignify at least some of his aristocratic sitters, and one or two of his actress clients (fig.7). In contrast, Surface defends his portraits as being characterised by an 'inveterate likeness – all stiff and awkward as the originals', thus entering contentious contemporary debates about portraiture and the function of 'likenesses'. While most of the rapidly auctioned portraits are those of eminent male ancestors, one of the cheapest on offer is of his great-aunt Deborah, by Sir Godfrey Kneller, 'a very formidable likeness. There she is … a shepherdess feeding her flock. You shall have her for five pounds ten – the sheep are worth the money.'[13]

The issues raised by this portrait-gallery-within-a-play have many resonances for this book. The scene signals the important symbiotic relationship between the visual and dramatic arts during the period. Both disciplines were

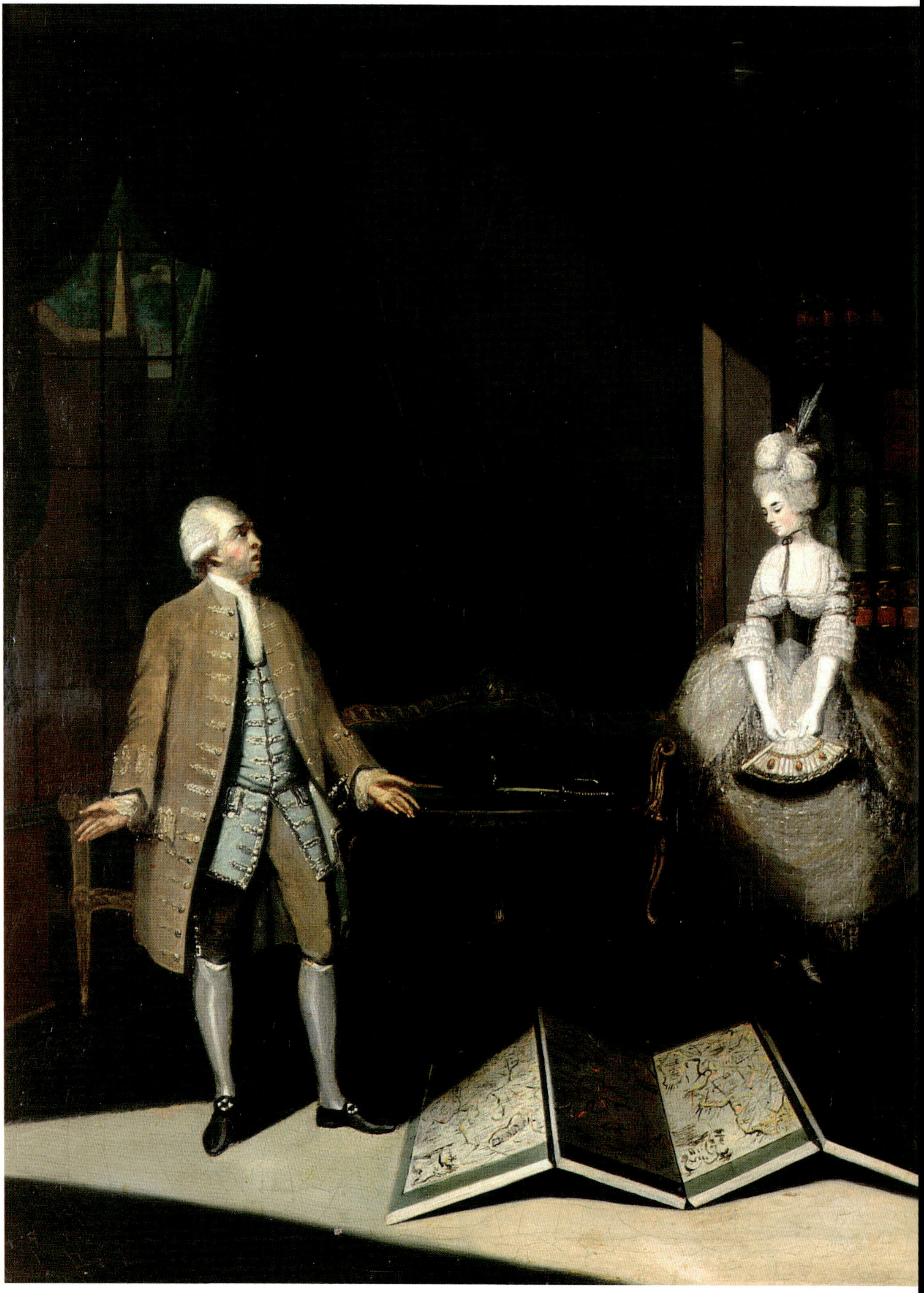

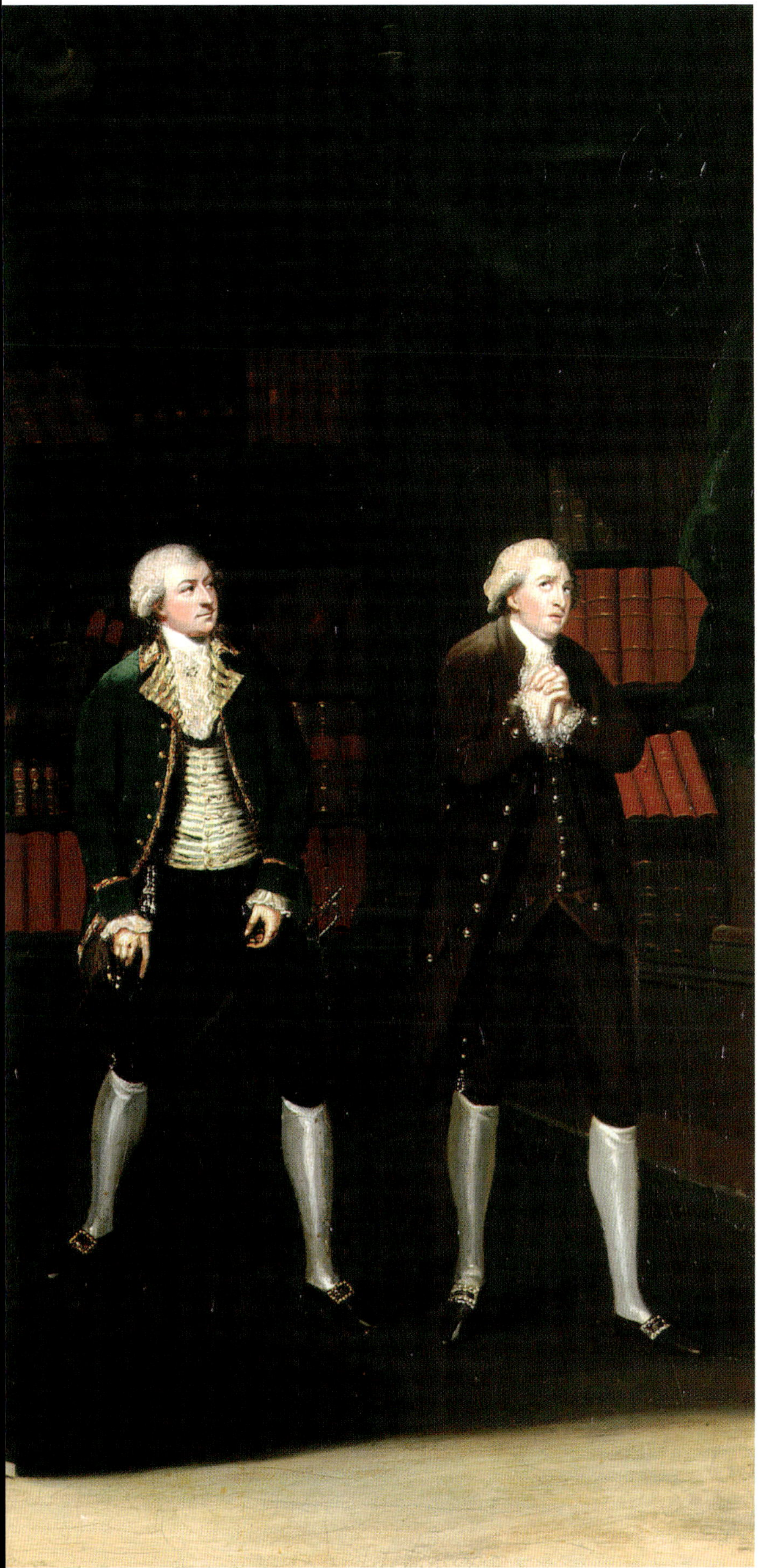

Fig.5

Frances Abington, Thomas King, John Palmer and William Smith in *The School for Scandal*
James Roberts, 1777

Fig.6 (right)

Playbill for Richard Brinsley Sheridan's *The School for Scandal*
9 May 1777

Fig.7 (opposite)

Frances Abington as Thalia
James Watson, after Sir Joshua Reynolds, 1769

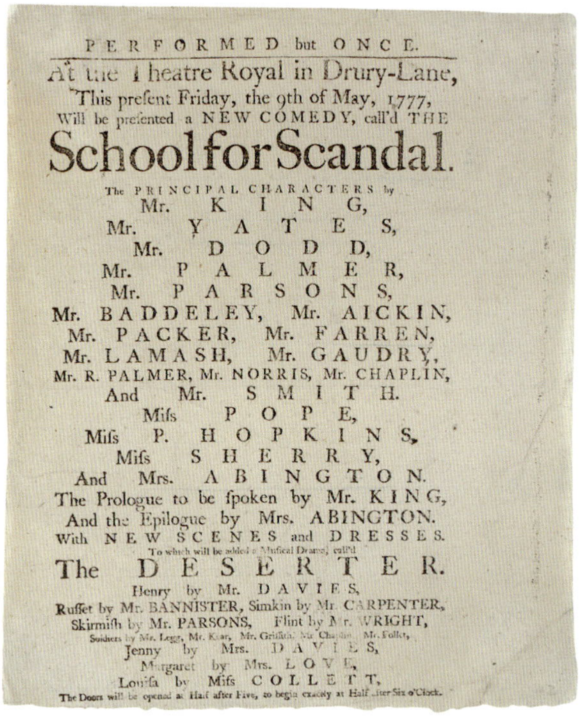

PERFORMED but ONCE.
At the Theatre Royal in Drury-Lane,
This prefent Friday, the 9th of May, 1777,
Will be prefented a NEW COMEDY, call'd THE
School for Scandal.
The PRINCIPAL CHARACTERS by
Mr. KING,
Mr. YATES,
Mr. DODD,
Mr. PALMER,
Mr. PARSONS,
Mr. BADDELEY, Mr. AICKIN,
Mr. PACKER, Mr. FARREN,
Mr. LAMASH, Mr. GAUDRY,
Mr. R. PALMER, Mr. NORRIS, Mr. CHAPLIN,
And Mr. SMITH.
Mifs POPE,
Mifs P. HOPKINS,
Mifs SHERRY,
And Mrs. ABINGTON.
The Prologue to be fpoken by Mr. KING,
And the Epilogue by Mrs. ABINGTON.
With NEW SCENES and DRESSES.
To which will be added a Mufical Drama, call'd
The DESERTER.
Henry by Mr. DAVIES,
Ruffet by Mr. BANNISTER, Simkin by Mr. CARPENTER,
Skirmifh by Mr. PARSONS, Flint by Mr. WRIGHT,
Soldiers by Mr. Legg, Mr. Kear, Mr. Griffith, Mr. Chaplin, Mr. Follet,
Jenny by Mrs. DAVIES,
Margaret by Mrs. LOVE,
Louifa by Mifs COLLETT,
The Doors will be opened at Half after Five, to begin exactly at Half after Six o'Clock.

preoccupied with the construction and representation of 'character'[14] and staged identities; and portraits of women attracted a voyeuristic form of criticism around the relative – and often lower – value attributed to their character, achievements and moral status (not to mention the lower value of their painted portraits). While Surface's great-aunt Deborah was given a metaphorical identity through disguise as a shepherdess, actress-portraits were often presented with reference to the roles and characters they played on stage. But actresses were also subject to the interventions and ambitions of those artists who represented them; visual images could both enhance and betray the identities enacted on stage or narrated through biography.

The growing demand for portraiture and the increase in the number of graphic images (including engravings and mezzotints, sometimes hand-coloured) in circulation during the mid- to late eighteenth century helped to construct and frame perceptions of the theatre. Popular satirical prints often disseminated subversive and mischievous identities for its celebrities, while high-art portraiture could, in theory at least, enhance claims for respectability and help to construct mythical identities. One of the most popular portrait subjects of his generation, the theatre manager and actor David Garrick (fig.12), recognised the publicity value and the social status to be accrued from this dynamic relationship between the dramatic and visual arts, a connection that was encouraged by the physical proximity of London's main theatres and exhibition spaces. The Royal Academy (established in 1768) was based at Somerset House on the Strand from 1780, only a short walk from the theatres of Drury Lane, Covent Garden and the King's Theatre on the Haymarket (fig.8). Portraits of well-known players were crowd-pullers at annual Royal Academy shows, where they were often hung cheek by jowl with those of upper-class and noble sitters, helping to enhance perceptions of the social and cultural status of dramatic art and its key players. Moreover, theatre and art critics shared an overlapping vocabulary, encouraging similar techniques of expression and 'performance'. Theatrical conventions and poses often informed portrait imagery, while the techniques of painting and sculpture, and the desire to produce a dramatic visual tableau, also influenced the presentation of theatrical spectacles.[15] From the age of Hogarth and Reynolds to the early nineteenth century, the theatre provided visual culture with some of its most pervasive and popular subjects.[16] Apart from prints, mass-produced objects such as porcelain figures, ceramic tiles, snuffboxes, fans and screens decorated with theatrical subjects also began to flood the market, contributing to the commodification of celebrity (figs 9, 10, 11).

Through both his painted and graphic work, William Hogarth was a key figure in the visual representation of the theatre and its female protagonists, and was one of the first artists to develop the popular subgenre of the so-called 'theatrical portrait', which depicted actors and actresses in role or on stage. His series of paintings of John Gay's popular *The Beggar's Opera* (see fig.52) have been identified as among the first to show a scene from an actual performance,[17] setting a model for the theatrical 'conversation piece' developed by artists such as Francis Hayman, Johan Joseph Zoffany, James Roberts and Samuel de Wilde (figs 12, 14, 15). In these theatrical portraits, famous scenes from popular plays were depicted, often with some artistic licence. As in Roberts's scene from Sheridan's play *The School for Scandal* (fig.5), which depicts the library scene, many of these works included celebrated women positioned centre-stage. The glamorous spectacle of a female star at the centre of a well-known dramatic moment could often help to promote the work and its visual appeal.

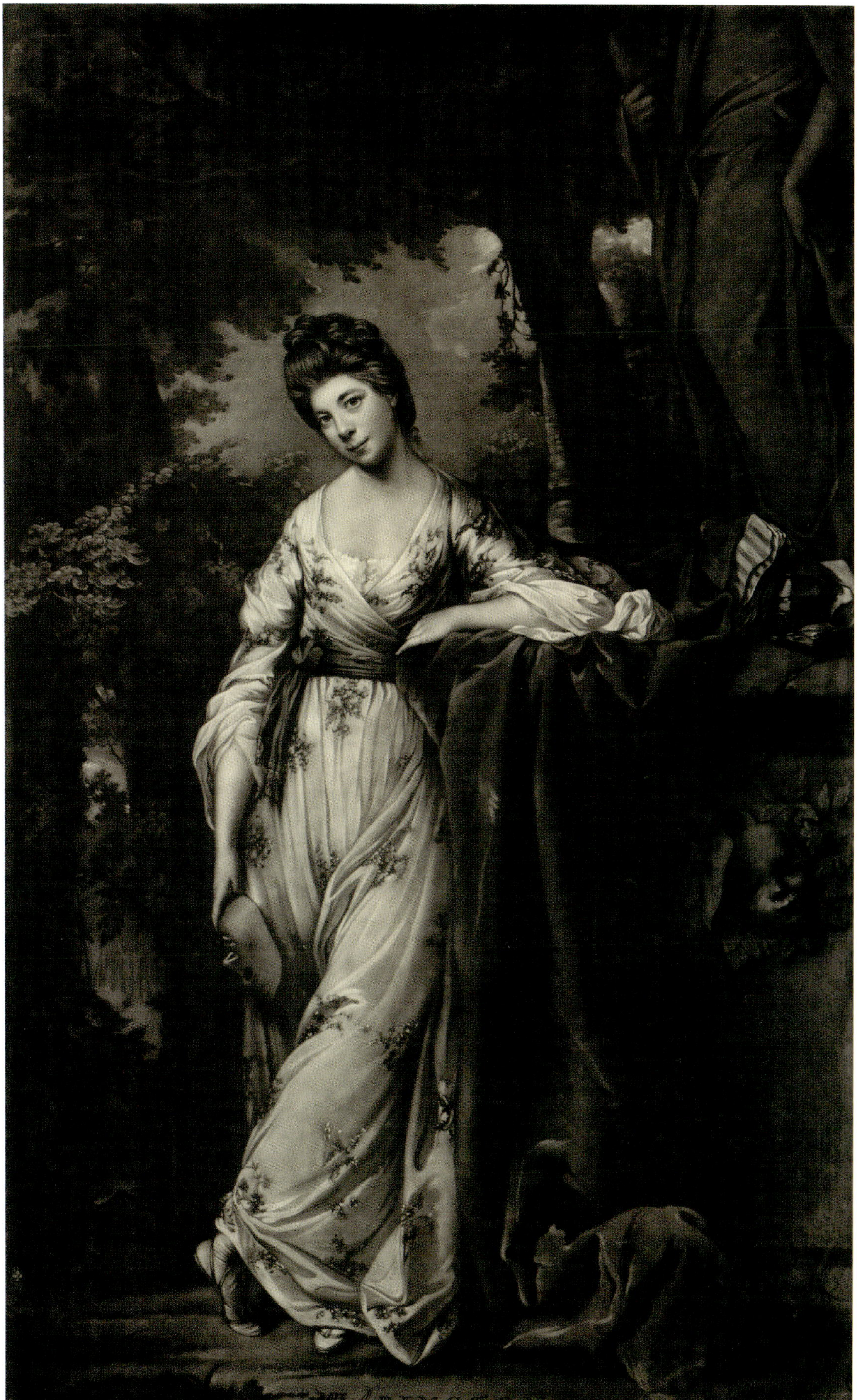
ABINGTON

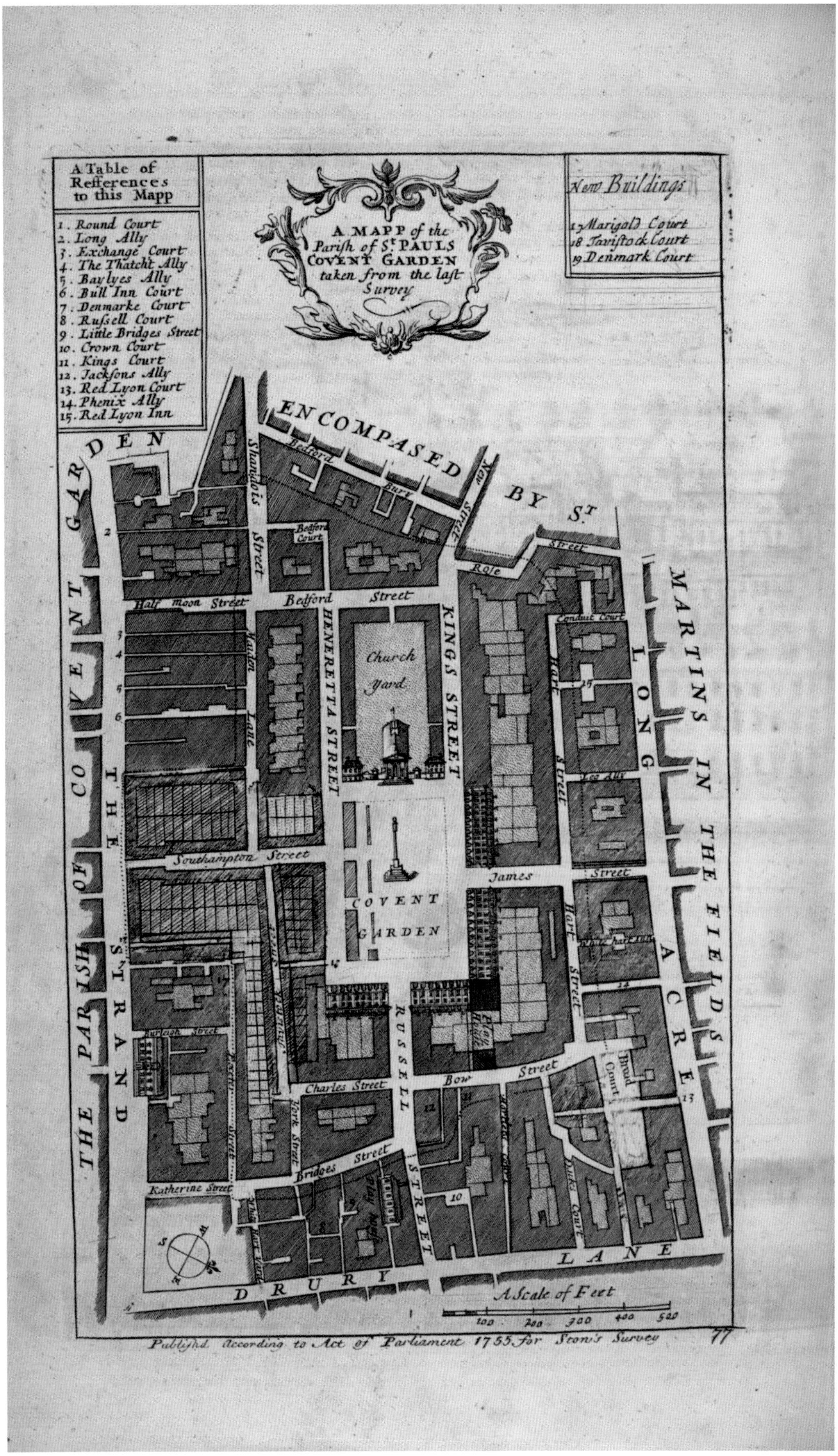
A Table of Refferences to this Mapp
1. Round Court
2. Long Ally
3. Exchange Court
4. The Thatcht Ally
5. Baylyes Ally
6. Bull Inn Court
7. Denmarke Court
8. Russell Court
9. Little Bridges Street
10. Crown Court
11. Kings Court
12. Jacksons Ally
13. Red Lyon Court
14. Phenix Ally
15. Red Lyon Inn
A MAPP of the Parish of St. PAULS COVENT GARDEN taken from the last Survey
New Buildings
17 Marigald Court
18 Tavistock Court
19 Denmark Court
THE PARISH OF COVENT GARDEN ENCOMPASED BY St. MARTINS IN THE FIELDS
THE STRAND
DRURY LANE
LONG ACRE
Bedford Street
Half moon Street
Southampton Street
HENERETTA STREET
KINGS STREET
Church Yard
COVENT GARDEN
James Street
Hart Street
Bow Street
RUSSELL STREET
Charles Street
Bridges Street
York Street
Katherine Street
Shandois Street
Maiden Lane
Rose Street
Broad Court
A Scale of Feet
100 200 300 400 500
Publishd according to Act of Parliament 1755 for Stow's Survey
77

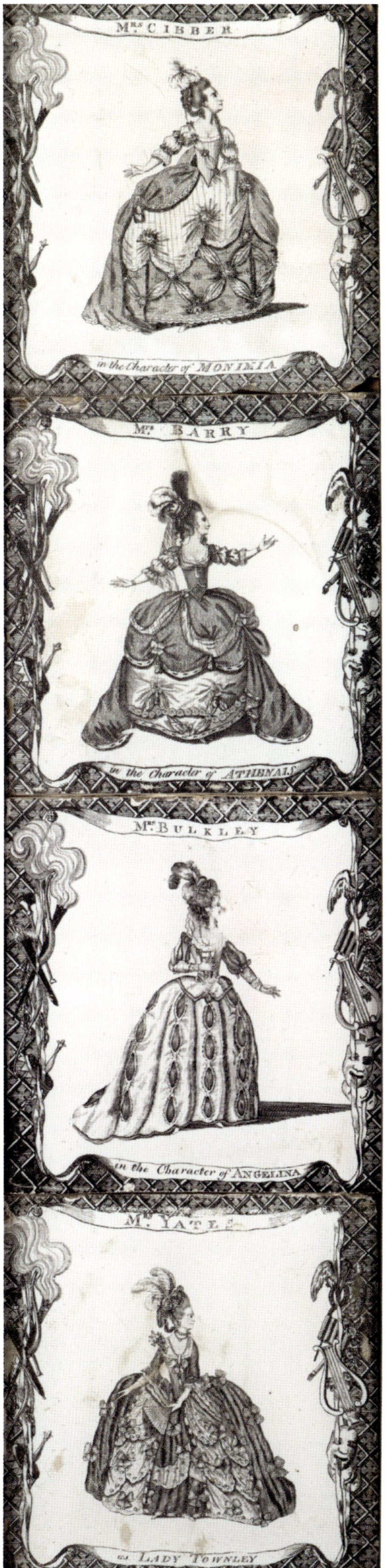

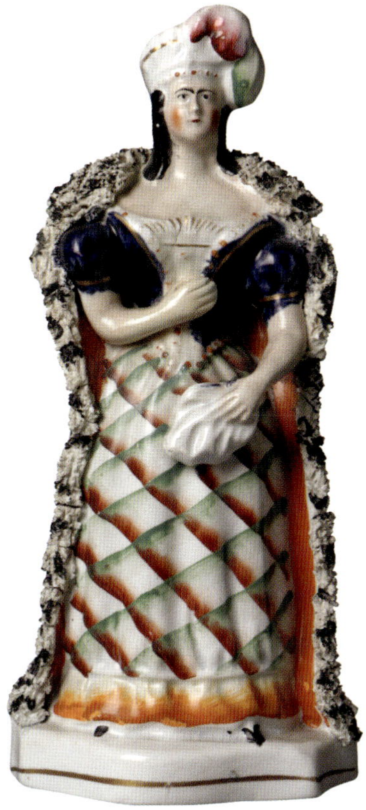

Fig.8 (opposite page)

A Map of the Parish of St Paul's, Covent Garden

from John Stow's Survey of London, 1755

Fig.9 (far left)

Tiles showing Mary Ann Yates, Mary Bulkley, Ann Barry, Susannah Cibber

Fig.10 (left)

Sarah Siddons as Lady Macbeth

*c.*1840

Fig.11 (below)

Catherine ('Kitty') Clive as Mrs Riot or The Fine Lady in *Lethe*

Charles Mosely, 1750

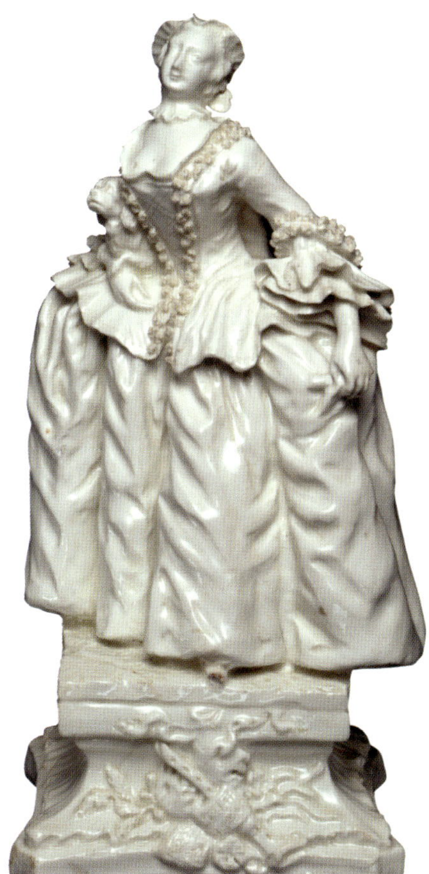

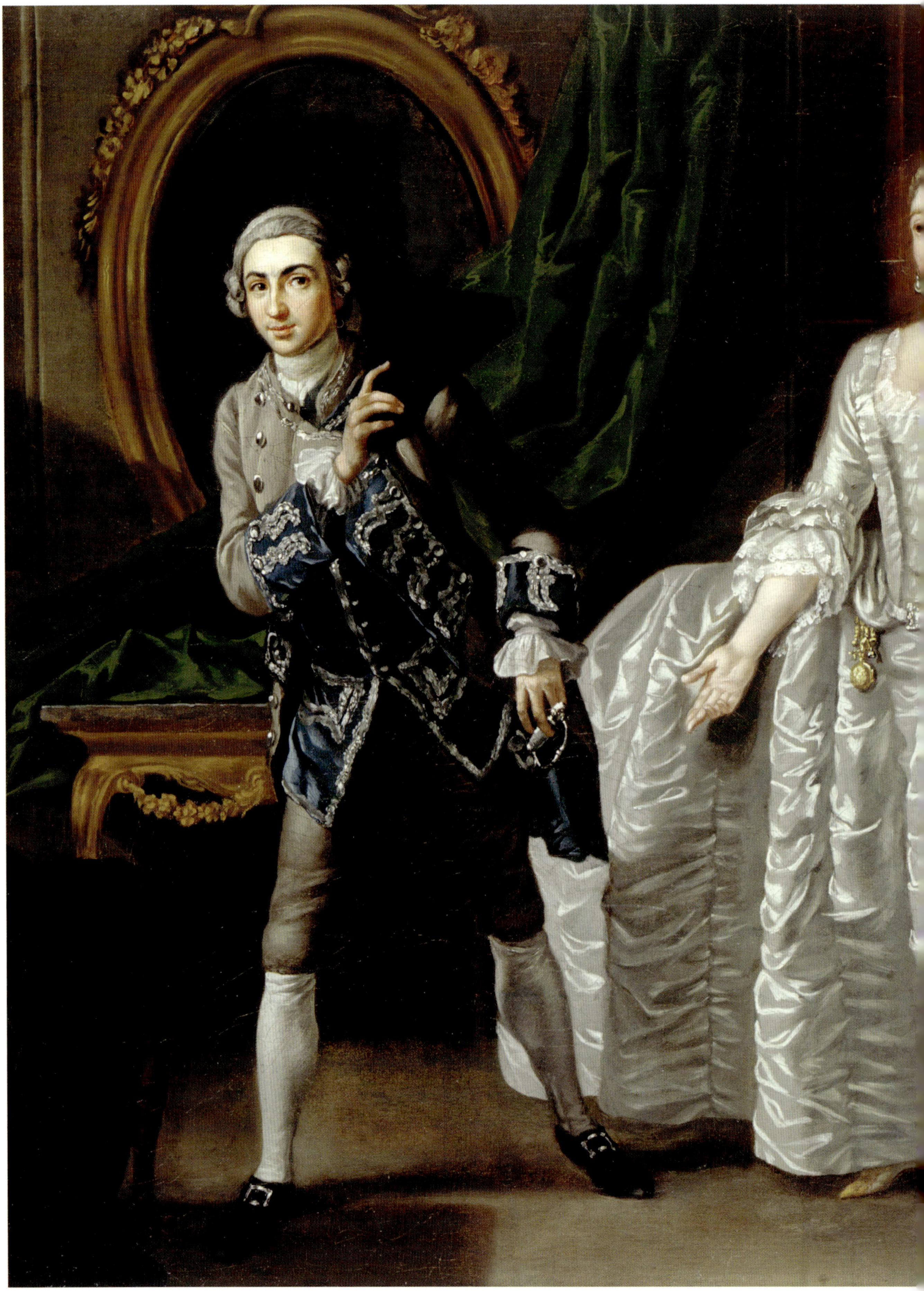

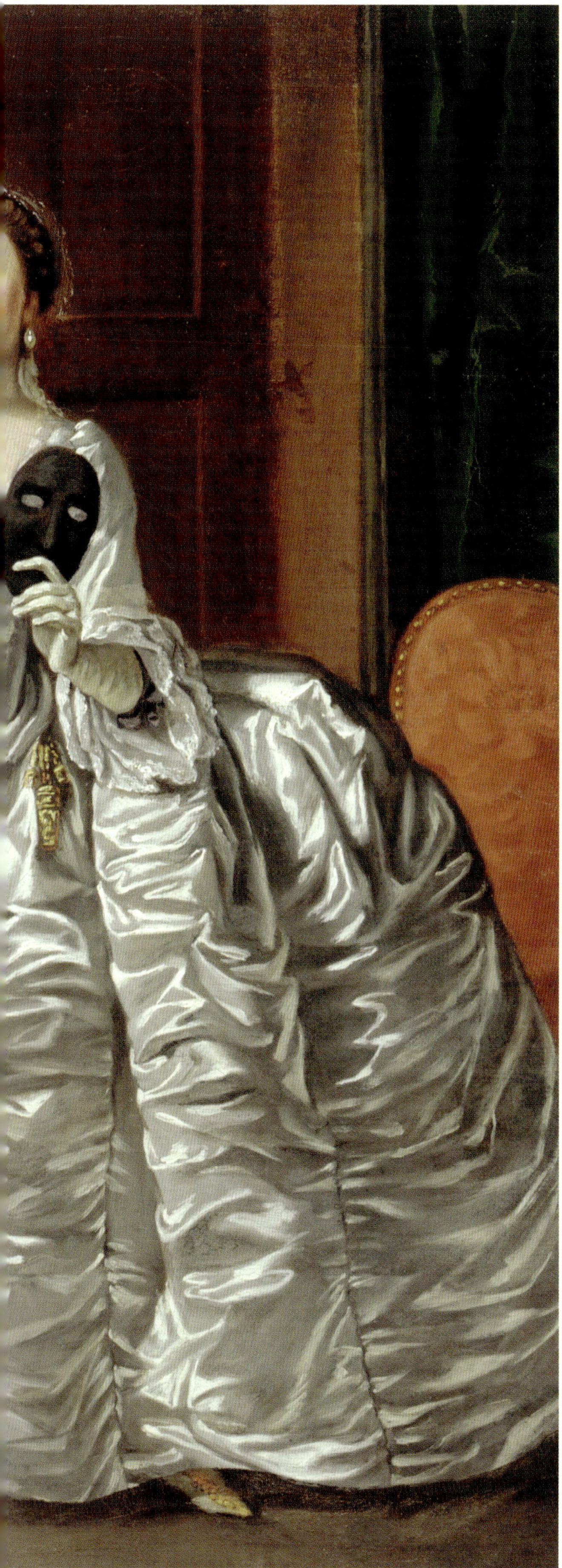

Fig.12

David Garrick as Ranger and Hannah Pritchard as Clarinda in *The Suspicious Husband*
Francis Hayman, 1752

And Hogarth was one of several eighteenth-century artists who deployed the image of the actress, especially through the medium of print, to make broader allegorical and satirical comments on eighteenth-century theatre and its political context. His engraving *Strolling Actresses Dressing in a Barn* of 1738 (fig.13) was printed the year after the notorious Licensing Act was passed by Parliament, making it illegal for companies to perform without royal patents, and empowering the Lord Chamberlain's office to censor all plays performed in licensed theatres. Initiated by Sir Robert Walpole's Whigs, the Act sought to eradicate the activities of strolling players and all unlicensed theatres, many of which were feared to be disseminating degenerate material and scurrilous attacks on the monarchy and Parliament. Set in a barn that appears as a makeshift women's dressing room, Hogarth's satirical image shows an almost exclusively female cast, preparing for the final performance by one of the actresses. Women strolling players were often viewed suspiciously and presumed to be prostitutes or what the cultural historian Kristina Straub has called 'sexual suspects'.[18] Mock heroic postures and pretentious role-playing dominate this grouping of semi-clothed players, depicted in the act of dressing up. Such posturing reinforces eighteenth-century perceptions of women as well suited to acts of masquerade and feminine deception, and echoes anxieties about women performing in the public sphere. It symbolises the theatre as a claustrophobic feminine space, replete with deception, masquerade and both visual and sexual intrigue. Yet it also marks the beginning of a period in which female performers could seek professional identities within major licensed theatres, albeit subject to forms of censorship.

Portraiture played an important role in establishing and constructing those identities, especially when displayed

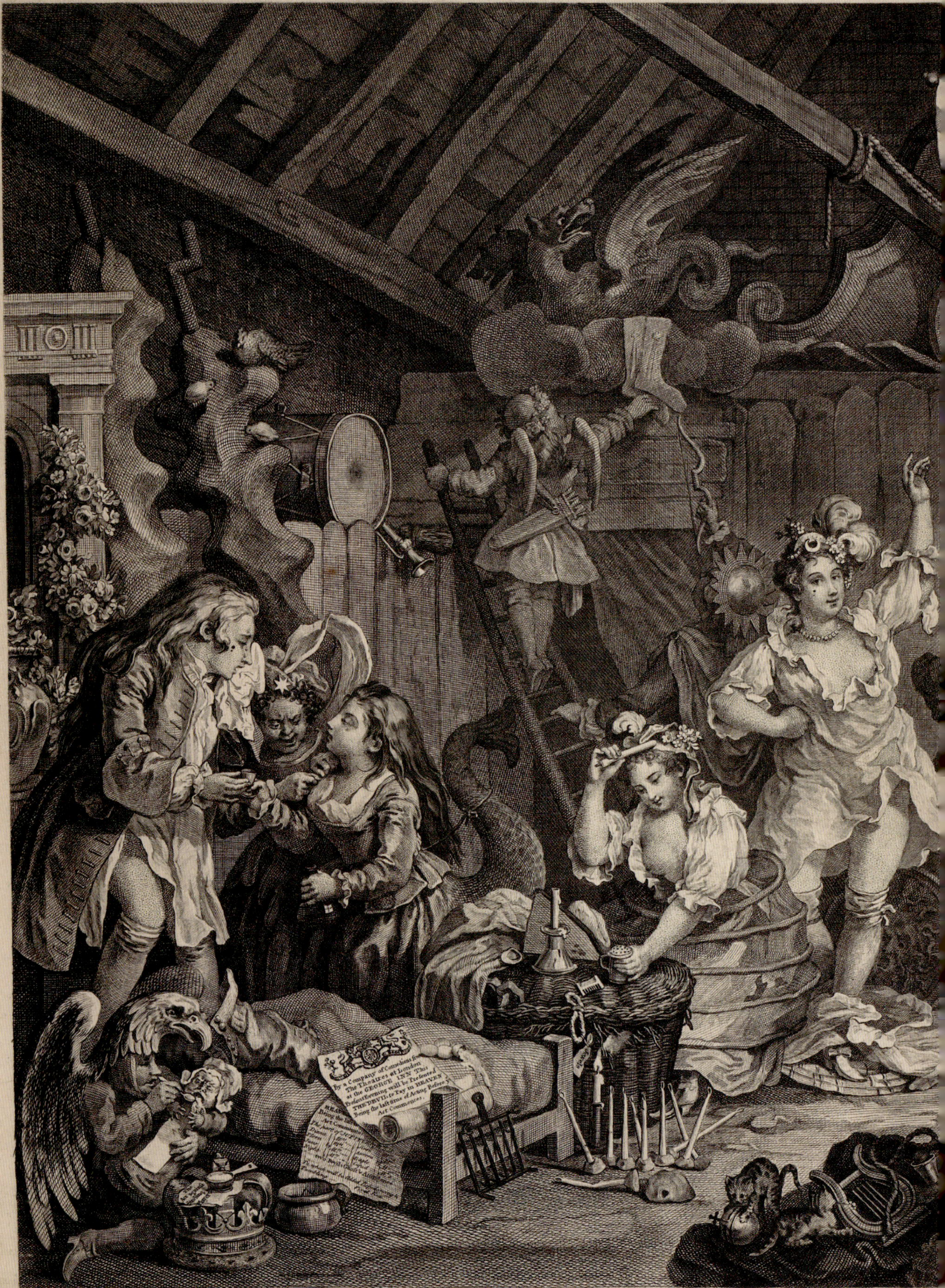

Invented, Painted, Engraved, & Publish'd, by Wm. Hogarth, March the 25, 1738. According to Act of Parliament.

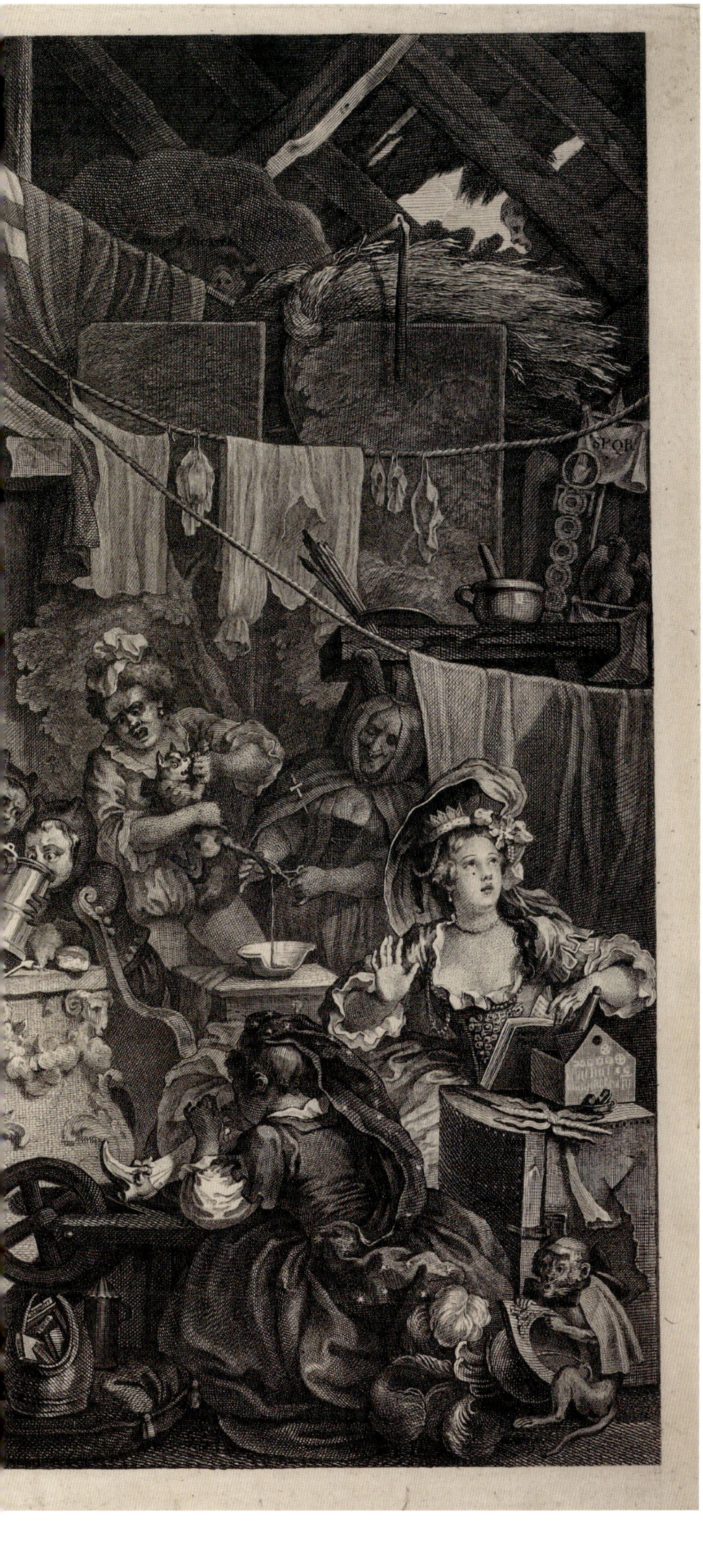

Fig.13

Strolling Actresses Dressing in a Barn

William Hogarth, 1738

Fig.14
Frances Abington as the Widow Bellmour in *The Way to Keep Him*
Johan Joseph Zoffany, 1768

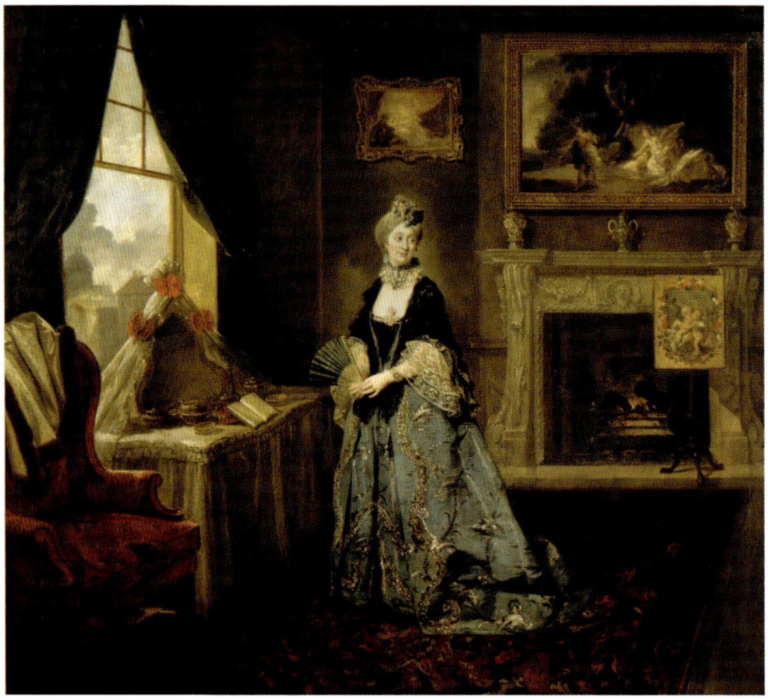

in public exhibitions or copied and disseminated through popular prints (fig.16). Portraits of well-known figures contributed to the popularity of annual Royal Academy exhibitions and encouraged identification and emulation.[19] Recognition and 'star-spotting' were key aspects of the viewing of these shows, as only members of the royal family were usually named in the catalogue until the late eighteenth century. Others were listed anonymously with the title *Portrait of a Lady*. Theatrical portraits could be identified through recognition of roles and performances. This encouraged the competitive display of knowledge of both art and theatre, anticipating some of the networking exchanges at the heart of modern celebrity culture. Marcia Pointon has shown that, foreshadowing the representational strategies of today's celebrity gossip magazines, 'the portrait painter of the late eighteenth century, in the words of writer and critic George Cumberland, "having discovered that the highest coloured pictures are those which attract publick notice most ... alters his style, or at least paints in that manner for the Exhibition." According to Cumberland, this manner involved emphasising rosy cheeks, bright red lips and dark eyebrows.'[20]

Actress-portraits were prominent among those seductive 'highly coloured pictures' in which the sitter was often in full make-up, seemingly poised to entice the viewer. As women performers were often defined by their role-playing, the themes of fashionable masquerade and beguiling, flirtatious femininity are frequently raised in reviews of their portraits. For example, Reynolds's portrait, *Mary Robinson – Perdita* of 1782 (fig.17), was widely reviewed in terms of its visual effects and the striking costume of black plumed riding hat, choker and dark bodice, itself reminiscent of Rubens's famous portrait known as the *Chapeau de Paille* (now in the National Gallery, London), which was known to the artist. Reynolds had, in a sense, depicted his subject 'in character', albeit an identity dignified by art history. But one reviewer of this work made a gendered comparison between portraits of '*celebrated* men' and those of '*celebrated* women', suggesting that because painters deal in appearances, they can produce adequate representations of famous women, but since men are renowned for their characters and achievements, they require the depth of written texts.[21] During her career as an actress Robinson was famous for her appearances in flamboyant costumes both on and off stage. Even her appearances in central London, which enthralled the gossip columnists, were perceived by contemporaries as forms of spectacular theatrical display involving multiple roles. According to the diarist Laetitia Hawkins, she was often seen in 'her chariot' in St James's Street and Pall Mall, where:

> Today she was a *paysanne*, with her straw hat tied at the back of her head ... Yesterday she perhaps had been dressed *belle* of Hyde Park, trimmed, powdered, patched, painted to the utmost powder of rouge and white lead; tomorrow she would be the cravatted Amazon of the riding house.[22]

Thus the actress's public identity was often confused with her costumed performances on stage, and the painted portrait was similarly conflated with the 'real' person. The struggle to define the actress's identity and sexual status runs throughout the writings on art and theatre of the period, and is enmeshed in the visual language of portraiture. And her notorious use of make-up (including the powder rouge and white lead apparently used by Robinson) is often seen to be at the heart of this shared strategy of the visual and dramatic arts – to dissemble and attract the viewer's attention. Such theatrical concerns could also be opposed to contemporary ideas of 'natural' femininity, sometimes

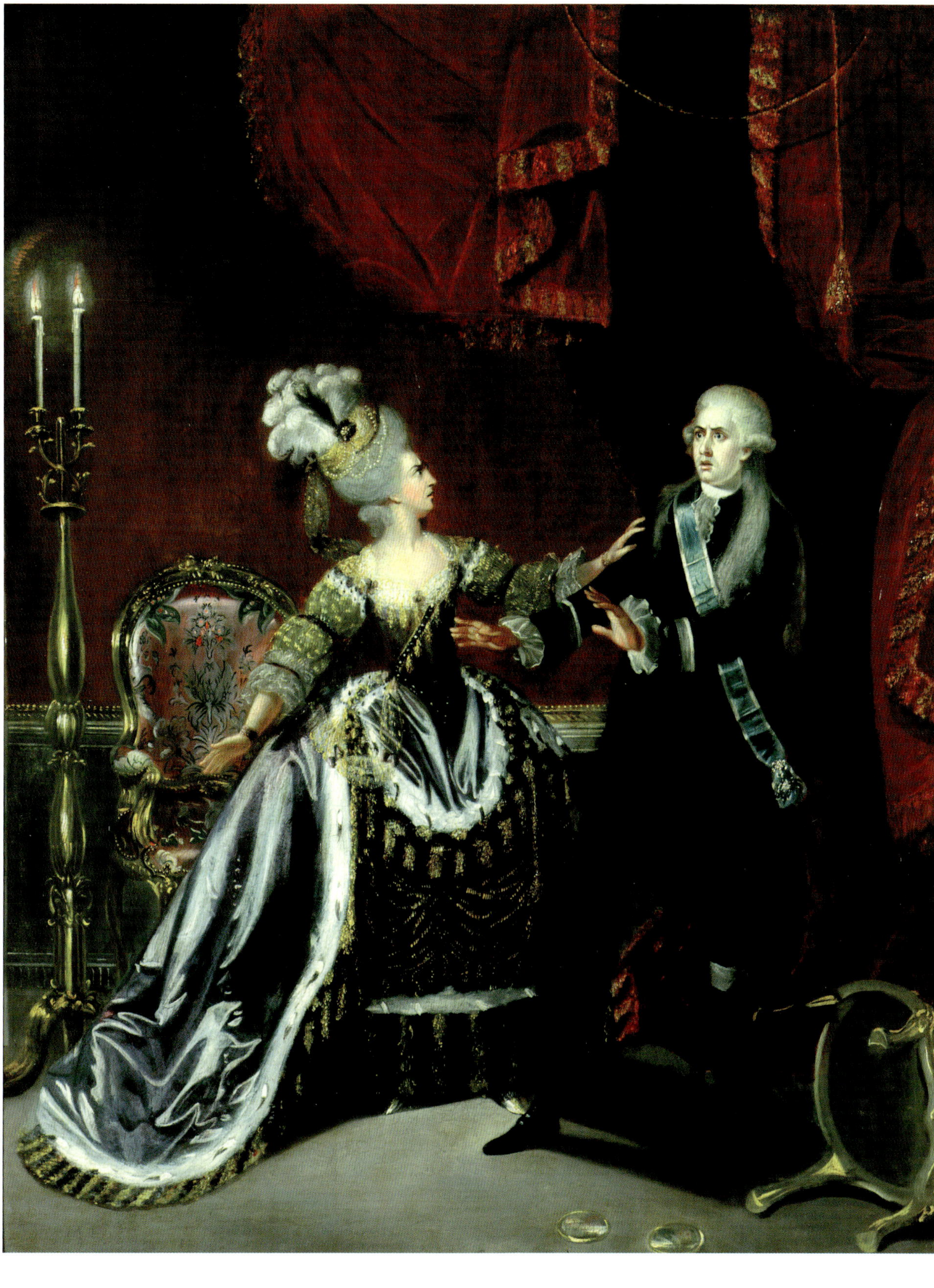

Fig.15

William Smith as Hamlet and Elizabeth Hopkins as Gertrude in *Hamlet*

James Roberts, 1777/8

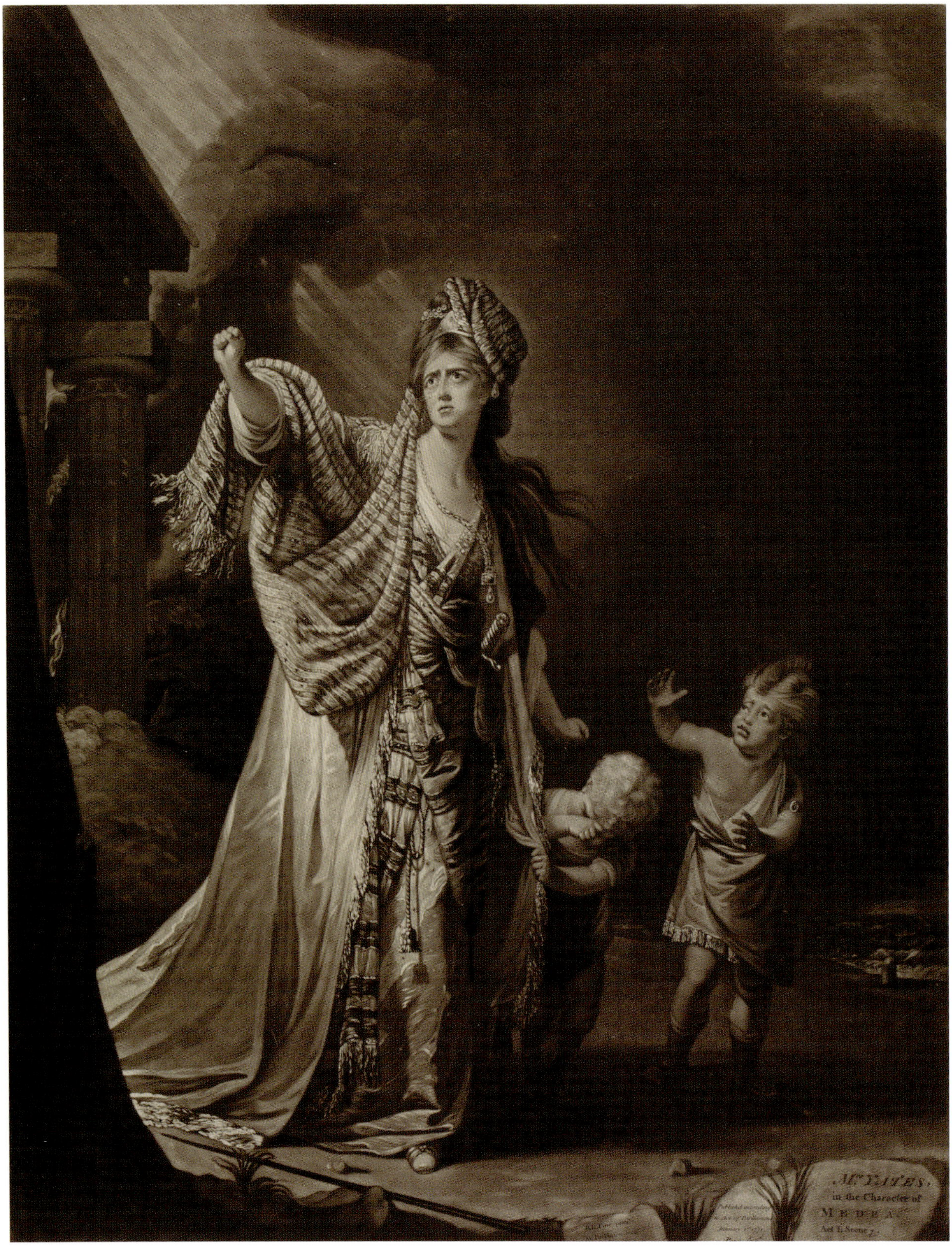

Fig.16

Mary Ann Yates as Medea

William Dickinson, after
Robert Edge Pine, 1771

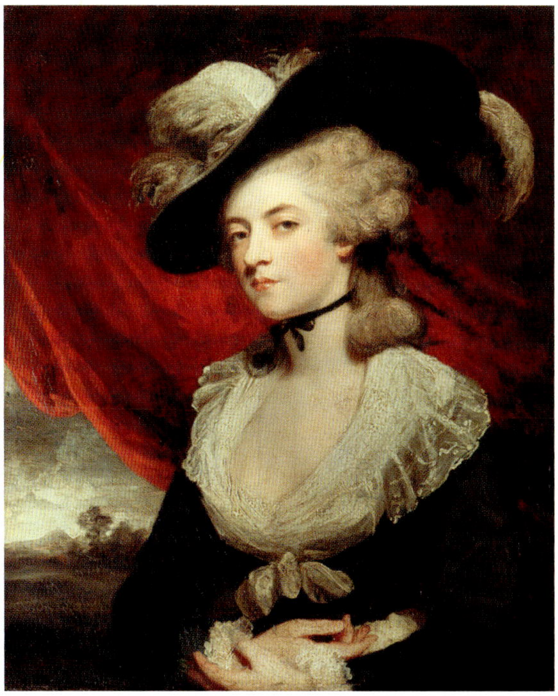

Fig.17

Mary Robinson – Perdita

Sir Joshua Reynolds, 1782

identified with a mythical English femininity, which was untainted by dissembling fashions from abroad. As we shall see later (pp.99–102), Gainsborough's portrait of the Italian-born dancer Giovanna Baccelli (see fig.30) was described by one reviewer as 'paint-painted', a reference to the painted representation of her heavy stage make-up. The portrait is thus seen to be doubly 'embellished'; paint has been laid on thickly to convey the sense that her face is also heavily painted. This idea of 'double embellishment', involving both the artifice of paint on canvas and the depiction of a made-up or disguised face, raises several issues central to our understanding of portraiture. Portraits purport to present a 'likeness' of the sitter, to reveal a recognisable individual with a lived history and presence. On another level, portraits are painted canvases or surfaces inscribed with many aesthetic, historical, cultural and political meanings, rather than mirror 'reflections' of the sitter. They tell us not just about the subject, her ambitions and how she wished to be seen (if the work was commissioned by the actress), but about the historical conventions of portrait painting, the artist's tastes, fashion, gender, social status and so on. And these meanings may emerge through dialogue with the perceptions and background knowledge of the viewer. The problematic issue of 'likeness' is particularly difficult to resolve in relation to theatrical portraits, which may depict the actress in role, or replete with references to role-playing, as in portraits of Robinson in flamboyant or theatrical dress, Isabella Mattocks as Catherine in David Garrick's *Catherine and Petruchio* (fig.18) or Sarah Siddons as the Tragic Muse (fig.73). Such portraits are themselves representations of a staged or pseudo-event, translated through the conventions and aesthetic preferences of the artist. They are, in a sense, twice removed from the supposedly 'real' person, drawing on the idea of 'double embellishment', or what I have called 'double mediation'.[23] These ambiguities encouraged eighteenth-century critics to confuse and conflate the personal, painted and public (theatrical) identities of these female stars, identities that were also often tinged with anxieties about their sexual status. Given these confusions, actress-portraits can provide an enormously rich resource for exploring the relationship between art, theatre and the broader social culture of the period.

Telling Tales: The Role of Biography

The anonymous reviewer of Reynolds's portrait of Mary Robinson (above) implied that written texts (rather than portraits) have the depth adequately to represent the lives of 'celebrated men'. While portraiture was seen to provide a visual trace of the physical presence of the famous and their performances, written texts in the form of short biographies, memoirs, diaries, puffs, scurrilous pamphlets and reviews in newspapers and journals, began to flood the market in the early eighteenth century, offering various tales and personalised narratives, which enhanced the 'well-knownness'[24] of celebrated men *and* women. Vast numbers of these publications had already begun to appear by the late seventeenth century, facilitated by the decreasing cost of printing. Many were short, witty and bawdy, and frequently attempted to capitalise on the popularity of the latest performer.[25] In combination with the increased dissemination of visual imagery, these biographies helped to produce a market of reputations, fuelling a public obsession with performers and their lives that can be seen as marking the beginning of a modern celebrity culture.[26] The increased visibility of portraits, prints and biographies enabled eighteenth-century audiences to claim access to deeper meanings of performances and the presumed 'real' identities of performers. For example, the knowledge, disseminated through biographies and reviews, that Sarah Siddons apparently pursued a morally upright family life,

Fig.18 (right)
Isabella Mattocks as Catherine in *Catherine and Petruchio*
Gainsborough Dupont, 1794

Fig.19 (opposite page, above)
A Narrative of the Life of Mrs Charlotte Charke
Charlotte Charke, 1755

Fig.20 (opposite page, below)
Faithful Memoirs of the Life, Amours and Performances ... of Mrs Anne Oldfield
Anne Oldfield, 1731

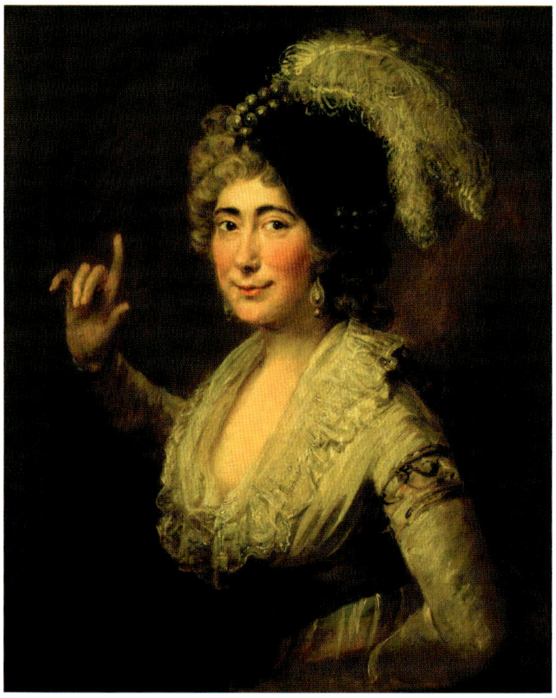

mixed in upper-class social circles and cultivated a dignified, queenly demeanour, informed the viewer's readings of both her tragic roles on stage and her painted portraits (as Shearer West will show later, pp.106–10).

One of the most important periods in the growing eighteenth-century market for theatrical memorabilia followed the spectacular success of John Gay's *The Beggar's Opera* in 1728, a musical play or 'ballad opera' (see pp.78–86) that satirised politics, poverty and corruption. It tells the story of the highwayman Macheath, who is involved in a love triangle with both Polly (the daughter of Peachum, the fence) and the jailer's daughter, Lucy. He is captured and confined to Newgate prison, where most of the comedy takes place. The main characters and performers were celebrated through a run of biographies, including that of Lavinia Fenton (1708–60) who played Polly Peachum (see fig.25). *The Life of Lavinia Beswick, Alias Fenton, Alias Polly Peachum* is widely identified as the first substantial actress-biography.[27] Fenton's contemporaries were drawn to her rags-to-riches story. She became the mistress of the Duke of Bolton shortly after the biography was published, and married him in 1751 after the death of his wife. The memoir, which sold well, has been seen by some as 'scurrilous' and 'probably untrustworthy'.[28] By being a public performer and a woman, the actress was often perceived as a contradiction within a society in which respectable women were expected to inhabit the supposedly 'private' domestic sphere.[29] Thus the anonymous author of the Fenton biography dwells on her sexual history, raising and denying the insinuations that she was 'ever a common Prostitute'.[30] The author also confuses her identity with that of her famous role, calling her 'Polly' and narrating her life as if it were a performance. Significantly, the role of Polly Peachum in *The Beggar's Opera* has been subject to conflicting interpretations as both innocent and shrewdly manipulative. This biography seems to echo these contradictions; like the stage role, the memoir portrays the actress as generous and good-natured, while privileging accounts of her many sexual encounters over her stage career.[31] At the same time, and despite her dubious past, she is presented as displaying acting talent and conversational skills, hinting at an acknowledged celebrity value as 'actress'.[32]

The construction of the actress as a celebrity brand was a fickle process, fraught with contradictions, and biographical accounts could demolish as well as enhance reputations. Actresses were targets of both eulogistic puffs and prurient tales, sometimes distributed as short books or pamphlets. At the turn of the eighteenth century Harriet Mellon (1777–1837), the daughter of strolling players, made her name at the Duke Street Theatre and took the town by storm in her role as Volante in *The Honeymoon* at Drury Lane in 1802. She famously attracted the attention of the elderly banker Thomas Coutts of Coutts & Co., whom she married after the death of his first wife. After his death in 1822 a castigatory biographical letter was published by a 'Mr Percy Wyndham', titled *Strictures on an Imposter, and Old Actress, Formerly Bet the Pot Girl, alias the Banker's Sham Widow*, which claimed Mellon had a dubious past in the workhouse and a sham marriage, using hyperbolic language to disparage 'the Indecent effrontery of this Vile, Wicked, Lying, Boasting, Puffing *She Pharisee*'.

Throughout the eighteenth and well into the nineteenth centuries, women performers were vulnerable to such vitriolic character assassinations. Thus many also adopted autobiographical strategies, along with commissioned portraits, to help control their own histories and identities. Actress-autobiographies from the period include memoirs by Charlotte Charke, Mary Robinson and George Anne Bellamy (fig.21). Charlotte Charke, the daughter of Colley Cibber,

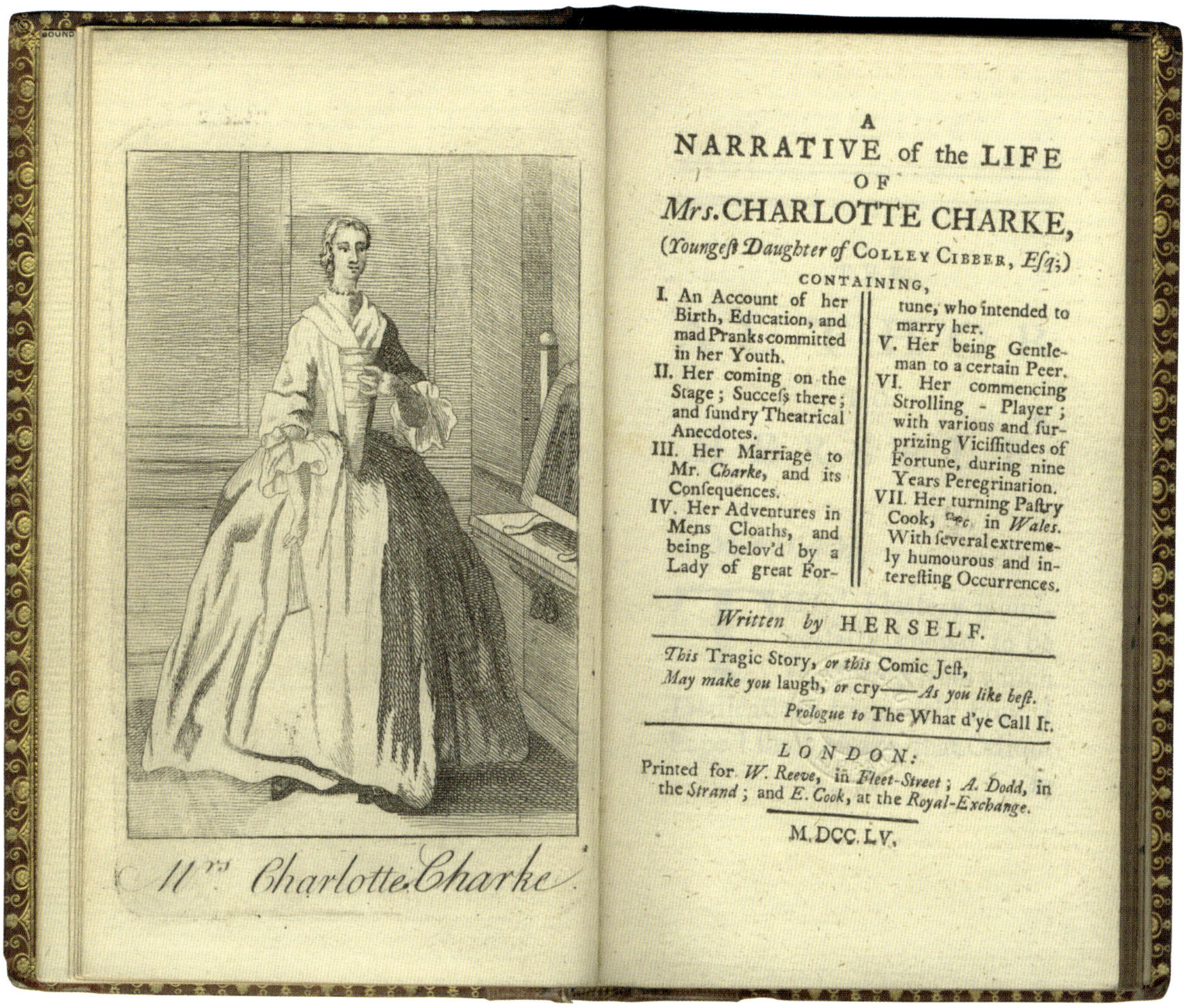

A

NARRATIVE of the LIFE

OF

Mrs. CHARLOTTE CHARKE,

(*Youngest Daughter of* COLLEY CIBBER, *Esq*;)

CONTAINING,

I. An Account of her Birth, Education, and mad Pranks committed in her Youth.

II. Her coming on the Stage; Success there; and sundry Theatrical Anecdotes.

III. Her Marriage to Mr. *Charke*, and its Consequences.

IV. Her Adventures in Mens Cloaths, and being belov'd by a Lady of great Fortune, who intended to marry her.

V. Her being Gentleman to a certain Peer.

VI. Her commencing Strolling - Player; with various and surprizing Vicissitudes of Fortune, during nine Years Peregrination.

VII. Her turning Pastry Cook, &c. in *Wales*. With several extremely humourous and interesting Occurrences.

Written by HERSELF.

This Tragic Story, *or this* Comic Jest,
May make you laugh, *or* cry——*As you like best.*

Prologue to The What d'ye Call It.

LONDON:

Printed for *W. Reeve*, in *Fleet-Street*; *A. Dodd*, in the *Strand*; and *E. Cook*, at the *Royal-Exchange*.

M.DCC.LV.

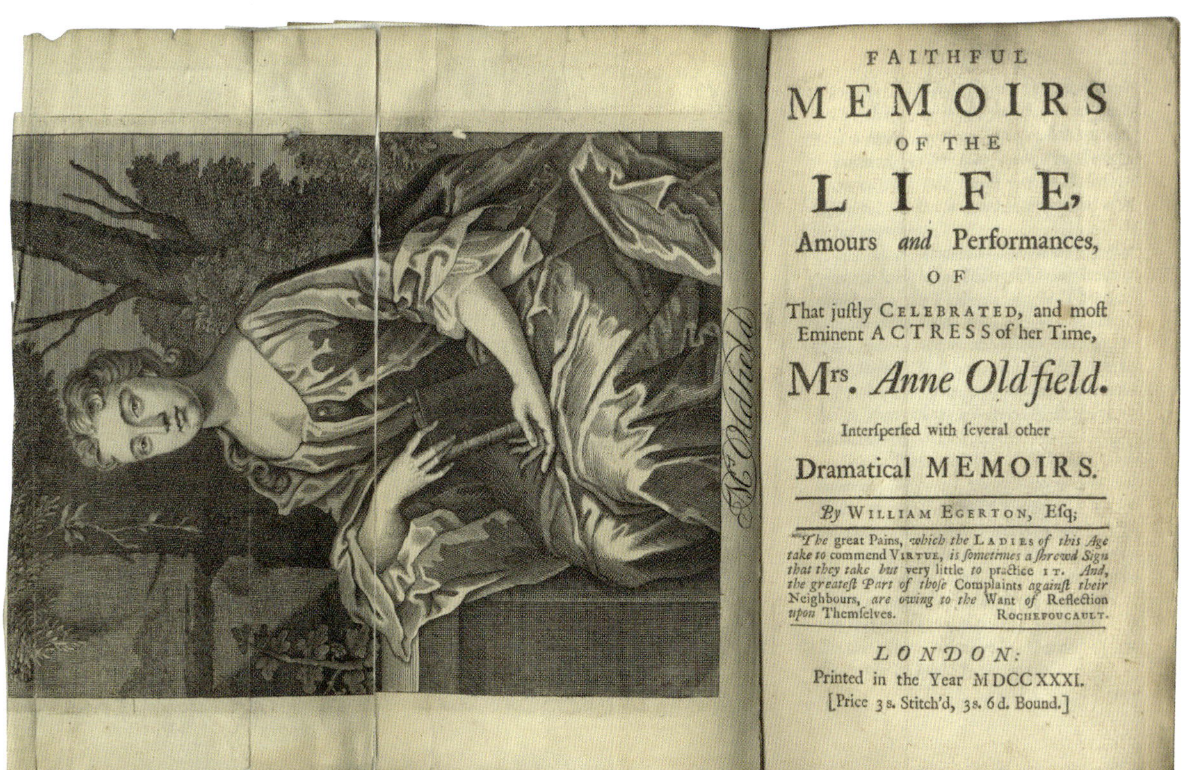

FAITHFUL

MEMOIRS

OF THE

LIFE,

Amours *and* Performances,

OF

That justly CELEBRATED, and most Eminent ACTRESS of her Time,

Mrs. *Anne Oldfield.*

Interspersed with several other

Dramatical MEMOIRS.

By WILLIAM EGERTON, Esq;

"*The* great Pains, *which the* LADIES *of this Age take to* commend VIRTUE, *is sometimes a shrewd Sign that they take but* very little *to* practice IT. *And, the greatest Part of those* Complaints *against their* Neighbours, *are owing to the* Want *of* Reflection *upon* Themselves. ROCHEFOUCAULT.

LONDON:

Printed in the Year MDCCXXXI.

[Price 3 s. Stitch'd, 3 s. 6 d. Bound.]

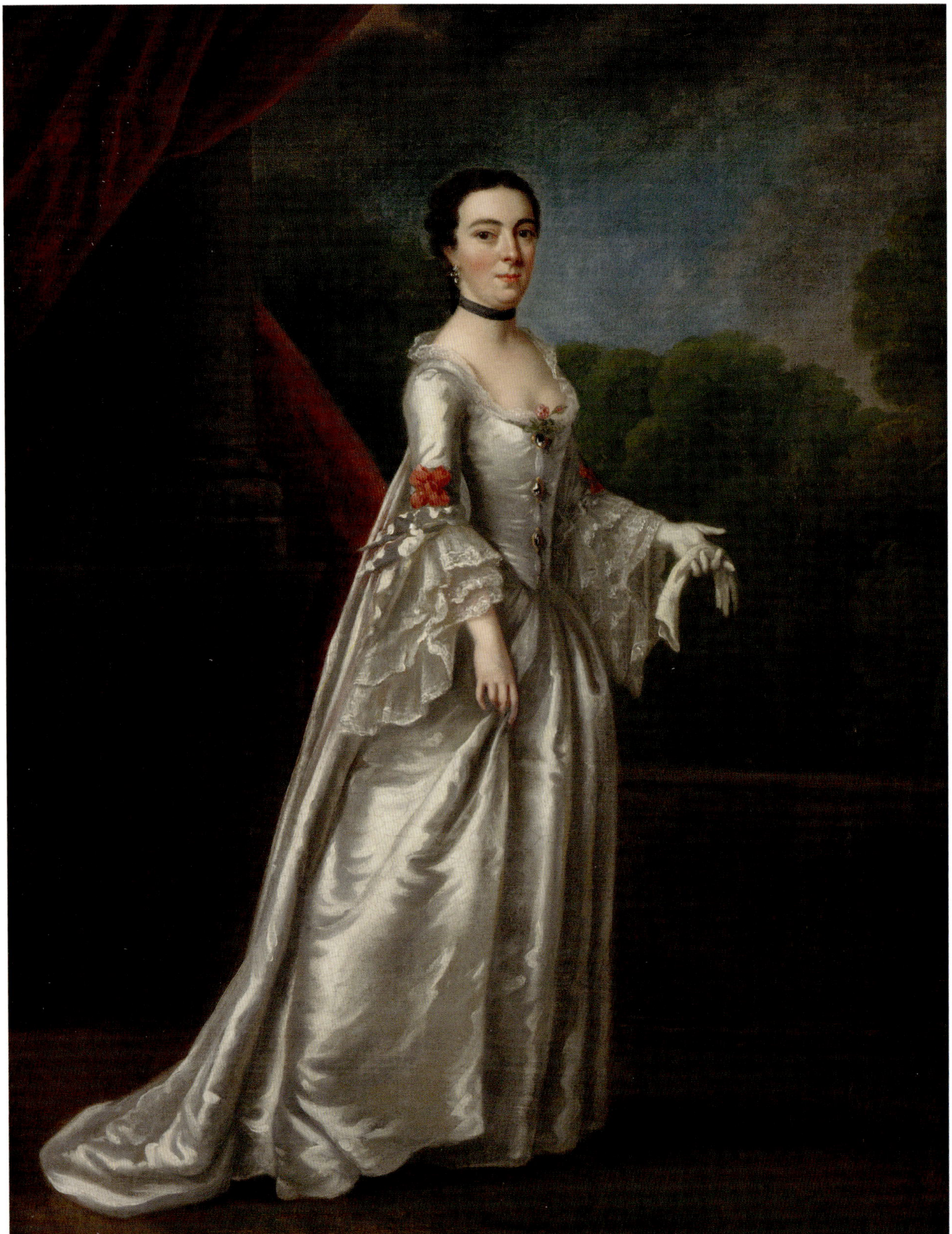

Fig.21

George Anne Bellamy

Francis Lindo, mid-1750s

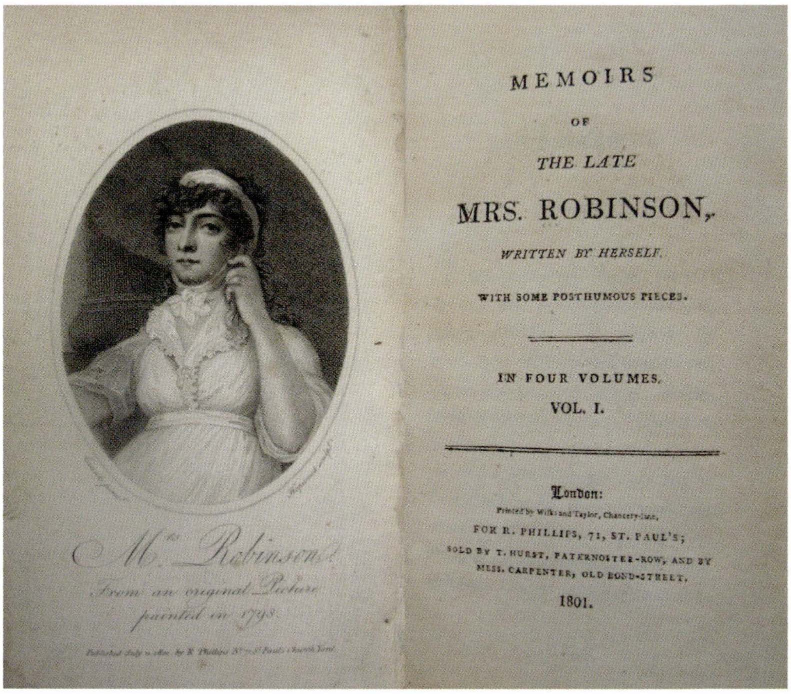

Fig.22

Memoirs of the Late Mrs Robinson

Mary Robinson, 1801

published one of the first actress-autobiographies, *A Narrative of the Life of Mrs Charlotte Charke*, in 1755 (fig.19). Charke describes her attempts to earn a living as actress and pastry cook, and boldly recounts her years spent impersonating a man. Many scholars have claimed this work as evidence both of gender ambiguity within theatrical culture, and of the problems encountered by actresses who refused to adopt a conventional femininity in their personal lives.[33] In anticipation of modern celebrity culture, Charke is now better known for her apparently intimate memoir than her theatrical performances. And her opening paragraph tells us much about mid-eighteenth-century perceptions of both female writers and actress-autobiography. She begs that her work be properly read before it is condemned: 'As the following History is the Product of a Female Pen, I tremble for the terrible Hazard it must run in venturing into the World, as it may very possibly suffer, in many Opinions, without perusing it.'[34]

Like portraiture, autobiography is, of course, a cultural practice that interprets and selectively tells tales, rather than holding up a mirror to its subject. And like portraiture it offers a feigned intimacy; it can seduce the reader into believing that he or she is being given access to the 'real' or private person described on the page or canvas, or what Joseph Roach describes on p.64 as 'public intimacy'. It can 'create the illusion of shared secrets'.[35] But for many women performers, writing one's own memoir offered a chance to negotiate history and shape a public identity that was vulnerable to misrepresentation, parody and moral disdain. Mary Robinson, who abandoned her acting career in the late eighteenth century for that of a writer and poet, was astutely aware of her own ability to shape her public identity. Apart from her early role-playing in outrageously fashionable outfits, she later wrote her own memoirs, edited by her daughter and first published in 1801 (fig.22), in which the original introduction maps out a recurring claim in actress-autobiographies, that 'a female of great personal and natural attraction, exposed to the gaze of libertine rank and fashion, under the mere nominal guardianship of a neglectful and profligate husband', is particularly vulnerable. Robinson sought to elicit both pity and admiration. She deployed a rhetorical strategy that echoed the conventions of theatrical portraiture; grandiose, sentimental or seemingly 'natural' effects could be integrated into the painted study to evoke a desired response in the viewer. Thus she also suggested that her memoir, while risking misinterpretation, purports to be a moral tale of 'the cold-hearted neglect which a woman of the most fascinating mental and personal attractions may encounter from those whose homage is merely sensual, and whose admiration is but a snare'. This book explores the multifarious ways in which portraiture and theatrical culture helped to construct and promote such 'fascinating personal attractions'.

THE ACTRESSES

A SELECTION OF BIOGRAPHIES

IN ORDER OF APPEARANCE:

NELL GWYN

HESTER BOOTH

LAVINIA FENTON

KITTY CLIVE

PEG WOFFINGTON

FRANCES ABINGTON

ELIZABETH INCHBALD

GIOVANNA BACCELLI

ELIZABETH ANN SHERIDAN

SARAH SIDDONS

MARY ROBINSON

ELIZABETH FARREN

DOROTHY JORDAN

ELIZABETH BILLINGTON

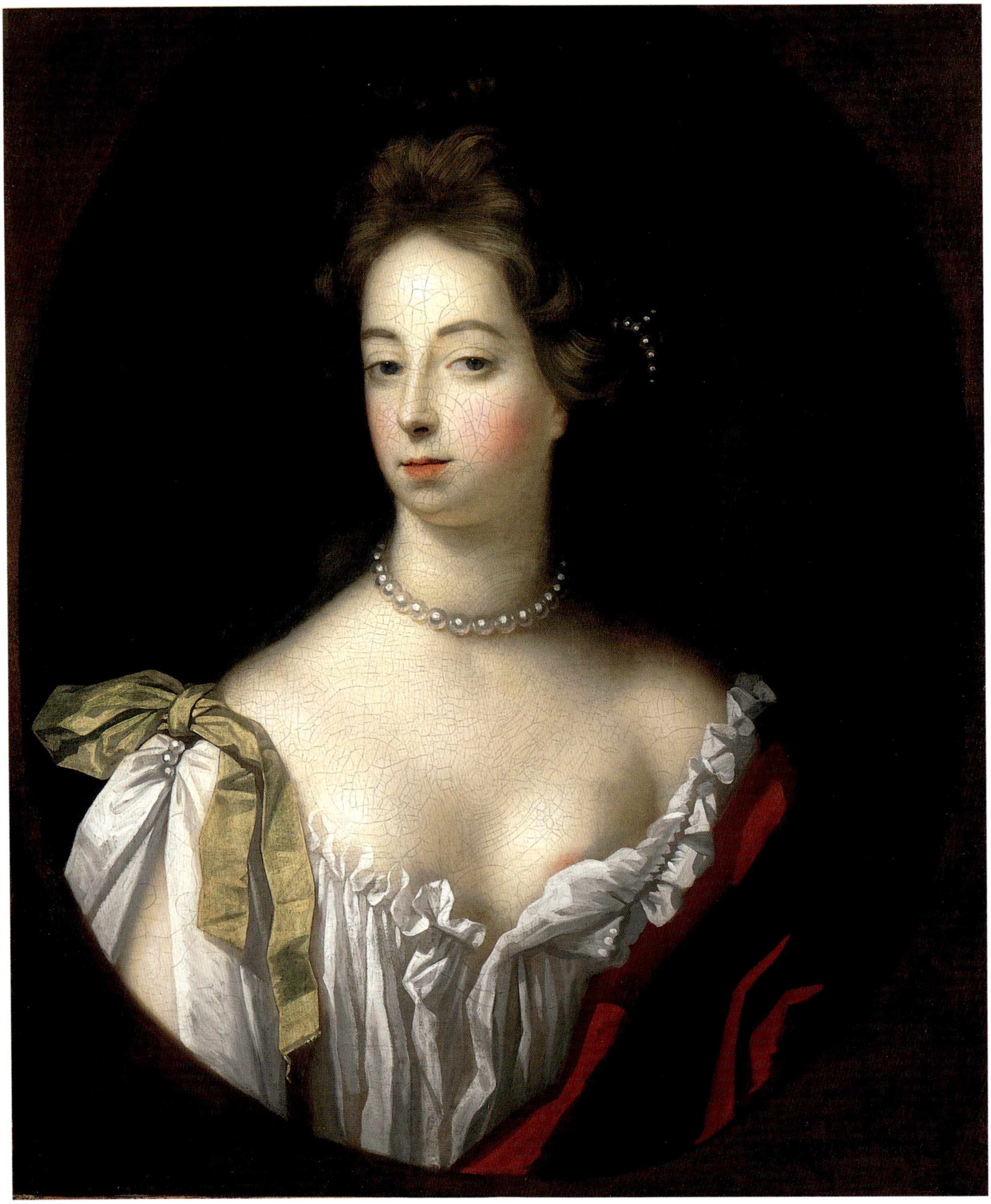

Fig.23

Eleanor ('Nell') Gwyn

Simon Verelst, *c.*1680

NELL GWYN

BORN IN 1651? – DIED IN 1687

The birthplace of Eleanor Gwyn, known as 'Nell', is unknown and her parentage obscure, but according to the diarist Samuel Pepys, she was raised in 'a bawdy house' where she served 'strong water' to the guests. Information on her early life is thin, but she is thought to have been an orange-seller at the Bridges Street Theatre in 1663, meeting actors and gentry before taking bit parts as an actress a year later. According to the playwright Colley Cibber, Charles Hart, leading actor in the King's Company, supported Gwyn, probably becoming her lover and starring opposite her on stage. She first came to the attention of Pepys in April 1665, when he noticed 'pretty witty Nell' in the audience at a play. When the theatres reopened following the plague of 1665–6, Gwyn's parts included Lady Wealthy in James Howard's *The English Monsieur* and the breeches part of Florimel in John Dryden's *The Maiden Queen, or Secret Love*, of which Pepys wrote that he could not hope to see such a performance again, 'by man or woman'. He felt that she was exceptional in comic roles, but less strong in serious parts.

After an affair with Charles Sackville, Lord Buckhurst, in 1667, Gwyn became a mistress of King Charles II, and was pregnant with her first child by the king in 1669. She stopped acting and gave birth to Charles, later Duke of St Albans, in May 1670. She returned to the stage to play in Dryden's *The Conquest of Granada* in 1670, but retired from the stage for good in 1671. She gave birth to her second son by the King in December 1671. In 1675 Gwyn became one of the ladies of the Queen's Privy Chamber and in 1677 the king gave her the freehold of a house in Pall Mall, although she never received a title. Her chief rival at court was the unpopular Catholic Louise de Kéroualle, Duchess of Portsmouth. During 1687 Gwyn became ill and partly paralysed. She died in November and was buried in St Martin-in-the-Fields.

Famous stage roles

1665–6: as Cydaria in John Dryden's *The Indian Emperour*; as Mirida in James Howard's comedy *All Mistaken, or the Mad Couple*; as Lady Wealthy in Howard's *The English Monsieur*
1667: in Richard Rhodes' *Flora's Vagaries*; as Florimel in Dryden's *The Maiden Queen, or Secret Love*; in Robert Howard's *The Surprisal*
1668: as a guardian angel in *The Virgin Martyr* by Thomas Dekker and Philip Massinger; in Dryden's *An Evening's Love, or The Mock Astrologer*; in John Lacy's *The Old Troop*
1669: as Valeria in Dryden's tragedy *Tyrannick Love*
1670–1: in Dryden's *The Conquest of Granada*

Key portraits

Sir Peter Lely, *c.*1664, oil on canvas, Weston Park; studio of Sir Peter Lely, *c.*1675, oil on canvas, National Portrait Gallery, London; Simon Verelst, *c.*1680, oil on canvas, National Portrait Gallery, London; Simon Verelst, *c.*1680–5, oil on canvas, private collection

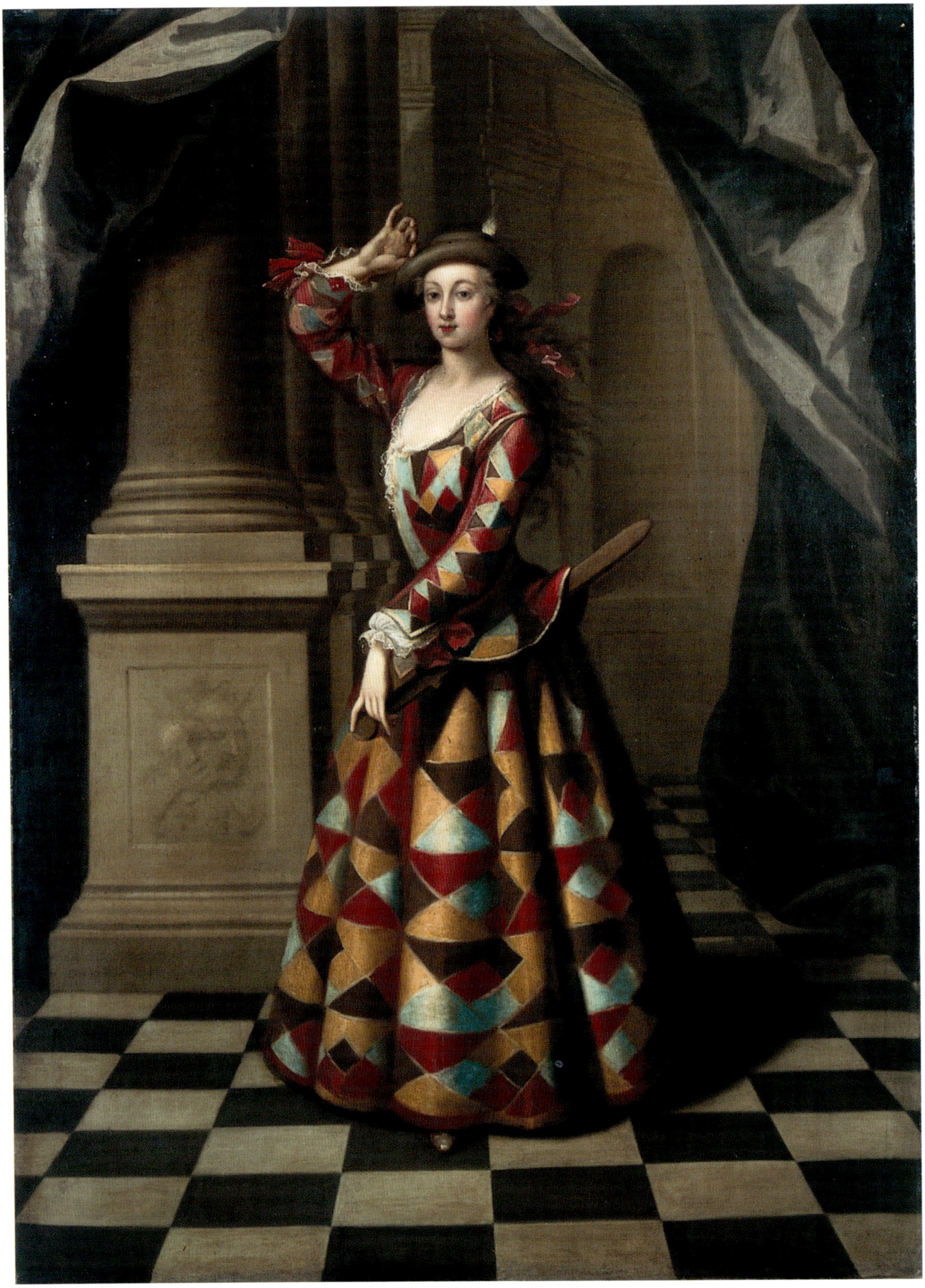

Fig.24

Hester Booth

John Ellys, *c.*1722–5

HESTER BOOTH

BORN CIRCA 1690/3 – DIED IN 1773

Hester Booth (née Santlow) made her name as a 'dancer-actress'. Born in London, very little is known of her early years, but 1706 marks her first performance as a dancer, aged sixteen, at Drury Lane, having been taught by the dancing-master René Cherrier. She made her debut as an actress in the same theatre three years later, in the part of Miss Prue in William Congreve's *Love for Love*. A visitor to the city, Zacharias Conrad von Uffenbach, wrote of her as 'universally admired for her beauty, matchless figure and the unusual elegance of her dancing and acting' in his journal, *London in 1710*. Between the 1707–8 and 1711–12 seasons she added a variety of roles to her repertory but was absent from the stage for most of 1712–13 as she gave birth to a daughter Harriot, fathered by James Craggs, private secretary to the Duke of Marlborough, in 1713. She resumed her stage career later that year, and extended her repertory of parts to include Angelica in George Farquhar's *The Constant Couple*, Cordelia in Shakespeare's *King Lear* and Desdemona in *Othello*, and Angelina in Colley Cibber's *Love Makes a Man*.

In 1719 she married the successful actor Barton Booth, after which she continued to act, playing around twenty parts a season. Alongside these roles, she also danced regularly in the entr'actes, or musical interludes, becoming famous for her solo *Harlequin Dance*. A favourite dancer of the choreographer John Weaver, she performed in several of his innovative dances – as Venus in *The Loves of Mars and Venus* (1717) and as Helen of Troy in *Judgment of Paris* (1733) – while in the 1720s she danced in the Drury Lane pantomimes. Ill health forced her husband to retire from the stage in 1728, and she cared for him until his death in 1733, later erecting a monument to his memory in Westminster Abbey in 1772. She died at her home in Bloomsbury, London in 1773, and was buried alongside her mother and husband in the Parish Church of St Laurence, Cowley, near Uxbridge.

Famous stage roles

1707–12: as Ophelia in Shakespeare's *Hamlet*; as Miranda in Susanna Centlivre's *The Busy Body*; as Gatty in George Etherege's *She Would if She Could*; as Miss Prue in William Congreve's *Love for Love*; title role in Charles Shadwell's *The Fair Quaker of Deal*
1713–14: as Angelica in George Farquhar's *The Constant Couple*; as Cordelia in *King Lear* and Desdemona in *Othello*; as Angelina in Colley Cibber's *Love Makes a Man*; as Celia in Ben Jonson's *Volpone*; as Selima in Nicholas Rowe's *Tamerlane*
1717–18: as Venus in John Weaver's *The Loves of Mars and Venus*
1720s onwards: as Fidelia in William Wycherley's *The Plain Dealer*; as Helena in Aphra Behn's *The Rover*; as Elvira in John Dryden's *The Spanish Fryar*
1733: as Helen of Troy in Weaver's *Judgment of Paris*

Key portraits

John Ellys, *c.*1722–5, oil on canvas, Victoria and Albert Museum, London; John Ellys, *c.*1720, oil on canvas, private collection; John Vanderbank, *c.*1725, oil on canvas, private collection

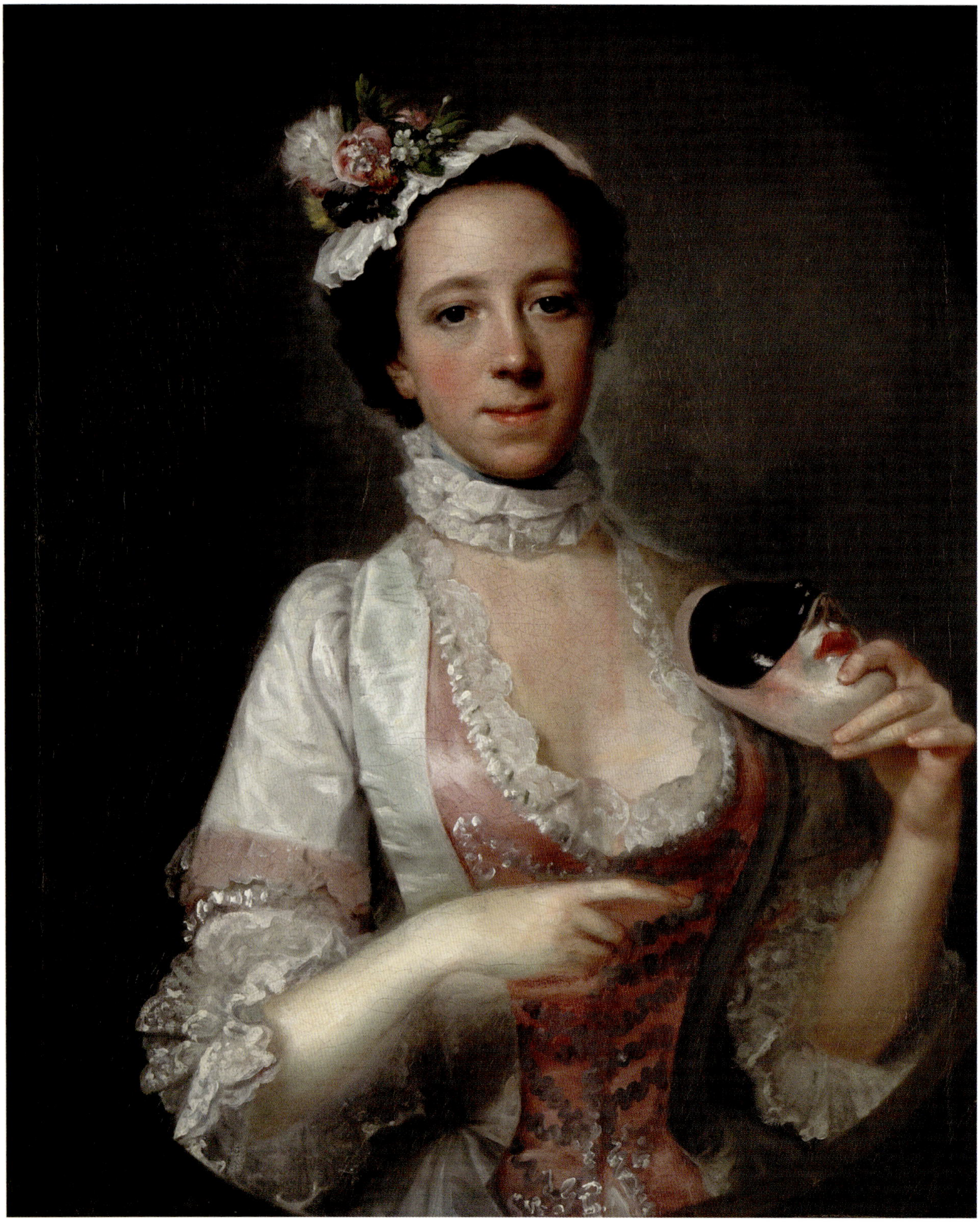

Fig.25

Lavinia Fenton

Possibly by George Knapton, *c.*1739

LAVINIA FENTON

BORN IN 1710 – DIED IN 1760

Lavinia Fenton (née Besswick) was alleged to be the illegitimate daughter of a navy lieutenant lost at sea, and her mother Elizabeth, who subsequently married a Mr Fenton. The Fentons opened a coffee house near Charing Cross, where Lavinia was reputedly a favourite with the customers because of her vivacious character and beauty. She was sent to boarding school for five years as preparation for a 'good marriage', before becoming briefly involved with a Portuguese nobleman. Fenton first appeared on stage in Thomas Otway's *The Orphan* at the New Theatre in the Haymarket. She then played at Lincoln's Inn Fields in 1726, performing Lucilla in William Davenant's *The Man's the Master*, before being employed by the impresario John Rich and taking the role of Mrs Squeamish in William Wycherley's *The Country Wife*. Fenton's great success as Polly Peachum in *The Beggar's Opera* in 1728 prompted Alexander Pope to remember her in a later edition of *The Dunciad*, writing that after being virtually unknown she 'became at once the great favourite of the town: her pictures were engraved and sold in great numbers, her life written, books of letters and verses to her published.'

During her short career Fenton performed several other roles, including Ophelia in *Hamlet* and a breeches part, Alinda, in Beaumont and Fletcher's *The Pilgrim*. She was the subject of endless satirical gossip and acquired many suitors, including Charles Powlett, 3rd Duke of Bolton, who is seen gazing at Polly from a box on the stage in Hogarth's painting of *The Beggar's Opera* (fig.52). She became the Duke's mistress and, after retiring from the stage in 1728, she lived with him for twenty-three years before they married in 1751, following the death of Bolton's first wife. They had three sons together. After his death she spent her last months with her lover, the Irish surgeon George Kelly. She died on 24 January 1760 and was buried at St Alphege, Greenwich.

Famous stage roles

1726: as Serina in Thomas Otway's *The Orphan*; as Lucilla in William Davenant's *The Man's the Master*; as Mrs Squeamish in William Wycherley's *The Country Wife*; as a country lass in Lewis Theobald's pantomime *The Rape of Proserpine*
1727: as Cherry in George Farquhar's *The Beaux' Stratagem*; as Lucy in Thomas Baker's *Tunbridge Walks*
1728 onwards: as Polly Peachum in John Gay's *The Beggar's Opera*; as Ophelia in *Hamlet*; as Betty in Susanna Centlivre's *A Bold Stroke for a Wife*; as Marcella in Thomas D'Urfey's *Don Quixote*; in Farquhar's *Love and a Bottle*; as Alinda in Beaumont and Fletcher's *The Pilgrim*

Key portraits

Possibly by George Knapton, *c.*1739, oil on canvas, private collection; William Hogarth, 1728, chalk sketch, Royal Library, Windsor Castle; William Hogarth, as Polly, in *The Beggar's Opera*, 1726–8, oil on canvas, Birmingham Museums and Art Gallery; Hogarth, *c.*1740–50, oil on canvas, Tate Britain

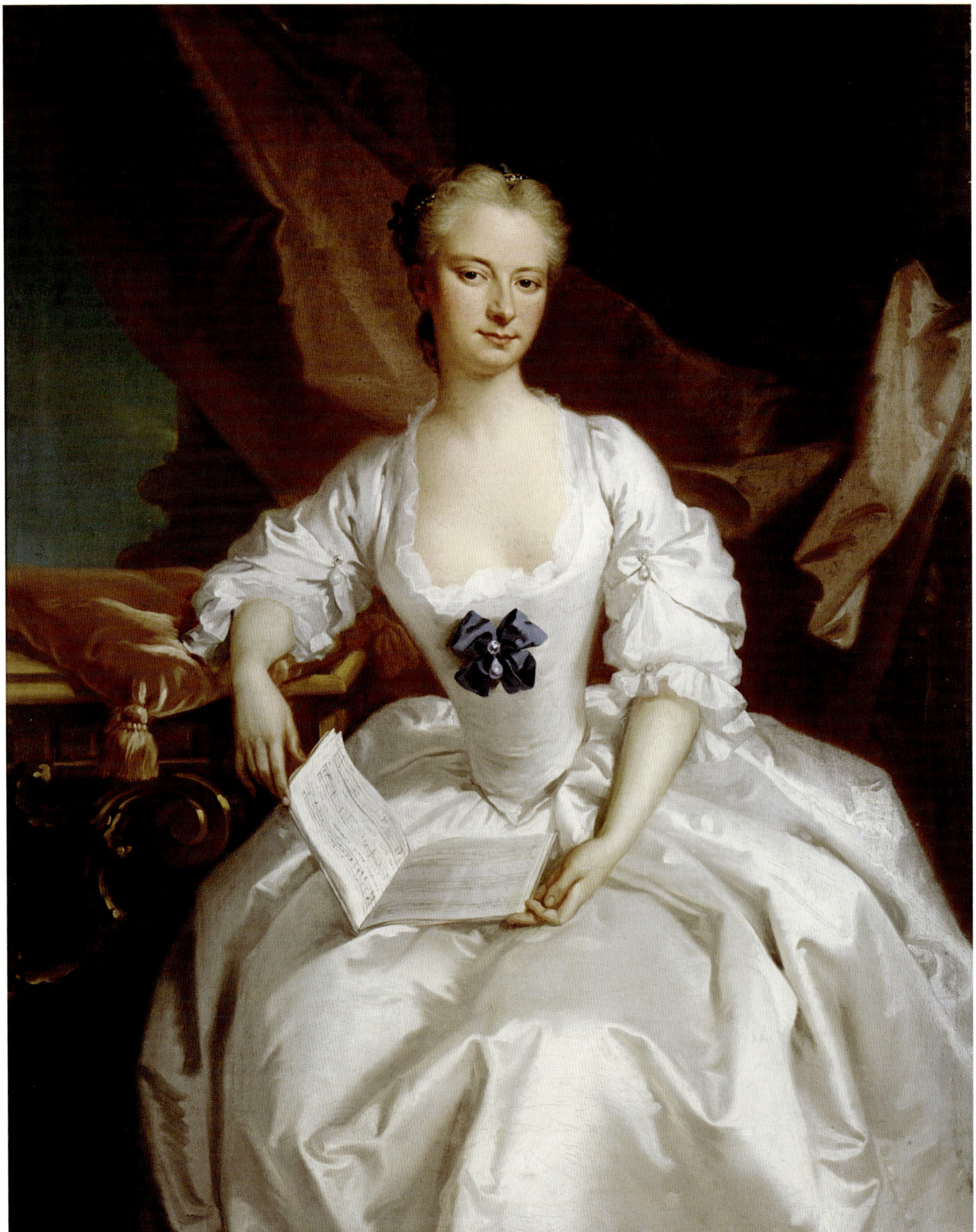

Fig.26

Catherine ('Kitty') Clive

Jeremiah Davison, 1735

KITTY CLIVE

BORN IN 1711 – DIED IN 1785

Catherine Clive (née Raftor), known as 'Kitty', was born in London, the the daughter of an Irish lawyer. She rose to become one of the most successful actress-singers of her time, with a career spanning forty years. She first appeared on the stage in 1728 in singing and acting roles under the management of Colley Cibber at Drury Lane, followed by a series of tragic parts such as Bianca in *Othello*. Kitty's brief marriage to the barrister George Clive took place around 1733; they parted by mutual consent in 1735. Her most popular early roles were in musical comedy and burlesque. In 1731 she played Nell in Charles Coffey's farce-opera, *The Devil to Pay*, and in 1732 played Polly in John Gay's *The Beggar's Opera*, when she was described by the *Daily Journal* as 'the Darling of the Age'. The role of Polly was also sought after by the actress Susannah Cibber (Colley's daughter-in-law), but after a bitter feud in 1736, known as the 'Polly War', Clive continued to play the role at Drury Lane. She befriended Handel and performed in several of his oratorios, including the part of Delilah in *Samson*. By 1744 Clive commanded a salary of £300 a year, plus earnings from her benefit performances (at which the profits went to the star performer), placing her among the best-paid actresses of her generation. In 1747 she became one of the founder members of David Garrick's acting company at Drury Lane. She also wrote farces for benefits, including *The Rehearsal or Boys in Petticoats* (1750), in which she played the breeches part.

Clive's acting was praised by Oliver Goldsmith, Samuel Johnson and David Garrick. She reputedly had a 'forthright temperament' and her rivalries with other actresses, such as Peg Woffington, were widely reported. She had numerous admirers but skilfully maintained a reputation for chastity. In 1769 Clive retired to a house known as 'Clive's Den' or 'Little Strawberry Hill', Twickenham, rented from her close friend Horace Walpole. She died in 1785 and was buried in St Mary's Church, Twickenham. Walpole had a poetic tribute inscribed on an urn in his garden, of which the last two lines are: 'The comic muse with her retired/ And shed a tear when she expired.'

Famous stage roles

1728–31: as Nell in Charles Coffey's *The Devil to Pay*; as Chloe in Henry Fielding's *The Lottery*; as Lappet in an adaptation of Molière's *The Miser*; as Bianca in Shakespeare's *Othello*; as Phillida in Colley Cibber's *Damon and Phillida*
1732: as Polly in John Gay's *The Beggar's Opera*
1734: title role in Fielding's *The Intriguing Chambermaid*
1738: as the Lady in John Milton's *Comus*
1747 onwards: as Mrs Cadwallader in Samuel Foote's *The Author*; as the Fine Lady in David Garrick's *Lethe*; as Lady Wishfort in William Congreve's *The Way of the World* and as Flora in Susanna Centlivre's *The Wonder*

Key portraits

Peter van Bleeck, as Phillida, 1735, oil on canvas, location unknown; Jeremiah Davison, 1735, oil on canvas, Longleat House, Wilts; Willem Verelst, 1740, oil on canvas, Garrick Club, London

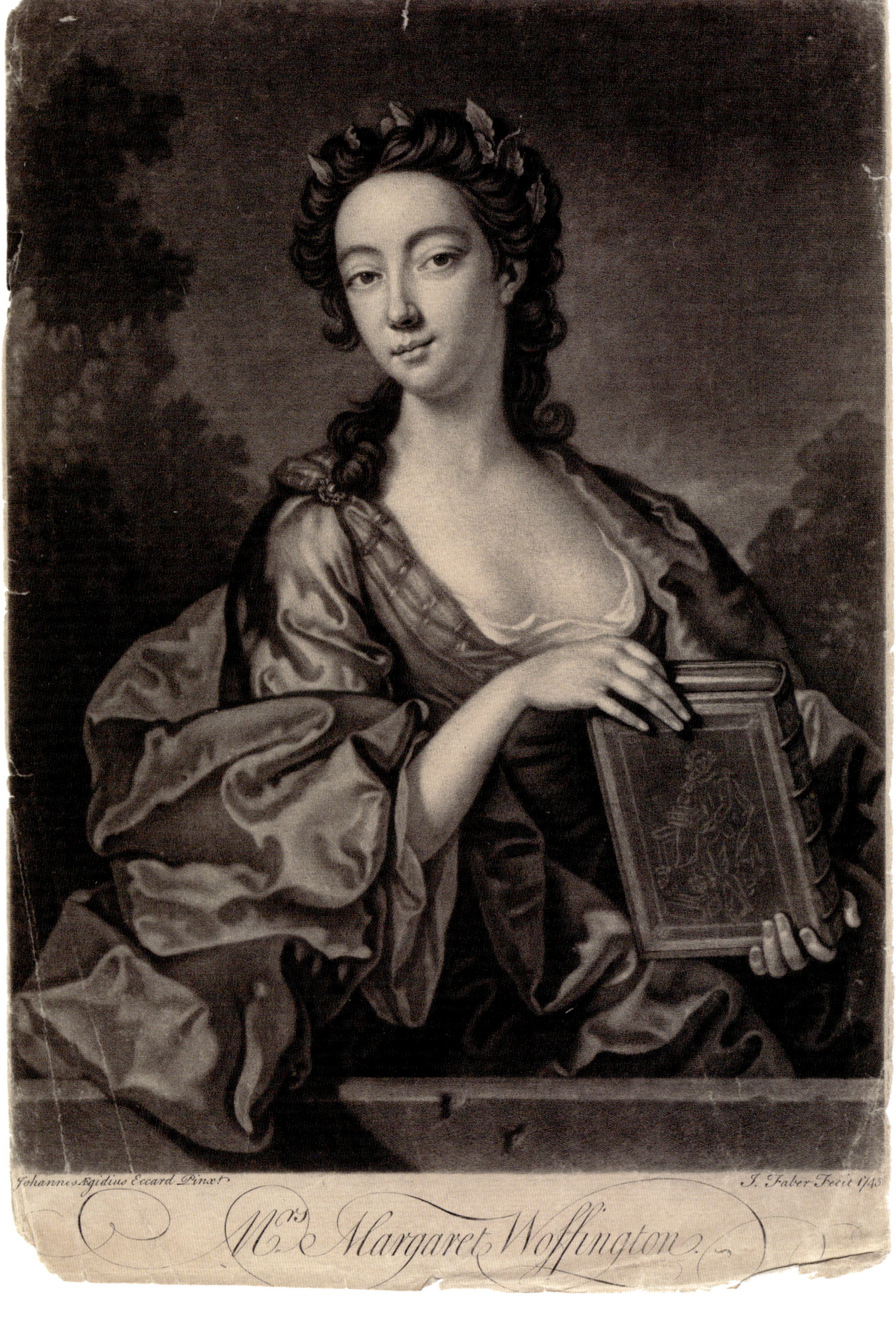
Johannes Ægidius Eccard Pinx.t
J. Faber Fecit 1745
Mrs Margaret Woffington.

PEG WOFFINGTON

BORN IN 1718/20 – DIED IN 1760

Margaret, known as 'Peg', was the daughter of John and Hannah Woffington, and first appeared on the Dublin stage as a juvenile in 1731. She played a cross-dressed role as Captain Macheath in a production of *The Beggar's Opera* by Signora Violante's company, the Lilliputians. The details of Woffington's early life are uncertain, but she is known to have taken acting, singing and dancing roles during her early career in Dublin. Her first major appearance was at Theatre Royal Dublin in 1735, playing Dorinda in an adaptation of *The Tempest* in which she sang and performed a 'pastoral dance'. After moving to London she was employed by John Rich at Covent Garden in November 1740. Woffington's slender physique enabled her to play many popular cross-dressed roles, including Silvia in Farquhar's *The Recruiting Officer*, and the libertine Sir Harry Wildair in Farquhar's *The Constant Couple*. She acted at Drury Lane from 1741 in both comic and tragic roles, including Garrick's revivals of Shakespeare. She played Cordelia opposite Garrick's *King Lear* and they were the success of the season in 1742 when she played Lady Anne to his Richard III. A relationship developed and they moved into the same lodgings in London, where they entertained eminent visitors including Samuel Johnson and Henry Fielding. Nevertheless, the couple parted within two years.

Many stories circulated of Woffington's numerous love affairs and of her rivalries with other actresses, especially Susannah Cibber, Kitty Clive and George Anne Bellamy, all of whom worked for the Drury Lane Theatre during Garrick's tenure as manager. In 1751 Woffington returned to Dublin and joined Thomas Sheridan's company at the Smock Alley Theatre for three seasons. She then retired to her country house in Teddington and, although born a Catholic, died a Protestant in 1760, probably because of terms associated with a large bequest from the Irish impresario Owen Swiny in 1754. She was buried at St Mary's Church, Teddington, where a memorial stone was laid, and most of her estate was bequeathed to her sister Mary.

Famous stage roles

1731: as Captain Macheath in John Gay's *The Beggar's Opera*
1735: as Dorinda in *The Tempest*
1739–40: as Polly in John Gay's *The Beggar's Opera*; as the central role in Charles Shadwell's *The Female Officer*
1740–1: as Sir Harry Wildair in George Farquhar's *The Constant Couple*; as Silvia in Farquhar's *The Recruiting Officer;* as Hellena in Aphra Behn's *The Rover*
1741–2: as Lady Brute in John Vanbrugh's *The Provok'd Wife*; as Lady Betty Modish in Colly Cibber's *The Careless Husband*; as Cordelia in *King Lear*
1742–3: as Lady Anne in *Richard III*
1746–7: as Kate Hotspur in *Henry IV* Part 1; as Cleopatra in John Dryden's *All for Love*
1754 onwards: as Jocasta in *Oedipus* by Dryden and Nathaniel Lee; as Roxana in Lee's *The Rival Queens*
1757: in *As You Like It*

Key portraits

John Lewis, 1753, oil on canvas, National Portrait Gallery, London; Rupert Barber, miniature on enamel, Victoria and Albert Museum, London

Fig.27
Margaret ('Peg') Woffington
John Faber Jr, after John Giles Eccard, 1745

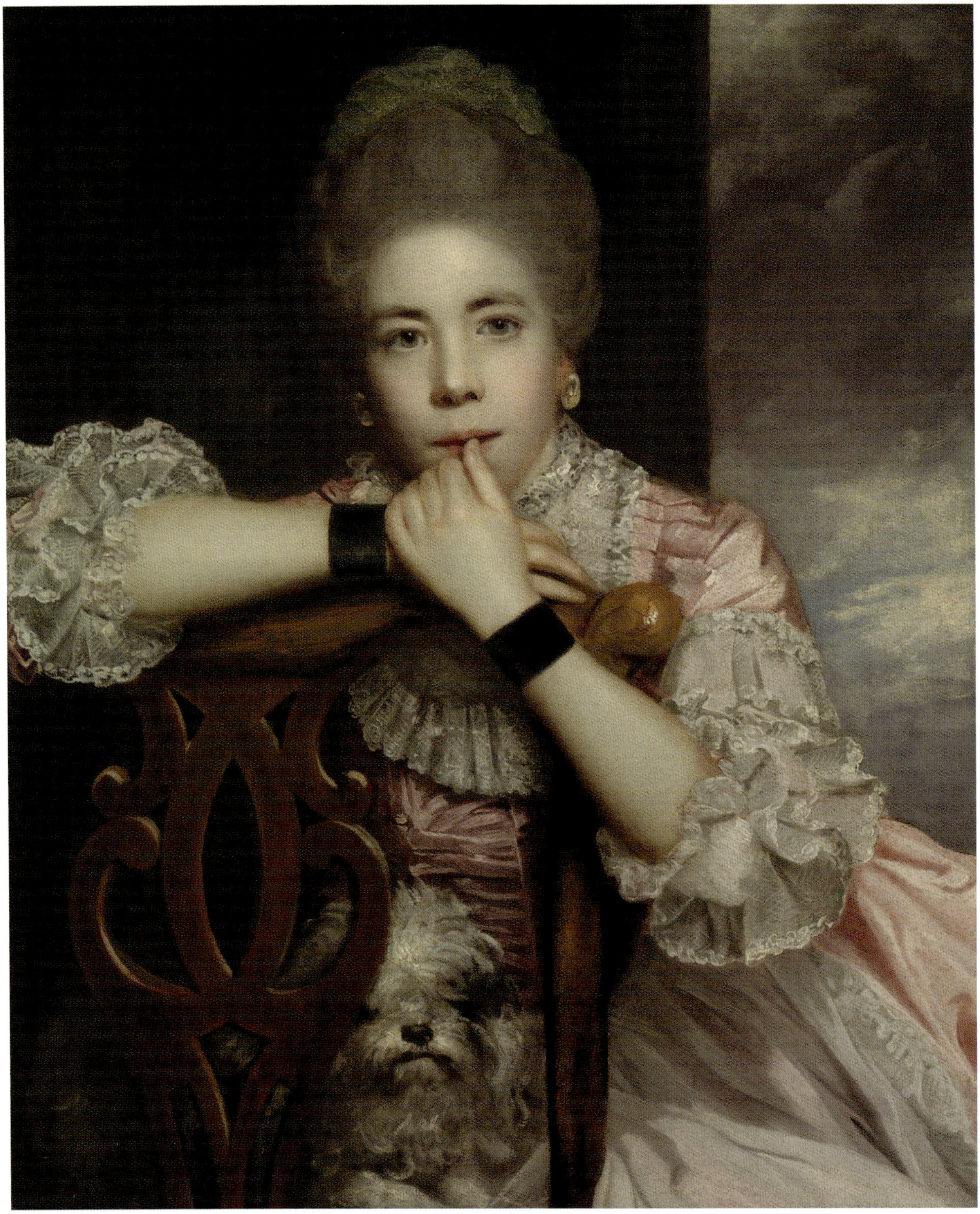

Fig.28

Frances Abington as Miss Prue in *Love for Love*

Sir Joshua Reynolds, 1771

FRANCES ABINGTON

BORN IN 1737 – DIED IN 1815

Frances Abington (née Barton) was the daughter of a soldier in the King's Guard. She grew up in a poor area around Drury Lane and her mother died when she was only fourteen. She worked as a flower girl and a street singer in Covent Garden, where she was known by the nickname 'Nosegay Fan'. She then worked as the servant of a French milliner, from whom she learnt French and a taste for elegant fashion. Contemporary accounts suggest that from an early age, she was determined to make a career on the stage, and made her first appearance at the Haymarket Theatre as Miranda in Susanna Centlivre's play *The Busy Body* in 1755. The following year, on the recommendation of the playwright Samuel Foote, she joined the Drury Lane company. In 1759 she married James Abington, one of the King's Trumpeters. She moved to Dublin in 1759 and took the town by storm in her performance as Lady Townley in John Vanbrugh and Colley Cibber's *The Provok'd Husband* at the Smock Alley theatre. Abington soon became a star and fashion icon in Dublin society and her famous 'Abington cap' was widely copied by milliners. By 1759 she had begun an affair with an Irish Member of Parliament, Mr Needham, and separated from her husband.

After five years in Ireland she returned to London to join the Drury Lane company under David Garrick. Needham died in 1765, leaving Abington well provided for in his will. She soon became one of the leading comic actresses of her day. Her famous roles included the Widow Bellmour in Arthur Murphy's comedy *The Way to Keep Him* and Lady Teazle in Sheridan's *The School for Scandal* (a part written especially for her), which opened to full houses in 1777. After seventeen years at Drury Lane, where she reputedly had a fractious relationship with Garrick, she played at Covent Garden and made her final appearance in 1799. She was a close friend of Sir Joshua Reynolds, who painted many portraits of her. In the late 1770s Abington had become the mistress of William Petty, 1st Marquess of Landsdowne, and she was able to retire on a comfortable income. She died at her Pall Mall home in 1815.

Famous stage roles

1755–6: as Miranda in Susanna Centlivre's *The Busy Body*; as Desdemona in Shakespeare's *Othello*
1756: as Lady Pliant in William Congreve's *The Double Dealer*
1759–60: as Lady Townley in John Vanbrugh and Colley Cibber's *The Provok'd Husband*; as Lucinda in Samuel Foote's *The Englishman in Paris*
1765 onwards: as the Widow Bellmour in Arthur Murphy's *The Way to Keep Him*; as Lady Betty Modish in Cibber's *The Careless Husband*; as Millamant in Congreve's *The Way of the World*
1777: as Lady Teazle in Richard Brinsley Sheridan's *The School for Scandal*
1786: as Scrub in George Farquhar's *The Beaux' Stratagem*
1799: as Lady Racket in Murphy's farce *Three Weeks after Marriage*

Key portraits

Sir Joshua Reynolds, as Miss Prue, 1771, oil on canvas, Yale Center for British Art; Johan Joseph Zoffany, as the Widow Bellmour, 1768, oil on canvas, Petworth House, Sussex; Thomas Hickey, as Lady Bab Lardoon, 1775, oil on canvas, Garrick Club, London

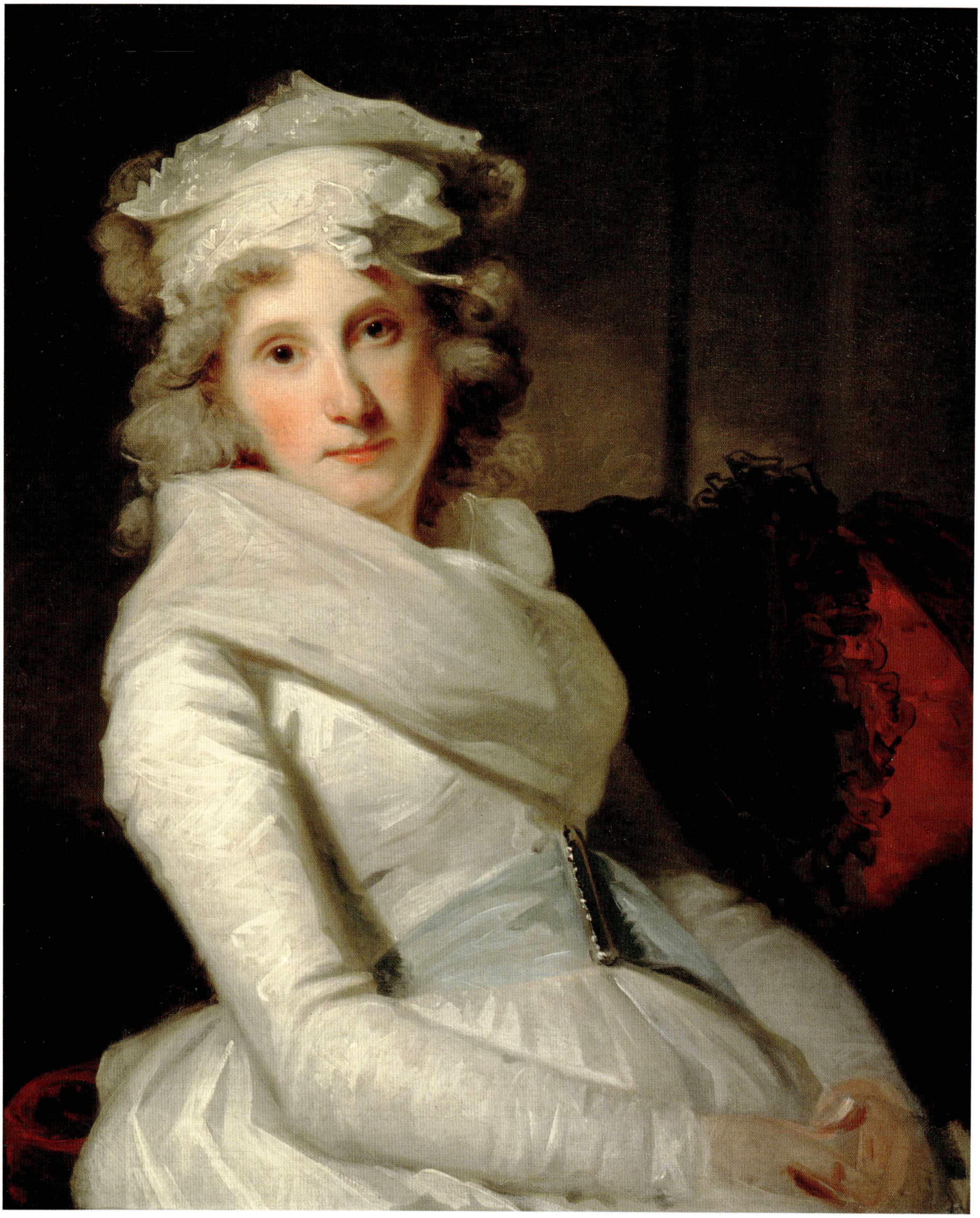

Fig.29

Elizabeth Inchbald

Attrib. John Hoppner, *c.*1789–95

ELIZABETH INCHBALD

BORN IN 1753 – DIED IN 1821

Elizabeth Inchbald (née Simpson) was born in Standingfield, Suffolk, into the large family of a Catholic farmer, John Simpson, and his wife Mary. She showed an early interest in literature and the theatre. Although her brother George became an actor in 1770, Elizabeth's family discouraged her ambition to act. Determined to work in the theatre, she left home in 1772 for London, and soon married the actor Joseph Inchbald. The couple moved to Bristol and Elizabeth made her first stage appearance as Cordelia to Joseph's King Lear in the same year. They toured Scotland with West Digges's theatre company in 1772–6, although Elizabeth's health suffered and her marriage was under strain. After leaving Digges's company the couple stayed briefly in France and Elizabeth began writing for the stage. Later in 1776 they found acting work in Liverpool, where she met Sarah Siddons. The two actresses became lifelong friends, supporting each other's intellectual ambitions. Over the next few years Joseph and Elizabeth acted with various English theatres, including Tate Wilkinson's company in Yorkshire.

After Joseph died suddenly in 1779 Elizabeth continued acting and her best-known leading roles included Desdemona in Shakespeare's *Othello* and the heroine of Nicholas Rowe's *The Tragedy of Jane Shore*. She performed in several new plays of the 1780s, including Hannah Cowley's *The Belle's Stratagem*. Drawing on her stage experience, she began to write plays, including the farce *The Mogul Tale*, which played at the Little Theatre in the Haymarket in 1784. She soon became a successful playwright and nineteen of her dramas were performed in London theatres between 1784 and 1805. Her *Lover's Vows* (1798), adapted from August Kotzebue's *Child of Love*, was the play famously performed in the private theatricals in Jane Austen's *Mansfield Park* (1814). She also began writing fiction and published a successful novel, *A Simple Story*, in 1791. She used some of her novels to criticise the corruption and hypocrisy of late eighteenth-century British society and politics, and her literary successes brought her considerable wealth. She was a well-known figure within London social circles, and her writings challenged dominant views on women's rights, the family and class relations. In old age she increasingly sought seclusion and she died at Kensington House in 1821.

Famous stage roles

1772: as Cordelia in Shakespeare's *King Lear*
1773–6: as lead role in Nicholas Rowe's *The Tragedy of Jane Shore*; as Calista in Rowe's *The Fair Penitent*; as Monimia in Thomas Otway's *The Orphan*; as Desdemona in *Othello*; as Juliet in *Romeo and Juliet*; as Hermione in *The Winter's Tale*; as Perdita in *Florizel and Perdita*; as Violante in Susanna Centlivre's *The Wonder*; as Angelica in George Farquhar's *The Constant Couple*
1780: as Bellario in Beaumont and Fletcher's *Philaster*
1780s: in Hannah Cowley's *The Belle's Stratagem*
1789: as Mrs Blandish in Burgoyne's *The Heiress*

Key portraits

John Russell, *c.*1788, oil on canvas, private collection; George Dance, 1794, pencil drawing, National Portrait Gallery, London; Sir Thomas Lawrence, *c.*1796, oil on canvas, private collection; Samuel de Wilde, as Lady Jane Grey, oil on canvas, Garrick Club, London; John Opie, oil on canvas, Petworth House, Sussex

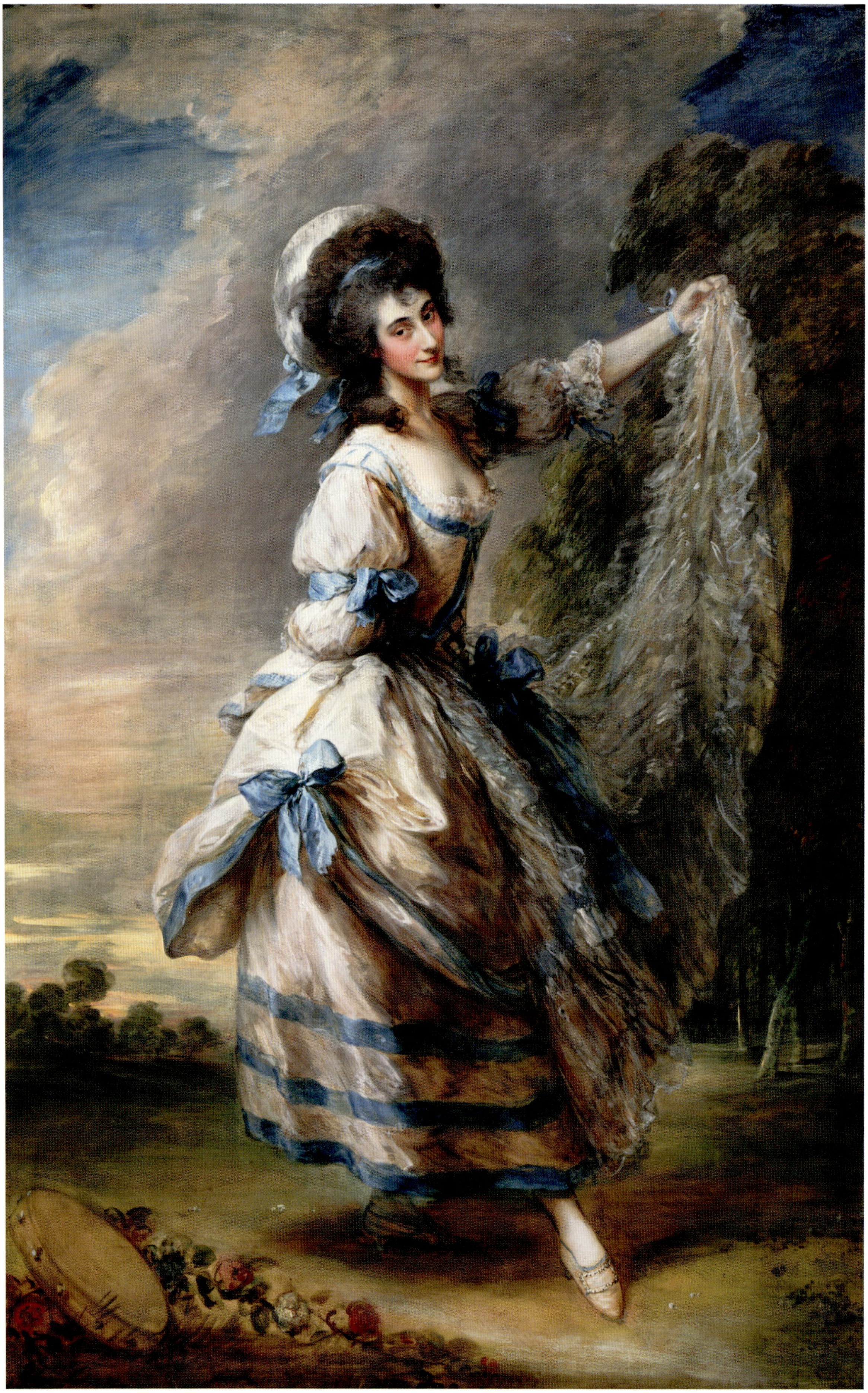

GIOVANNA BACCELLI

BORN CIRCA 1753 – DIED IN 1801

Giovanna Baccelli (née Zanerini) was born in Venice to an itinerant Italian theatrical family. Little is known of her early life, but her sister 'Argentine' Zanerini was a popular actress at the Comédie-Italienne in Paris. Baccelli's mother, Antonietta Rosa Baccelli, remarried after her husband's death and it may be that Giovanna took the name of – or was the daughter of – the second husband. Giovanna (also known as 'Gianetta' or 'Janetta') may have trained in France, and was fluent in Italian and French as well as speaking English, which suited the international itinerary of a travelling performer. Baccelli first appeared in London in November 1774 when she danced as the Rose in 'Le ballet des fleurs', from Rameau's opera *Les Indes galantes* at the King's Theatre, Haymarket. She remained at the Haymarket, apart from performances in Paris and Italy, until 1789, becoming one of London's most popular dancers. By 1779 Baccelli had become the mistress of John Frederick Sackville, 3rd Duke of Dorset, and moved in with him at the family seat – Knole, in Kent. She accompanied the Duke to Paris when he was appointed British ambassador there in 1783 where, according to *The Morning Herald*, she lived 'in great splendour', and 'her house is the resort of all the fashionable English in that gay metropolis' (9 February 1785). During this period she also continued to dance at the Paris Opéra.

The Duke's health began to suffer and the events of the Revolution caused the couple to return to Knole, although Baccelli left the house for good in 1789, leaving her son behind with the Duke. During their relationship the Duke commissioned portraits of Baccelli by Sir Joshua Reynolds, Ozias Humphry, the sculptor Giovan Battista Locatelli and Thomas Gainsborough, who painted her in the ballet *Les amans surpris*, one of her most famous roles of the 1781–2 season. After her separation from the Duke, Baccelli enjoyed a close friendship with Henry Herbert, Earl of Pembroke, who died in 1794. After this she settled in Sackville Street, Piccadilly with a James Carey. She died a wealthy woman in 1801.

Famous stage roles

1774: as the Rose in 'Le ballet des fleurs' from Rameau's opera *Les Indes galantes*
1775: as Galatea in Bougueton's *Pigmalion amoureux de sa statue*; as Clytemnestra in Vallouis's *Oreste et Electre*; as the Victim in *Le Triomphe d'Euthime sur le genie de Libas*
1779: as Atalante in *Hippomene et Atalante*
1780–1: principal ballerina, King's Theatre, Haymarket; as Creusa in *Médée et Jason*
1781–2: in *Les amants surpris* (the Surprised Lovers), staged by French ballet-master Jean-Georges Noverre

Key portraits

Thomas Gainsborough, exhib. 1782, oil on canvas, Tate Britain; Sir Joshua Reynolds, 1783, oil on canvas, and Giovan Battista Locatelli, *c.*1781, marble sculpture, both Sackville Collection, Knole Estate, Kent

Fig.30
Giovanna Baccelli
Thomas Gainsborough, exhib. 1782

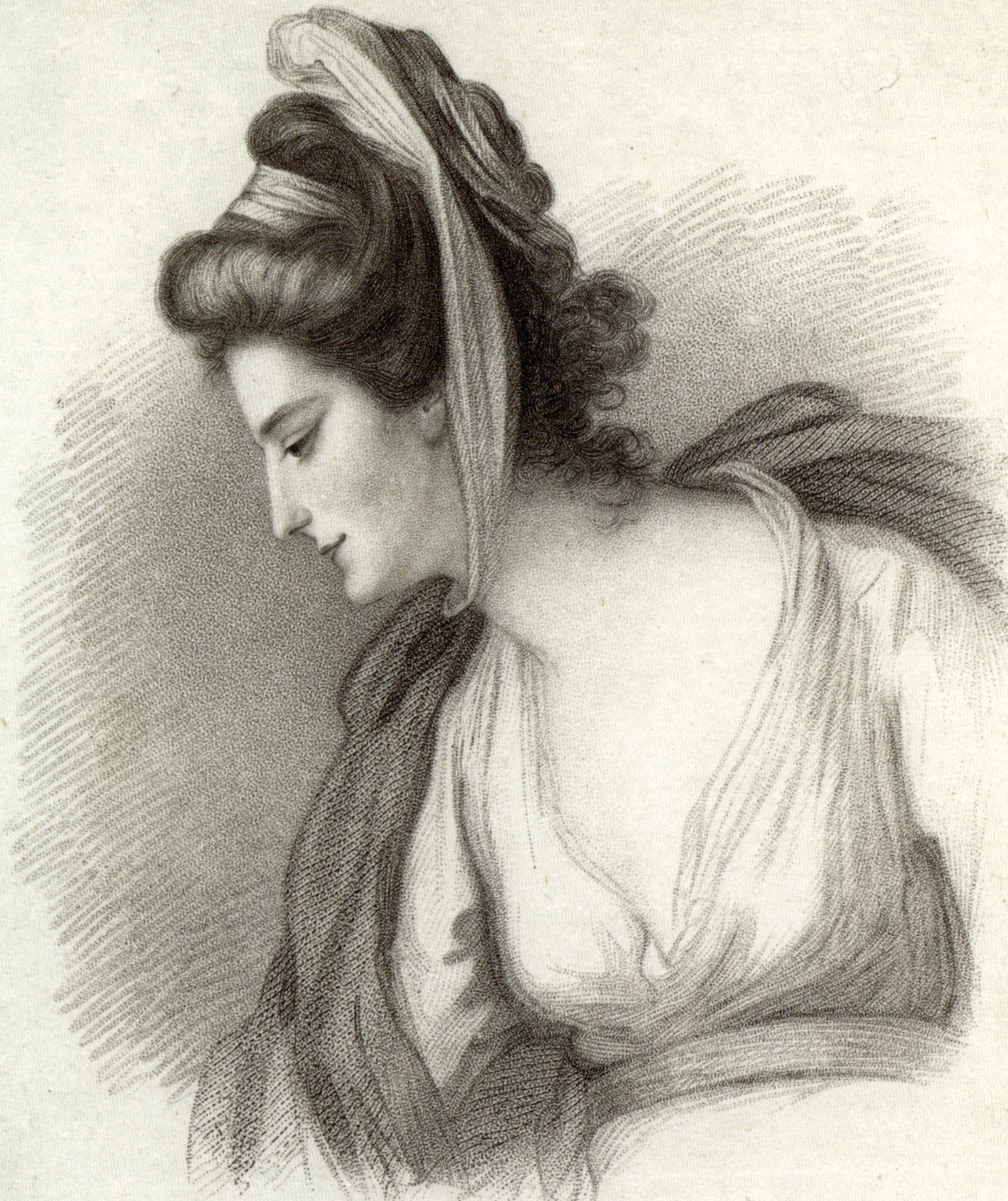

Mrs. Elizabeth Sheridan.

Engraved by H. Meyer, from a Drawing by Ozias Humphry, R.A.

London Published by Henry Colburn Conduit Street 1816.

ELIZABETH ANN SHERIDAN

BORN IN 1754 – DIED IN 1792

Elizabeth Ann Sheridan (née Linley) was the eldest surviving daughter of Thomas Linley, a conductor, composer and music teacher, and his wife, Mary Johnson, all of whose children became talented musicians. Trained by her father, Elizabeth sang in Bath's weekly concerts from the age of twelve. In the early 1770s she performed with her sister Mary and brother Thomas in Oxford, Chester, Worcester and London. Elizabeth was renowned for her voice, beauty and intelligence, and David Garrick affectionately called her 'the Saint'. The novelist Fanny Burney praised her voice, and when Thomas Linley took his family to London for the oratorio season in 1773, Burney wrote that the whole town seemed to be absorbed with her: 'Miss Linley alone engrosses all eyes, ears, hearts' (*Early Journals and Letters*, vol. 1, p.249). She attracted numerous admirers; one was satirised in Samuel Foote's comedy based on her life, *The Maid of Bath*, performed between 1772 and 1775 at the Haymarket. Linley received many marriage proposals, but eloped to France in 1772 with Richard Brinsley Sheridan. On their return Sheridan fought two duels with another of his wife's admirers, Captain Thomas Mathews.

The Bath Chronicle estimated that Linley's father made nearly £10,000 from her voice, but on her official marriage to Sheridan in April 1773 her public career ended, as Sheridan insisted that his new wife could no longer perform in public. He declined the large sums of money that were offered for her performances, believing that her appearance in public concerts would compromise his own reputation (her sister Mary also 'retired' on marriage). Sheridan, Thomas Linley and a Dr Ford bought Garrick's share in the Drury Lane Theatre in 1776 and were assisted as theatre managers by Elizabeth, who kept accounts, auditioned singers, and helped with Sheridan's compositions and manuscripts, composing her own music for *Robinson Crusoe*. She suffered from fragile health and several miscarriages. In 1775 she gave birth to one surviving son, Tom, but died from tuberculosis in June 1792, at the age of 37. She was buried at Wells Cathedral.

Famous stage roles

1763 onwards: Bath concerts
1767: in Thomas Hull's *The Fairy Favour*
1770s: Concerts and oratorios nationwide including Handel's *Samson*
1773: London oratorio season

Key portraits

Thomas Gainsborough, double portrait (with her brother), *c.*1768, oil on canvas, Sterling and Francine Clark Art Institute, Williamstown, Mass.; Gainsborough, double portrait (with her sister Mary), *c.*1771–2, oil on canvas, Dulwich Picture Gallery, London; Gainsborough, *c.*1775, oil on canvas, Philadelphia Museum of Art; Sir Joshua Reynolds, as St Cecilia, 1775, oil on canvas, Waddesdon Manor, Bucks; Gainsborough, *c.*1785–7, oil on canvas, National Gallery of Art, Washington, D.C.

Fig.31

Elizabeth Ann Sheridan

Henry Meyer, after Ozias Humphry, 1816

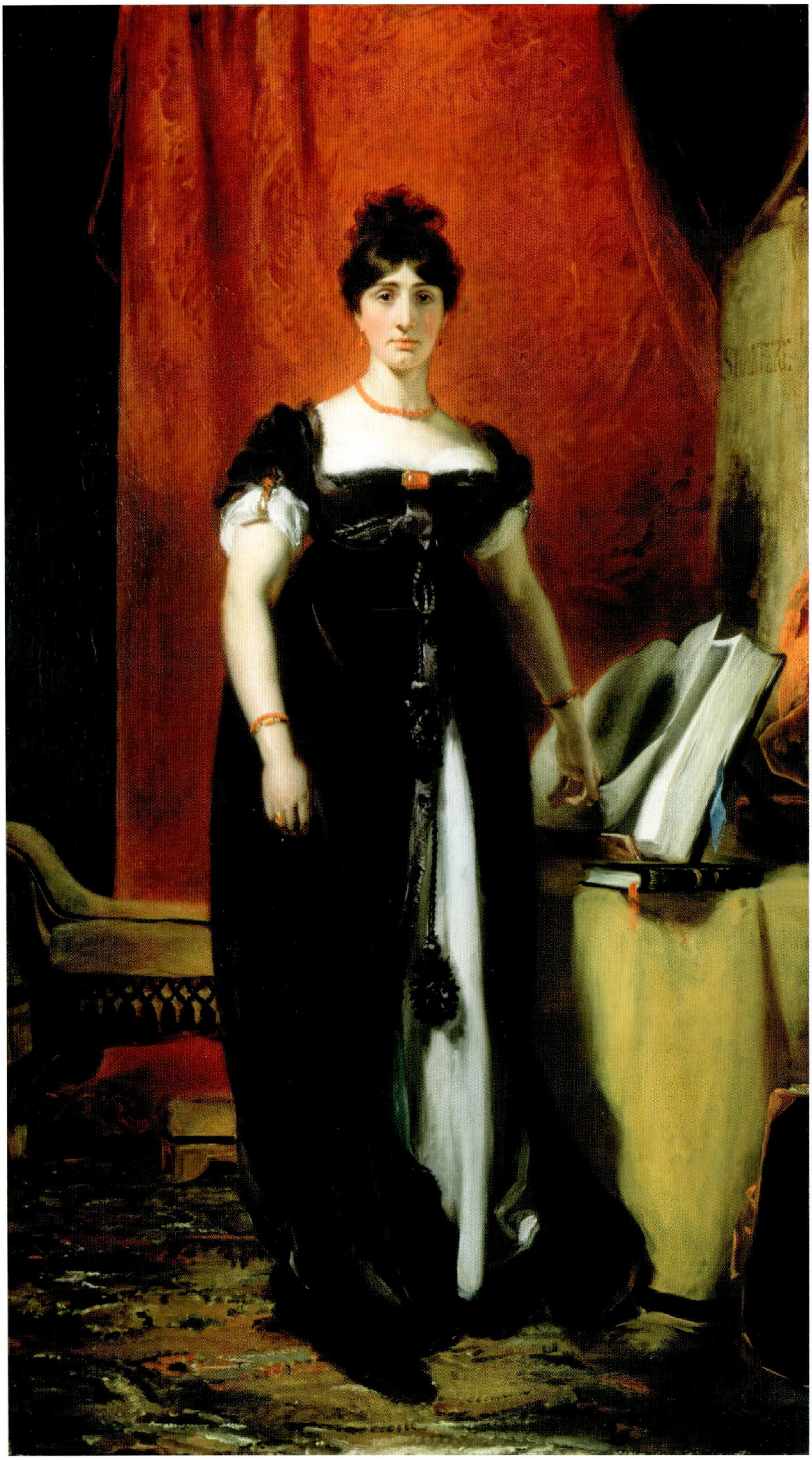

SARAH SIDDONS

BORN IN 1755 – DIED IN 1831

Sarah Siddons (née Kemble) was the daughter of Roger Kemble, a provincial actor and theatre manager, and the actress Sarah Ward. Seven of her brothers and sisters went onto the stage, of whom John and Charles Kemble were the best known. Born in Brecon, most of Sarah's childhood was spent travelling with her father's theatre company. At the age of eighteen she married the actor William Siddons, with whom she had worked in the provinces. After being spotted by Lord Bruce of Tottenham, and recommended to David Garrick, she first appeared at Drury Lane in December 1775, although her contract was not renewed for the following season. In her memoirs Siddons recalls the hardships and disappointments of those early years, when she continued working in poor health for the sake of her children. By 1782 she already had four children (a fifth had died in infancy) and had become established as the leading actress of the Bath Theatre Company. She accepted a contract from Richard Brinsley Sheridan to return to the Drury Lane stage in London for the 1782–3 season, and soon established a reputation as the leading tragic actress of her day, playing an important role in helping to raise the social and professional status of the theatre.

Siddons achieved particular renown for her performances as Isabella in David Garrick's adaptation of Thomas Southerne's *Isabella or, The Fatal Marriage*, Belvidera in Thomas Otway's *Venice Preserv'd*, and the title role in Nicholas Rowe's *The Tragedy of Jane Shore*. Siddons's acting reputedly had a powerful impact on her audiences. Her biographer James Boaden recorded that during her performance as Isabella, when she was about to plunge a dagger into her bosom, most of the audience were too overwhelmed and distraught to use their hands to applaud. Later she became famous for her Lady Macbeth, which she played for her farewell appearance in June 1812. She was respected for her intelligence and supposedly 'moral' character, and became a close friend of Samuel Johnson, Horace Walpole and Sir Joshua Reynolds. She was painted by many successful portraitists, among them Thomas Gainsborough, Sir William Beechey, George Romney, Sir Thomas Lawrence, and Reynolds. She outlived five of her seven children, and several younger members of her family established successful careers on the stage, including her son Henry and her niece Fanny Kemble.

Fig.32
Sarah Siddons
Sir Thomas Lawrence, 1804

Famous stage roles

1766: as Ariel in Shakespeare's *The Tempest*
1774: as Belvidera in Thomas Otway's *Venice Preserv'd*
1775: as Portia in *The Merchant of Venice*; as Rosalind in *As You Like It*
1779–80: as Queen Katharine in *Henry VIII*; as Lady Macbeth
1782: the title role in David Garrick's *Isabella, or, The Fatal Marriage*
1783: in Edward Moore's *The Gamester*; as Constance in *King John*, opposite her brother John Kemble as the King
1787: as Volumnia in *Coriolanus*
1801–2: as Hermione in *The Winter's Tale*
1811–12: the title role in Nicholas Rowe's *The Tragedy of Jane Shore*

Key portraits

Sir Thomas Lawrence, as Mrs Haller, 1796–8, oil on canvas, Tate Britain; George Romney, 1783, oil on canvas, private collection; Sir Joshua Reynolds, Sarah Siddons as the Tragic Muse, 1784, oil on canvas, The Huntington Art Gallery, California; Thomas Gainsborough, *c.*1785, oil on canvas, National Portrait Gallery, London; Sir William Beechey, 1793, oil on canvas, National Portrait Gallery, London; Richard Westall, as Lady Macbeth, oil on canvas, Garrick Club, London

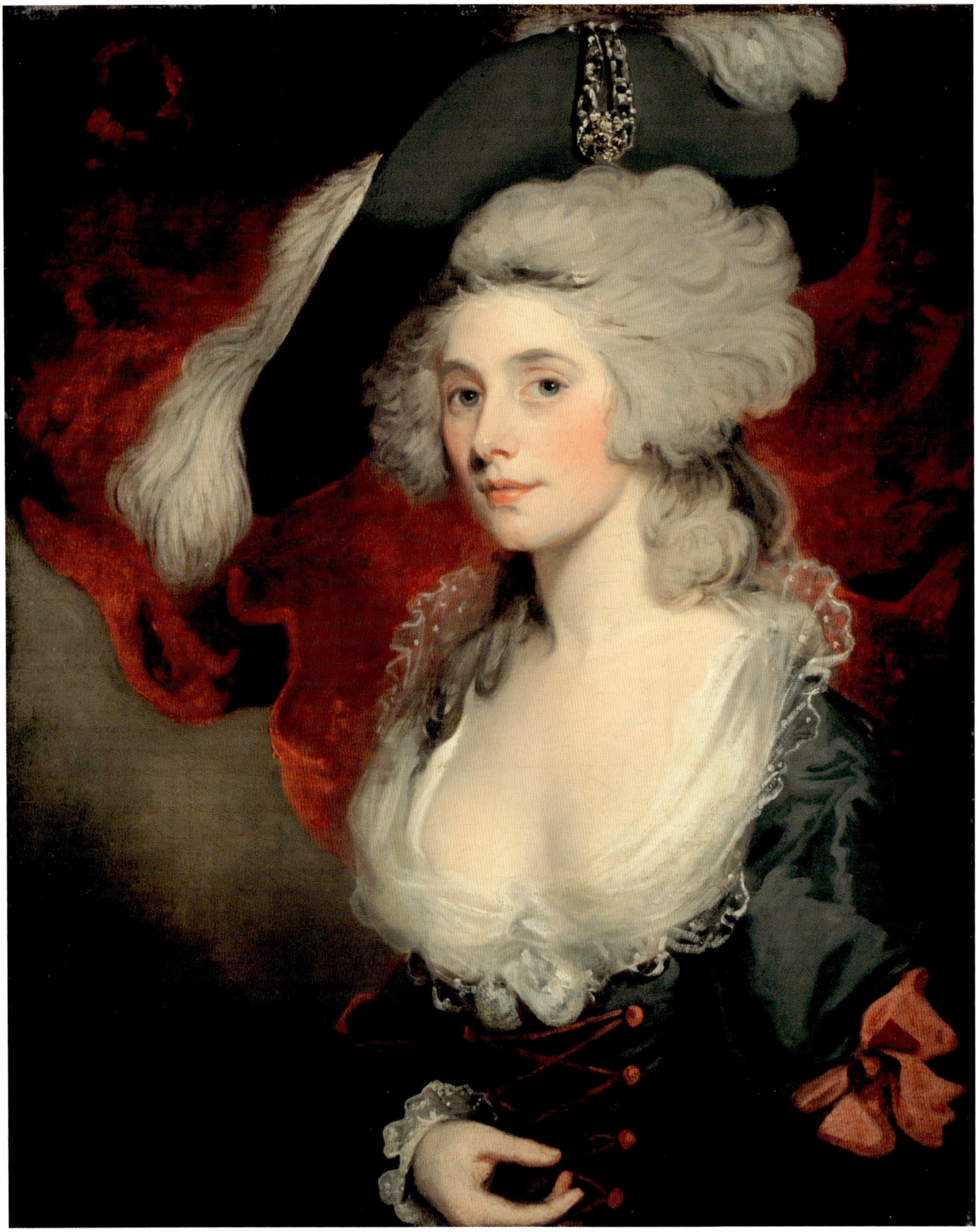

Fig.33

Mary Robinson – Perdita

John Hoppner, 1782

MARY ROBINSON

BORN IN 1756/8 – DIED IN 1800

Mary Robinson (née Darby) was born in Bristol, the daughter of a merchant and sea captain, Nicholas Darby, and his wife Hester. Her father was often away, developing ill-conceived financial schemes, and became increasingly remote, until eventually he separated from his wife. Mary and her brother John were sent to London, where Mary was taught by a woman called Lorrington, and learned several foreign languages. In 1771 her mother opened a boarding school in Chelsea, where Mary taught English, but they were forced to close the establishment under pressure from her father. Mary showed an early interest in acting and David Garrick took her on as his protégée at Drury Lane. In 1773 she married Thomas Robinson, an articled clerk, and their daughter Maria Elizabeth was born in 1774. The following year Thomas Robinson was confined to the King's Bench Prison for bankruptcy as a result of his profligate life within fashionable society. This encouraged Mary to pursue an independent income by publishing her poems, which attracted the attention of Georgiana, Duchess of Devonshire.

Robinson then pursued her early interest in acting, with the support of Garrick, and first appeared at Drury Lane in 1776. She soon became an acclaimed actress renowned for her beauty and her love of fashion. After a famous royal command performance as Perdita in *The Winter's Tale* in 1779, she was pursued by the young Prince of Wales, with whom she became involved in 1780, although the affair was short-lived. Robinson separated from her husband and gave up her stage career. By 1783 she had been painted by many famous portraitists, including Sir Joshua Reynolds, George Romney and Thomas Gainsborough, and her private life had been featured regularly in the satirical press, including her much publicised affairs with Sir Banastre Tarleton and the Whig politician Charles James Fox. In the summer of 1783 Robinson's health was undermined by a stroke, and she was later crippled by rheumatism, but she continued writing poems, plays and novels. In 1799 she published an influential pamphlet on women's rights, *A Letter to the Women of England, on the Injustice of Mental Subordination*. Left exhausted by work and illness, her health deteriorated and she died in 1800.

Famous stage roles

1776: as Juliet in Shakespeare's *Romeo and Juliet*
1776–7: as Amanda in Richard Brinsley Sheridan's *The Trip to Scarborough*; as Fanny in *The Clandestine Marriage* by David Garrick and George Colman the Elder
1777–8: as the Lady in John Milton's *Comus*; as Araminta in John Vanbrugh's *The Confederacy*; as Octavia in John Dryden's *All for Love*; as Lady Macbeth
1778–9: as Palmira in James Miller's *Mahomet*; as Jacintha in Benjamin Hoadly's *The Suspicious Husband*; as Fidelia in William Wycherley's *The Plain Dealer*
1779–80: as Viola in *Twelfth Night*; as Perdita in *The Winter's Tale*; as Rosalind in *As You Like It*; as Oriana in George Farquhar's *The Inconstant*, and Eliza Campley in Lady Craven's comedy *The Miniature Picture*

Key portraits

George Romney, 1781, oil on canvas, Wallace Collection, London; John Hoppner, 1782, oil on canvas, Waddesdon Manor, Bucks; John Hoppner, 1782, oil on canvas, Chawton House Library, Hants; Sir Joshua Reynolds, exhib. 1782, oil on canvas, Waddesdon Manor, Bucks; attrib. Johan Joseph Zoffany, as Rosalind, oil on canvas, Garrick Club, London

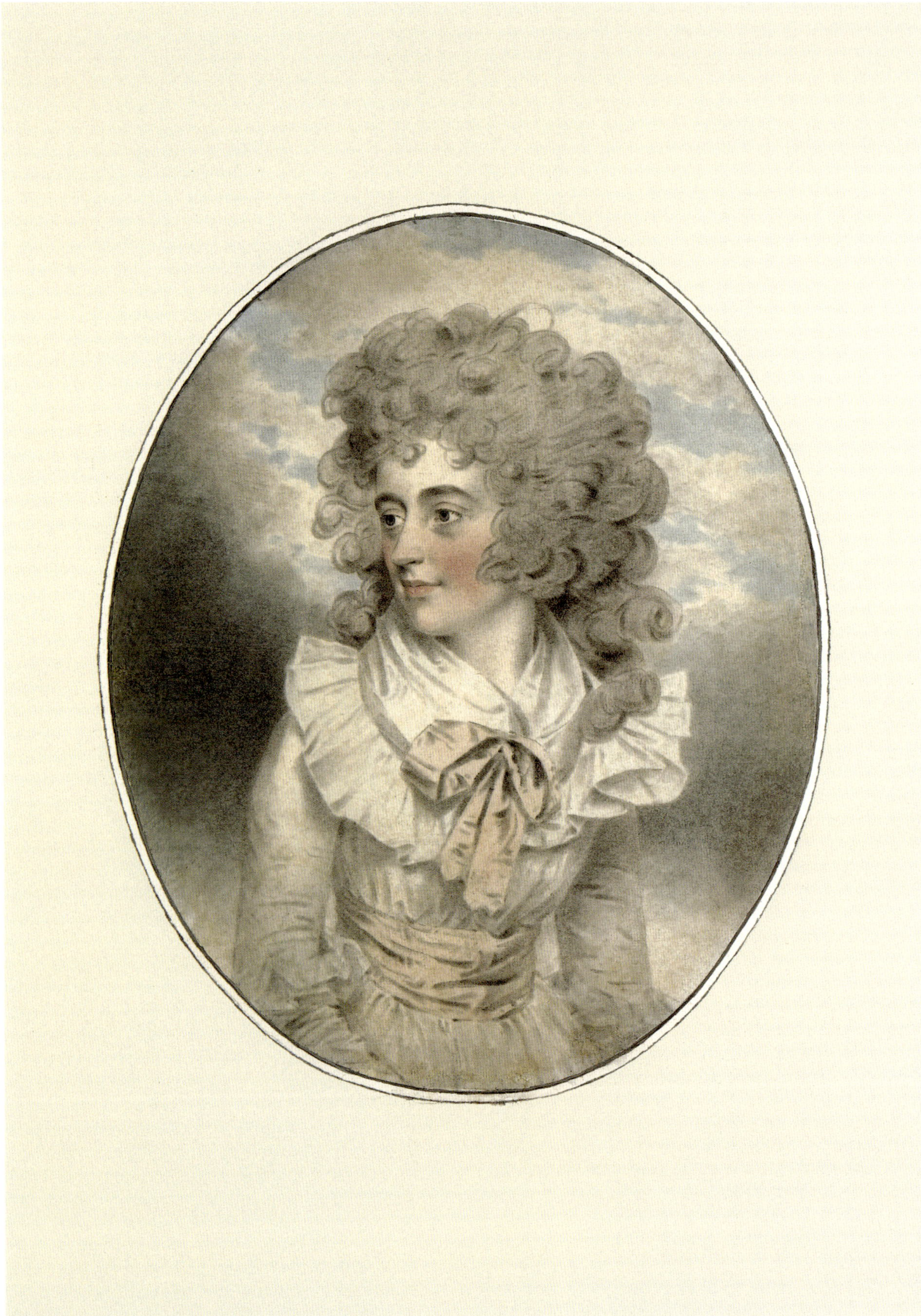

Fig.34

Elizabeth Farren, later Countess of Derby

John Downman, 1787

ELIZABETH FARREN

BORN IN 1759 – DIED IN 1829

Elizabeth Farren (or Farran) was born in the West Country, the daughter of George and Margaret Farren, who ran a touring company until George died in 1770, leaving four daughters. Elizabeth acted her first part at the age of ten, and by 1773 she was working with her mother and sisters for James Whitley, manager of a Midlands theatrical circuit. Farren's earliest performances consisted of singing entr'acte songs and appearing in pantomimes. Her best-known early roles included Rosetta in Isaac Bickerstaff's *Love in a Village* and Lady Townley in *The Provok'd Husband* by Colley Cibber and John Vanbrugh, at the Theatre Royal, Liverpool. Farren's first London appearance was as Miss Hardcastle in Oliver Goldsmith's *She Stoops to Conquer* in 1777, after which *The Morning Chronicle* praised her performance, claiming 'Miss Farren is ... more perfect than most of the theatrical ladies who have been initiated into the profession in country seminaries' (10 June 1777).

For the next twenty years Farren was one of the leading comic actresses at Drury Lane, and her famous Shakespearean roles included Hermione in *The Winter's Tale*, Beatrice in *Much Ado about Nothing*, and Lady Teazle in Sheridan's *The School for Scandal*. Farren became the mistress of Edward, 12th Earl of Derby, in 1785 or 1786. She helped to manage the Duke of Richmond's private theatricals at Richmond House – attended by George III and Queen Charlotte, along with famous figures from the theatre, art and politics – in 1787–8. Sir Thomas Lawrence's full-length portrait of Farren was exhibited at the Royal Academy in 1790 (fig.83), next to his portrait of Queen Charlotte. Following the death of the Countess of Derby, Farren made her farewell appearance as Lady Teazle at Drury Lane in April 1797; the performance brought record takings at the box office. On 1 May she married Lord Derby and soon afterwards was presented to the Queen. Farren had four children and was known for her vivacious entertaining at the family seat, Knowsley Hall, until her death in 1829.

Famous stage roles

1774 onwards: as Rosetta in Isaac Bickerstaff's *Love in a Village*
1777: as Kate Hardcastle in Oliver Goldsmith's *She Stoops to Conquer*; as Rosina in the première of George Colman the Elder's adaptation of Beaumarchais's *Le barbier de Séville*
1778: in Colman's *The Suicide*; as Lady Townley in John Vanbrugh and Colley Cibber's *The Provok'd Husband*
1780s: as Hermione in *The Winter's Tale*; as Beatrice in *Much Ado about Nothing*
1797: as Lady Teazle in Richard Brinsley Sheridan's *The School for Scandal*

Key portraits

Johan Joseph Zoffany, *c.*1780, oil on canvas, National Gallery of Victoria, Melbourne; John Downman, 1787, chalk drawing, National Portrait Gallery, London; Sir Thomas Lawrence, exhib. 1790, oil on canvas, Metropolitan Museum of Art, New York; Edward Francisco Burney, as Olivia, ink and wash drawing, British Museum, London; Johann Heinrich Ramberg, drawing, as Desdemona, British Museum, London

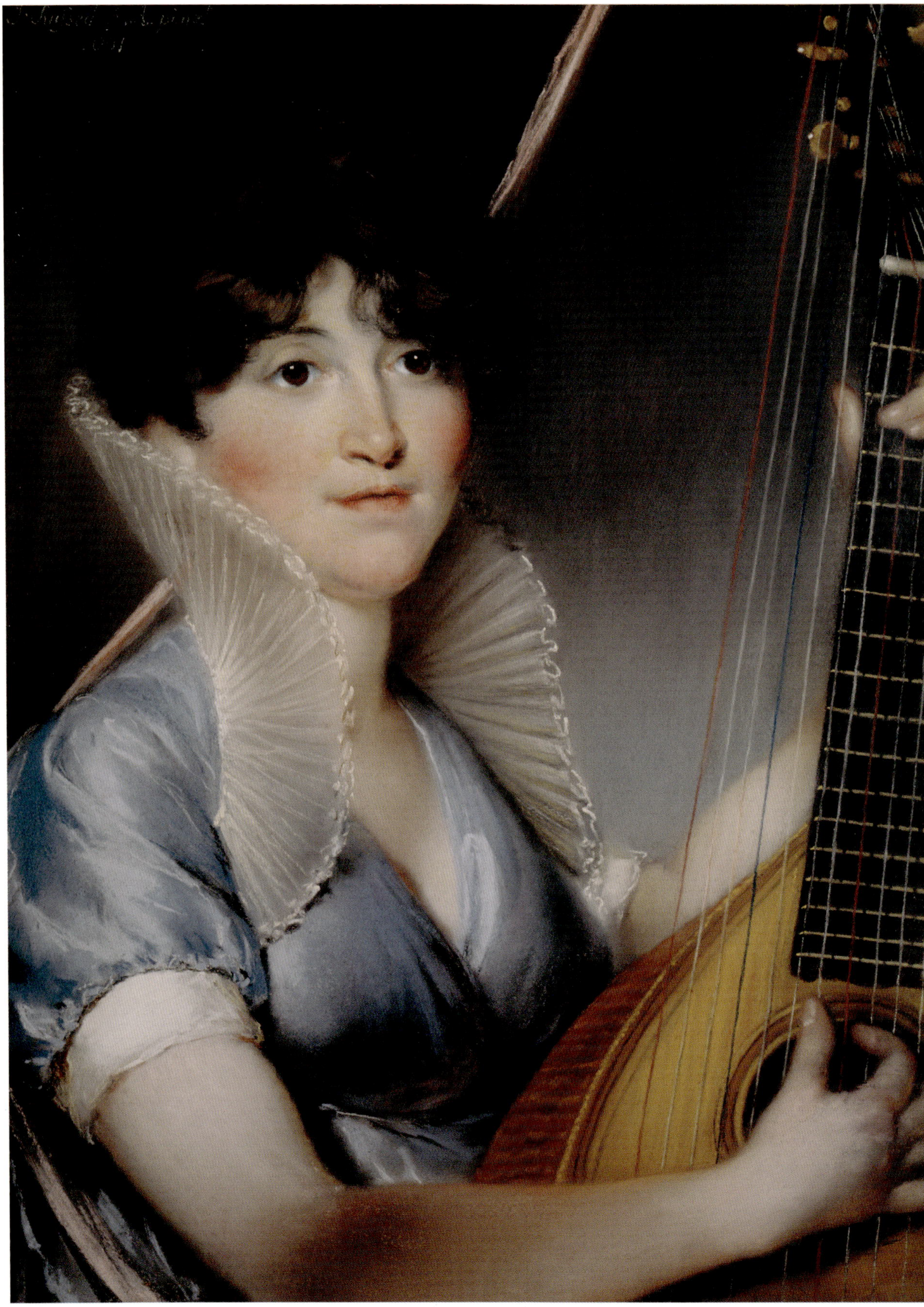

Fig.35

Dorothy Jordan

John Russell, 1801

DOROTHY JORDAN

BORN IN 1761 – DIED IN 1816

Dorothy Jordan (née Phillips) was born in London in 1761 to an Irish father, Francis Bland, and Welsh mother, Grace Phillips, both of whom worked on the Dublin stage, but whose marriage was invalid as they were under-age. After her father abandoned the family, to marry an heiress when Dorothy was thirteen, she became the main breadwinner, working in a hat shop. She soon followed her mother onto the stage and became pregnant by the Dublin theatre manager Richard Daly. Her daughter Fanny was born in 1782. Along with her mother, she left Ireland for Yorkshire and was given work by the stage manager Tate Wilkinson, adopting the stage name 'Mrs Jordan'. While touring in Wilkinson's company she won a reputation for her acting abilities, especially her comic roles. In 1785 she moved to Drury Lane, where she was an instant success, renowned for her skills in speaking verse, singing, comic timing and breeches parts. She was best known for roles such as Peggy in David Garrick's *The Country Girl*, Viola in Shakespeare's *Twelfth Night* and Hypolita in Colley Cibber's comedy *She Would and She Would Not* (fig.71).

Jordan's popularity provoked a so-called 'Jordan-mania' in London, and during her twenty-four years as one of the stars of the Theatre Royal, Drury Lane, she enjoyed a high salary and was painted by many famous portraitists, including John Hoppner, George Romney and Sir William Beechey (figs 71, 75). In 1786 Richard Ford, a young lawyer, became her lover, and their child, Dora, was born in 1787. By 1790 Jordan was being wooed by Prince William, Duke of Clarence (later King William IV), and she parted from Ford. In 1791 she began a relationship with the Duke, which was to last twenty years. They lived together at Bushy House, an estate near Hampton Court Palace, and had ten children. Jordan continued working on the stage, helping to support her family. In 1811, under pressure from the royal family, Prince William broke off the relationship. Jordan accepted the loss with dignity, but never recovered from the blow. She continued to work to support her children, but suffered tragedy at the end of her life. She was cheated by a son-in-law and was probably forced to flee to France, where she died alone and in relative poverty in 1816.

Famous stage roles

1779 onwards: as Rosalind in Shakespeare's *As You Like It*; as Viola in *Twelfth Night*; as Sir Harry Wildair in George Farquhar's *The Constant Couple*; as Priscilla Tomboy in Isaac Bickerstaff's *The Romp*; as Anne in *Richard III* and Adelaide in Robert Jephson's *The Count of Narbonne*
1785 onwards: as Peggy in David Garrick's *The Country Girl;* as Hoyden in *The Relapse* by John Vanbrugh; as Widow Cheerly in Andrew Cherry's comedy *The Soldier's Daughter*; as Angela in Matthew 'Monk' Lewis's *The Castle Spectre*; as Lady Teazle in Richard Brinsley Sheridan's *The School for Scandal*; as Hypolita in Colley Cibber's comedy *She Would and She Would Not*

Key portraits

George Romney, as the Country Girl, 1786–7, oil on canvas, Waddesdon Manor, Bucks; Sir William Beechey, as Rosalind, 1787, oil on canvas, private collection; John Hoppner, as Hypolita, exhib. 1791, oil on canvas, National Portrait Gallery, London; John Hoppner, as Viola, *c.*1796, oil on canvas, Kenwood House, London; John Russell, 1801, oil on canvas, Fenton House, London; Sir Francis Chantrey, statue, 1834, Royal Collection; Samuel de Wilde, as Phaedra, oil on canvas, Garrick Club, London

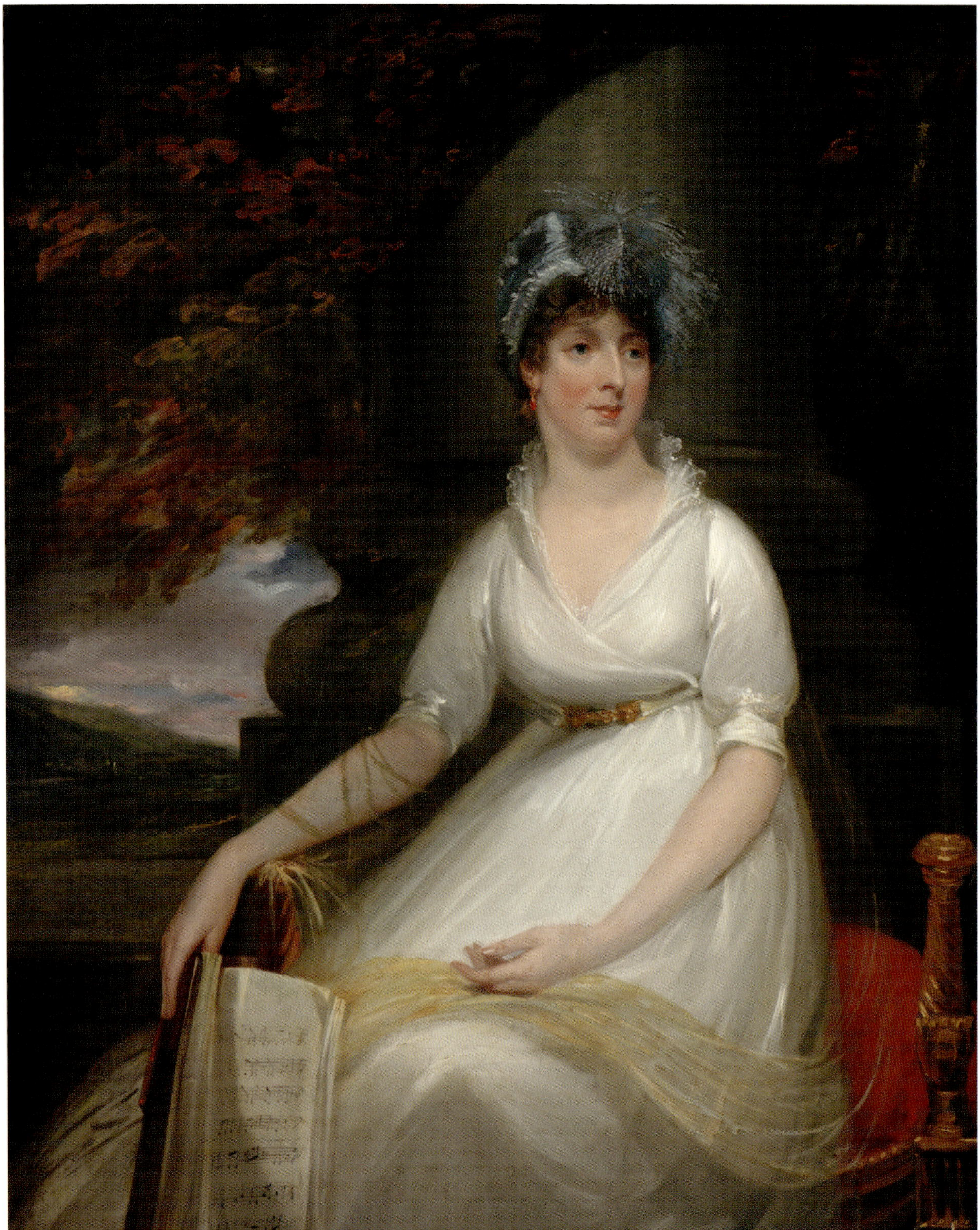

Fig.36

Elizabeth Billington

John Hoppner, *c.*1801

ELIZABETH BILLINGTON

BORN IN 1765 – DIED IN 1818

Elizabeth Billington (née Weichsel) was the daughter of a German musician, Carl Friedrich Weichsel, who was the principal oboist at the King's Theatre, and Fredericka Weirman, a singer at Vauxhall. Born in London, Elizabeth and her brother Charles were child prodigies and performed concertos on piano and violin respectively. Elizabeth became a fine pianist and composer of sonatas for both violin and piano. She married a voice teacher and double bass player, James Billington, in 1783, and began her theatrical career in Gluck's *Orfeo ed Euridice* in Dublin in 1784. Her only daughter was born in 1784 but died shortly afterwards. Billington's many affairs, including one with the theatre manager Richard Daly, were the subject of much scurrilous gossip. In 1786 she was wildly successful as Rosetta in Thomas Arne's *Love in a Village* at Covent Garden. As Fanny Burney reported in her journal, 'no song seems too high or too rapid for her execution' and she possessed an 'exquisitely sweet tone' and 'considerable knowledge of music.' Billington performed in the Handel Jubilee commemorations in Westminster Abbey in 1786, and made regular appearances at Vauxhall Gardens and in Lenten oratorios.

In 1793 Billington travelled to Italy with her husband and brother. Here she met Sir William and Lady Emma Hamilton and the King and Queen of Naples, and made her debut in Bianchi's *Ines de Castro,* a part that was written especially for her. Following the sudden death of her husband, Billington toured Italy with her brother between 1796 and 1799, winning the highest European reputation of any English singer at that time. While in Milan she met the man who was to become her second husband, a Frenchman named Felican. Their relationship rapidly deteriorated because of his violence towards her. Billington returned to England and made a famous appearance as Mandane in Arne's *Artaxerxes* at Covent Garden in 1801. She sang at Drury Lane and Covent Garden, and for the Italian Opera Company at the Queen's Theatre from 1802 to 1806, receiving an unprecedented salary of £2600 for her final season. Billington retired to her villa in Fulham in 1811 for health reasons and died in Venice in 1818.

Famous stage roles

1784: in Gluck's *Orfeo ed Euridice*
1786: as Rosetta in Thomas Arne's *Love in a Village*; Handel Jubilee commemorations
1786–8, 1791–2: professional concerts; Concerts of Ancient Music; Lenten oratorios
1794: in Bianchi's *Ines de Castro*
1796–9: in roles created for her by Paisiello, Paer, Nasolini, Himmel, and other leading composers
1801: as Mandane in Arne's *Artaxerxes*
1804: in Peter von Winter's *Il trionfo dell'amore fraterno*
1806: as Vitellia in Mozart's *La clemenza di Tito*

Key portraits

Sir Joshua Reynolds, as St Cecilia, 1789, oil on canvas, Beaverbrook Art Gallery, Fredericton, New Brunswick; James Gillray, 1801 and 1803, etchings, National Portrait Gallery, London; John Hoppner, *c.*1801, oil on canvas, Peter Moores Foundation

NELL GWYN

AND COVENT GARDEN GODDESSES

by Joseph Roach

NELL GWYN

AND COVENT GARDEN GODDESSES

Even though she made a spectacle of herself in an age of painted beauties, there has always been more to Nell Gwyn's image than meets the eye. Born into obscure poverty, Eleanor Gwyn pioneered modern celebrity, living her private life in public as a theatrical and social icon. For someone who was arguably the single most important prototype for the culture of charismatic celebrity in which we now live, her time on the boards was remarkably brief: she debuted at the Theatre Royal in 1664 aged fourteen and retired for good in 1671 at twenty-one. During that exciting seven-year run, which included interruptions caused by the Great Plague and the Fire of London, along with an absent-without-leave hiatus from the stage in the keeping of a titled admirer (in this instance, Charles Sackville, Lord Buckhurst), Gwyn drew an inordinate degree of public attention to herself. The glamour and scandal of the roles she played carried over into her off-stage persona, and vice versa, never to be relinquished, neither during her lifetime nor after it (fig.37).

Image-Making and 'Public Intimacy'

The attention paid to Nell Gwyn has always mixed the personal with the professional, notoriety with celebrity, so that her name has become a catch-all for miscellaneous guilty pleasures, prefiguring the concept of what today we call an 'image'. An image in this sense, which Gwyn pioneered, means that the idea of a celebrity – character, life-story and look – circulates in the absence of her person. Few of the anecdotes by which Gwyn is best remembered can be verified beyond the shadow of a doubt, but enough of them persist (and enough of them *fit*) that, taken together, they reliably mark the passage of an extraordinarily vivid personality through the imaginative life of her tribe. That journey, comet-like, continues its ascending arc; but the same caveats pertain to the visual record as to the archival. The shaky iconography of her portraits, like the anecdote-rich, document-poor narrative of her life, paradoxically proves the durability and power of her after-image, which persists as legend even in the historical darkness, like the shape of a flame that glows in the retina after the candle has gone out.[1]

Only a few portraits exist in which Gwyn can be securely identified as the sitter, but that embarrassment has not stopped generations of hopefuls from trying. As long ago as 1963, David Piper ruefully observed of the connoisseurship on the late seventeenth-century female subject, 'The iconography has been confused almost beyond hope by the continuous baptism of portraits of unknown women of the late seventeenth century with Nell Gwyn's name.'[2] Problems of identification and misidentification persist.[3] Despite the dearth of unassailable fact, eked out by scraps of gossip drawn largely from the diary of the indispensably prurient Admiralty clerk Samuel Pepys (fig.38), the titillating image of Nell Gwyn still prospers as an idea.

The verifiable Gwyn portraits, at least one of which Pepys owned as a print, do flesh out popular fantasies of her by showing her emphatically *décolletée*. In Simon Verelst's feigned oval portrait of circa 1680 (see fig.23), for instance, she appears to have experienced the sort of wardrobe malfunction that models call a 'nipple slip', preventable today by double-sided lingerie tape. This was a visual code that often marked the late seventeenth-century subject as a courtesan, and wholly or partially bared breasts typify images of Gwyn. A long-reigning favourite is the role portrait in the pastoral mode, seen in Gerald Valck's line engraving after a picture by Sir Peter Lely (fig.39). Other portraits of her, or presumed to be of her, such as the reclining nude in the seventeenth-century engraving marked 'Ellen Groinn', would call for more than a bit of tape to chasten them (fig.40). Falling somewhere between Titian's idealised *Venus of Urbino* and Manet's gritty *Olympia*, the *Ellen Groinn*

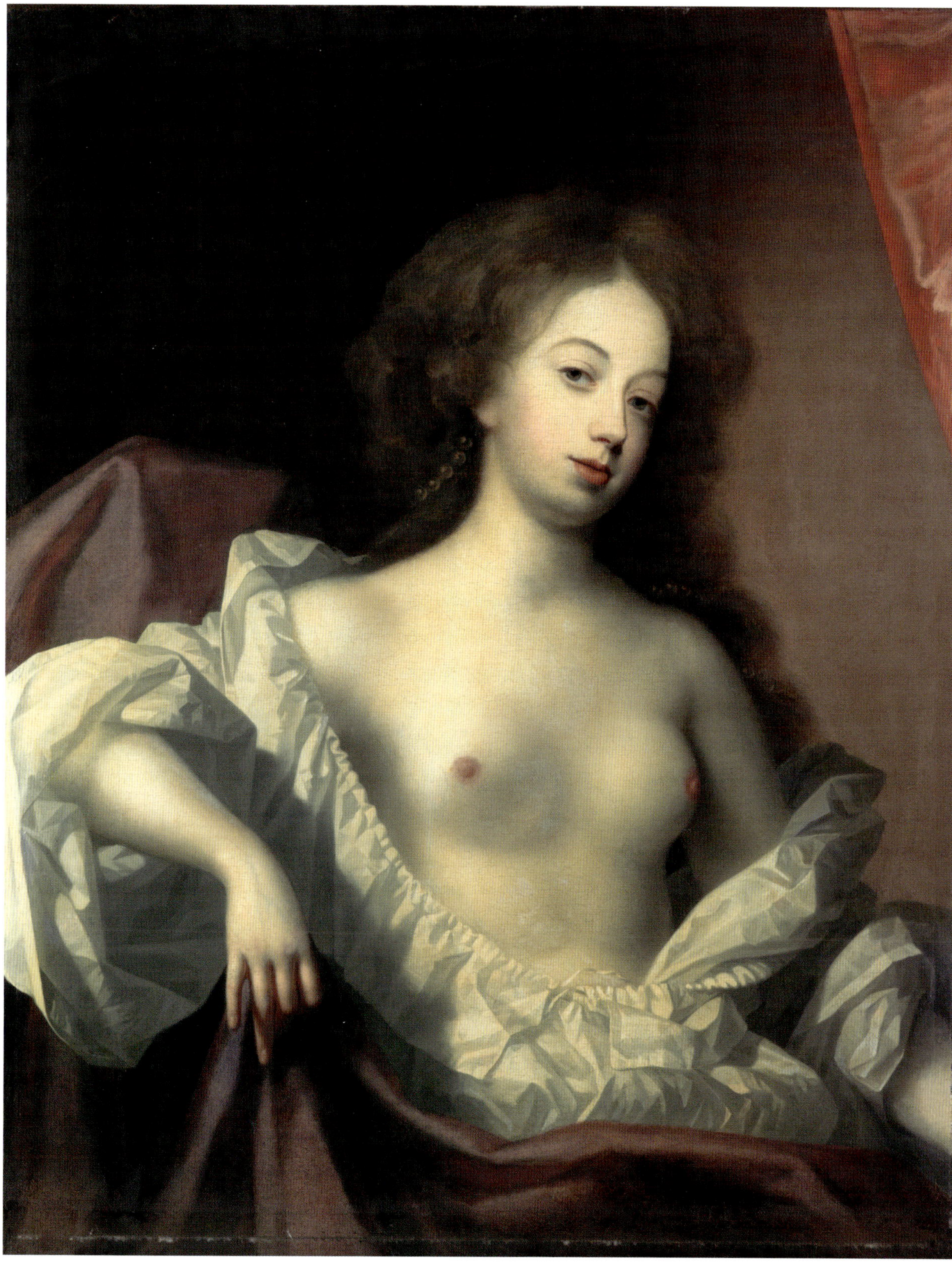

Fig.37

Eleanor ('Nell') Gwyn

Simon Verelst, *c.*1680–5

Fig.38 (right)
Samuel Pepys
John Hayls, 1666

Fig.23 (opposite page, left)
Eleanor ('Nell') Gwyn
Simon Verelst, *c.*1680

Fig.39 (opposite page, right)
Eleanor ('Nell') Gwyn
Gerard Valck, after Sir Peter Lely, *c.*1673

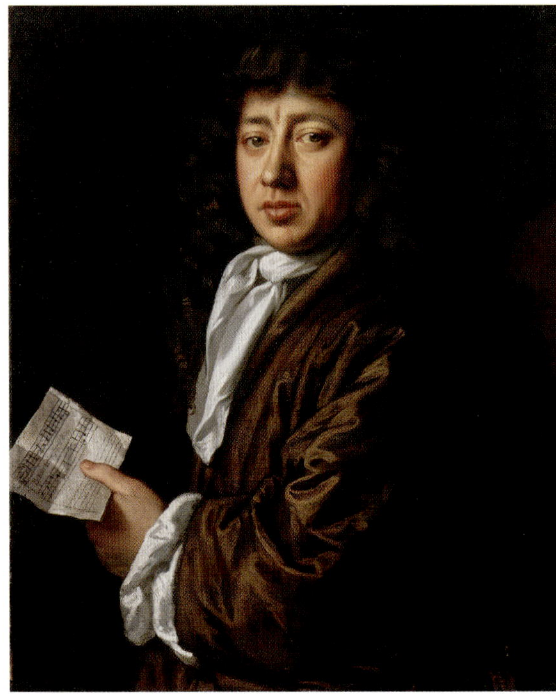

shows the actress reclining on a leafy bank attended by winged *putti*, representing her illegitimate sons. In the print that Pepys kept as a pin-up,[4] Gwyn herself appears bare-breasted and winged. Naked or clothed, she may have spent relatively little time in direct public view, but people keep seeing her everywhere. What Shakespeare's Enobarbus says of Cleopatra – 'Other women cloy/ The appetites they feed, but she makes hungry/ Where she most satisfies'[5] – suits Gwyn in death as it did in life. Why is that?

Part of the endless fascination that Gwyn exerts originates in the irreconcilable contradictions she embodied or was believed to have embodied. She came from origins more humble and circumstances more tenuous than any of the other women whom King Charles II (fig.42) notoriously flaunted as mistresses, but she outlasted all of them in his affection, and, more remarkably, in his esteem. Even though Charles seems to have favoured brunettes – other royal mistresses such as Lady Castlemaine, the Duchess of Portsmouth and the actress Moll Davis (fig.43) were 'brown' – Gwyn trumped her rivals as a red-head with hazel eyes. Before training for the stage by hawking oysters in the streets and selling oranges in the pit of the playhouse, she had already prepared for her ultimate role in life – 'concubine' to the well born – by being 'brought up in a bawdy-house to fill strong water to the guest[s]'.[6] She bravely realised her ambitions, rising from the degradation of her childhood as the daughter of a drunken procuress to see her illegitimate sons well educated and ennobled; but in doing so, she placed her fate in the hands of three wilful men: the actor Charles Hart, who took her as a mistress when she was fourteen years old and who, Pygmalion-like, coached her until she was presentable on the stage; Charles Sackville, Lord Buckhurst, who first took her from the stage as a short-lived trophy mistress; and Charles II, who took her from the stage for good, fathered her two sons, and may have infected her with the sexually transmitted disease that probably shortened both their lives.

In every category of experience, her life ran to paradox. Apparently no more than semi-literate, she possessed an abundant and much-admired 'wit', the highest intellectual attribute among women as well as men at the time of the Restoration. She wrote nothing that survives except the letters that she probably dictated to an amanuensis, but she remains the most famous woman of her age, rivalled only by the playwright Aphra Behn and surpassed by none. Cast as the well-spoken lady in high comedy, she cursed off-stage with a vulgarity sufficient to raise a blush even in the cheeks of Pepys, who dealt regularly with sailors. Cast in tragedy, she could not keep a straight face. Cast as an angel in a play called *The Virgin Martyr*, she played the first four acts in breeches, showing off her legs. Cast as a whore, she reversed the paradox by her Magdalene-like performance of penitence, turning a whiff of sex into the odour of sanctity.

Despite being castigated for her indiscretions by moralists such as Bishop Gilbert Burnet and the diarist John Evelyn, she entreated Dr Thomas Tenison, Rector of St Martin-in-the-Fields and future Archbishop of Canterbury, to eulogise her at her funeral, and she was not refused. Tenison took as his text the verses from Luke's Gospel about the sheep that once was lost but now is found again. Perhaps he remembered or consulted the Valck engraving after Lely's portrait depicting Nell Gwyn as shepherdess, nuzzled by a happy, though not visibly penitent, sheep (fig.45). Again like Shakespeare's pagan Cleopatra, Gwyn could win over even her pious critics and, like a Christian saint, appear all the more sanctified in their eyes because she appeared in the nude, 'for vildest things/ Become themselves in her, that the holy priests/ Bless her when she is riggish.'[7] Men of the cloth, alert to the strength of the human spirit as well as the weakness of the flesh, were no

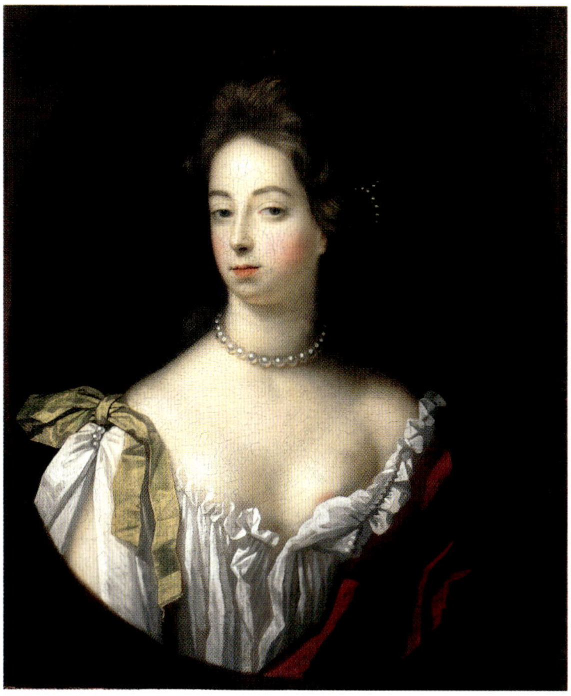

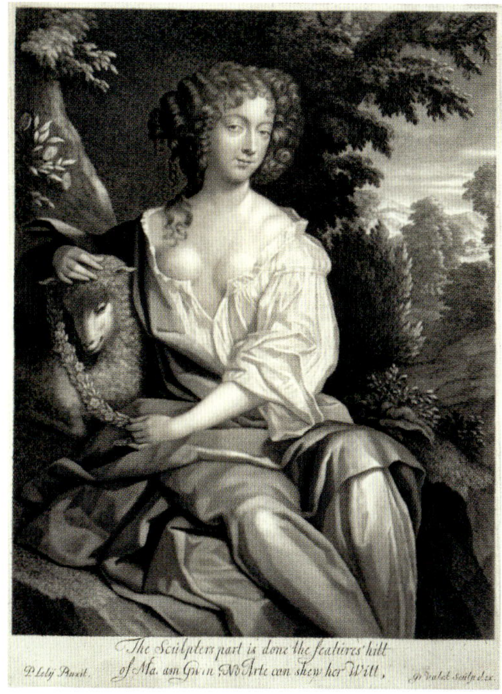

more immune to her fascinating contradictions than other men. In the seventeenth century, the word 'riggish' could mean lewd, wanton or debauched; but it also could mean gay, gallant or cheerful. All of these synonyms describe qualities attributed to Gwyn: the first three account for the soft-pornographic appropriation of her image in the eighteenth and nineteenth centuries as a precedent for the involvement of successive royal courtesans in political and religious intrigues[8]; but the latter three qualities also show through brightly, then and now. Gwyn apparently liked men, while they, in their simple-minded way, have liked her in return. But so have women, including Aphra Behn, who wrote an affectionate encomium to 'Mrs Ellen Gwynn' in the dedication to *The Feigned Courtesans: or, A Night's Intrigue* (1679): 'you never appear but you glad[den] the hearts of all that have the happy fortune to see you, as if you were made on purpose to put the whole world into good Humour.'[9] So she did – and continues to do.

Gwyn's most recent biographer, Charles Beauclerk, presents her, apparently without irony, as a 'People's Princess' *avant la lettre*: 'Here was a woman who brought the monarchy to the people and the people to the monarchy, indeed symbolised the union of King and subject, and what wouldn't the present-day House of Windsor give for such a force to set to work in the nation's psyche?'[10] Beauclerk's comparison need not be wholly credited in order to be judiciously savoured. Neglected as a child by her alcoholic mother, Gwyn carefully protected her two sons by the philandering king. Pimped out by a succession of agents acting in their own selfish interests, she became a philanthropist, noted for her thoughtfulness, playing a part in the founding of Chelsea Hospital and remembering in her last will and testament the most abject of the people, clothing the naked of the parish and releasing debtors from prison on Christmas Day. Adored by the multitudes, she was despised by them too, sometimes by the same ones at the same time, in a way that made her seem to belong to them all the more, even when she slept every night in her own palace on a custom-built silver bed. Ever in possession of the common touch, she famously distinguished herself from the King's despised Catholic mistress, the Duchess of Portsmouth, and won over an angry mob of anti-Papists that had mistakenly assaulted her carriage by loudly identifying herself to them as 'the *Protestant whore!*'[11] But the most telling detail about her status is the familiarity with which she was and is addressed. Within months of her acting debut, she had already become known by her first name to people she had never met, and so she has been intimately and loyally remembered by fans and favourite subject of biographers ever since.[12]

Once reserved to royals and divines alone, universal first-name recognition has now become an attribute of modern celebrity writ large. This is true in part because of a new potential that the first actresses, led by Gwyn, primitively but innovatively exploited: public intimacy, or the general circulation of their images in the absence of their persons. Like images of the gods and goddesses of ancient myth or the heroes and heroines of folklore, they appear in imagination and memory with the celerity of dreams, bidden or unbidden, living on in a mental mélange of half-remembered public appearances, painted or graphic portraits and bits of anecdotal gossip.

The felicitous association of these mixed materials with one abnormally interesting personality, however, lets a single given name stand in for an entire idea, especially when commercial motives intensify deeply rooted cultural values. Literary scholars would say that a proper name used in this way functions metonymically (as in the question, 'Have you read your Milton?'), a function that might best be translated into the terms of today's mass-mediated culture by the

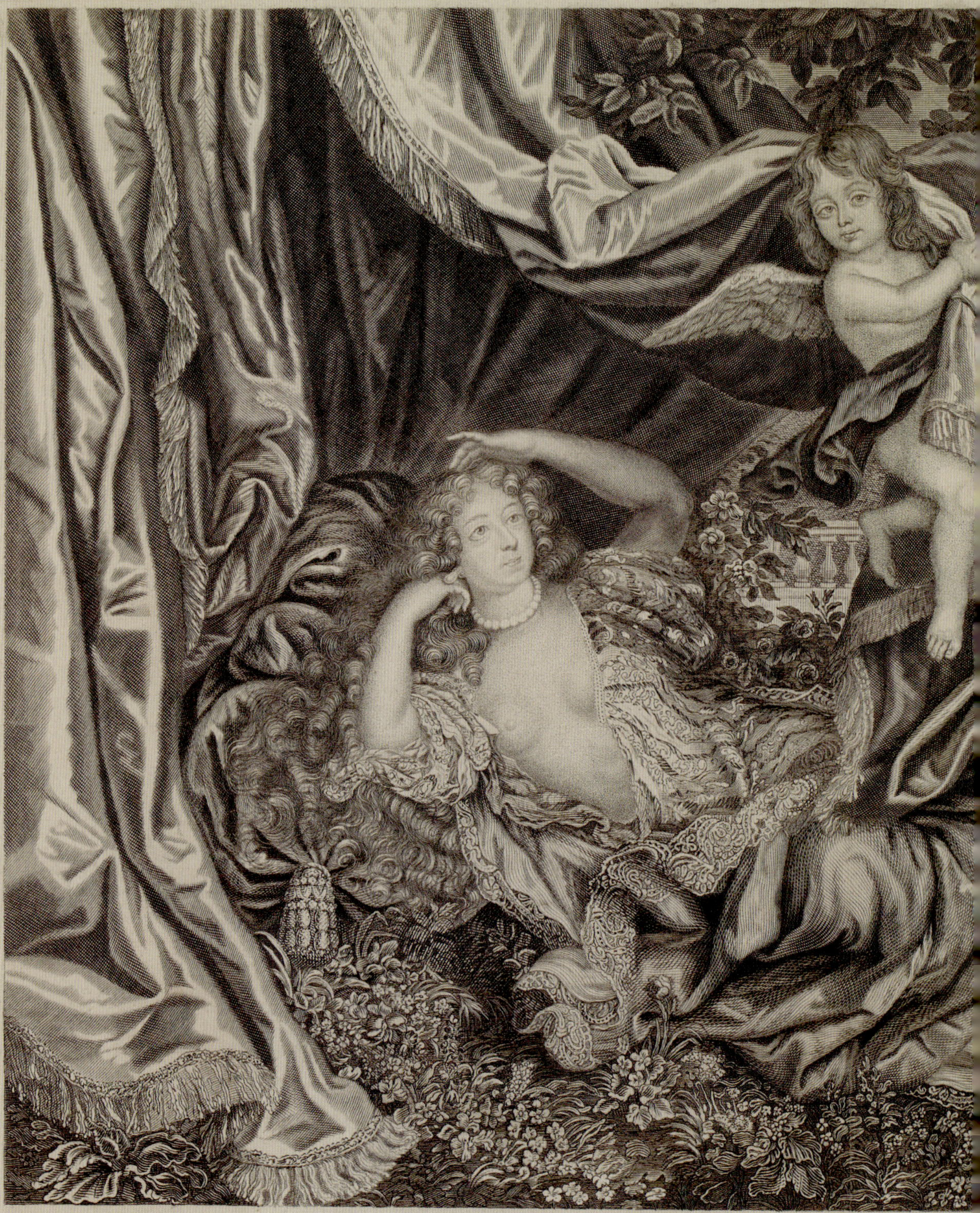

Madame Ellen Groinn and h
Earl of Beaufort and Jame

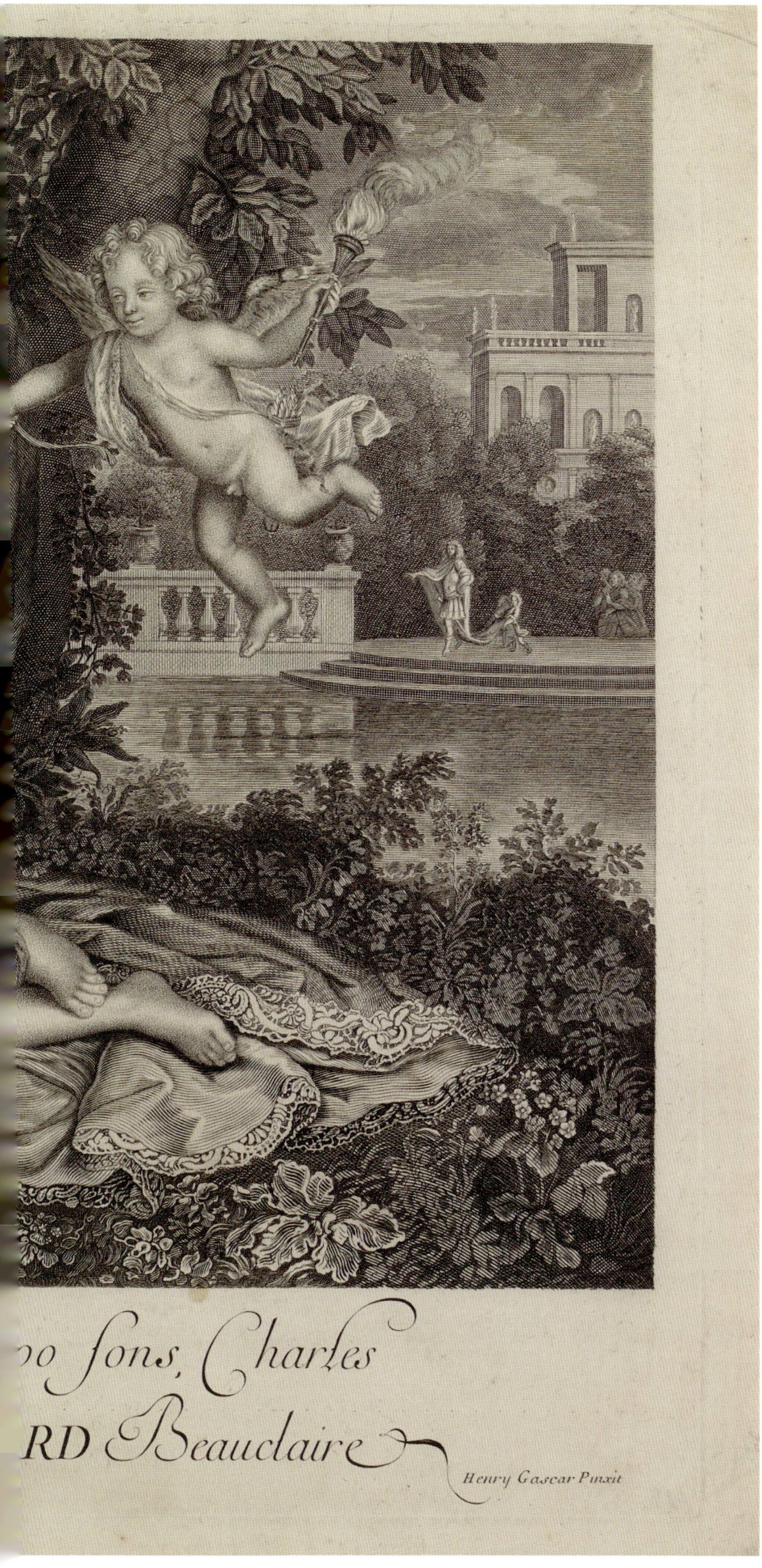

Fig.40

Madame Ellen Groinn and her troo sons, Charles, Earl of Beaufort and James, Lord Beauclaire

Unknown artist, after Henry Gascar, 1677–80

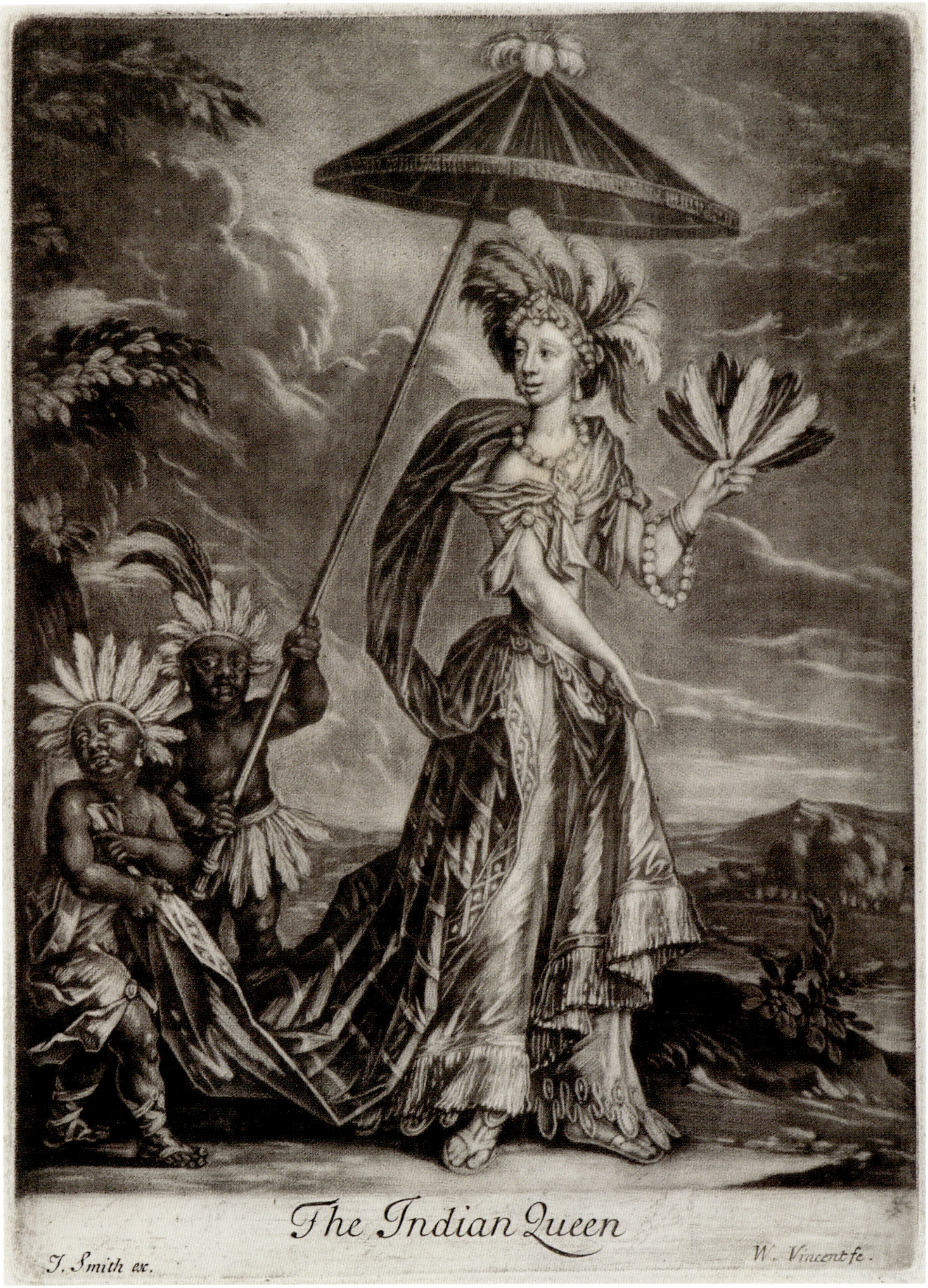
The Indian Queen
J. Smith ex.
W. Vincent fe.

Fig.41
'The Indian Queen' (Anne Bracegirdle)
William Vincent, *c.*1685–95

word *brand.* A brand is a metonym strategically deployed by marketeers to focus our attention and, if possible, command our allegiance. This may seem unremarkable now, when the commercialisation of leisure (and just about everything else) pervades society, but long before 'Beyoncé' or 'Kylie', there was 'Nell'.

Goddesses and 'It Girls'

What did 'Nell' mean to the contemporaries who summoned her image by using that name, and what does that image mean to us today? Another question follows the first one implicitly: what peculiar personal magnetism made the image of 'Nell' so efficacious, and why does it retain its power across the centuries? Similar questions arise in connection with many other actresses, of course, from 'Becke' (Rebecca Marshall) and 'Perdita' (Mary Robinson) to 'Cara' (Anne Bracegirdle) (fig.41), but Gwyn has priority among these Covent Garden goddesses because she fashioned her unique personality into a repeatable model for the new professional career of actress-celebrity, blazing a trail for others to follow. In so doing, she accomplished more than anyone else in renovating the apparently settled tradition of male transvestite theatre that had predominated from the age of Sophocles to the age of Shakespeare.

Gwyn was not literally the first actress to step onto the English stage, but she was the first starring one, and she remains the most popularly referenced. A comparison of the strength of her goddess-like image with the weakness of that of 'Ianthe' (Mary Betterton, née Saunderson, called Ianthe by Samuel Pepys after her first and most famous role), her close contemporary, is revealing: based on the surviving performance records, 'Nell' is credited with approximately twenty roles in seven years; 'Ianthe' is credited with over sixty roles in more than thirty years on the stage.[13] 'Ianthe' was both respectable and talented, but she is remembered only by specialists. 'Nell' was not respectable, but she is folkloric, even mythic, the subject of many historical novels and a dozen feature films;[14] plaques mark her places of residence, and pubs bear her name.

There is no evidence to suggest that Gwyn intended to tap into mythical or folkloric archetypes to project her image to the public, but she succeeded in doing so nonetheless. Scholars have cited the scandal of her personal life to explain her pre-eminence, and no one would contest the fact that, in the words of a distinguished historian of the first actresses, her sexuality 'became the central feature of her professional identity as a player'.[15] But not the only feature: people not only wanted to see her or hear about her, they also wanted her to succeed, perhaps after suffering appropriate tests and ordeals, like the heroine of a folk tale. She activates poignant associations with Cinderella, for instance, the abject working girl who wins the heart of a prince, and like Cinderella, Gwyn was admired for her tiny feet, a fact lingered over by her biographers.[16] She also recalls Galatea of the Pygmalion myth, the lump of common clay who becomes hyper-animate in the hands of her self-absorbed lover. More darkly, she evokes the mythic figure of Philomela, who, raped and deprived of her tongue, became emblematic of the silenced survivor of sexual abuse whose eloquence transcends victimhood by finding another way to express itself besides speech.

Part of Gwyn's magic resided in her ability to make her personality a conduit for the jolt of social energy that flows whenever something useful and accessible, like a 'bar wench' in a brothel, turns into something ornamental and exclusive, like a royal concubine, but still completes the circuit by 'remembering where she came from'. That is the sure-to-be electrifying Cinderella action, whereby 'Nell' underwent a proper royal makeover and still came out 'Nell'. The putative agents of her transformation were the

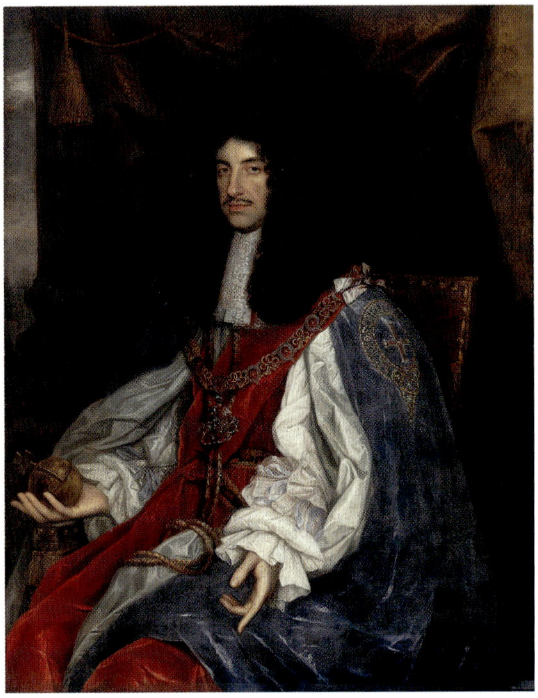

Fig.42
King Charles II
John Michael Wright, *c.*1660–5

men who trained her to suit their pleasure on the stage and off – Charles Hart and Charles Sackville, Lord Buckhurst. They played the sculptor's part in the Galatea action, but, as George Bernard Shaw acknowledged in his afterword to *Pygmalion* (1912), the modern Galatea shows more agency than did her Ovidian precursor. Shaw modelled Eliza Doolittle's plucky ascent on the social mobility demonstrated by the self-fashioning actress in English theatrical history: 'Such transfigurations have been achieved by hundreds of resolutely ambitious young women since Nell Gwynne set them the example by playing queens and fascinating kings in the theatre in which she began by selling oranges.'[17]

'Nell' delivered value as an actress and a lover, but she drove a hard bargain. Sharp-witted and sharp-tongued, she could speak truth to power with breath-taking impudence, as when she reputedly dubbed her royal lover, who had followed in the steps of Hart and Buckhurst, 'Charles III'.[18] Unlike the aristocratic drama queens the Duchesses of Cleveland and Portsmouth, however, she tactfully left rants and soliloquies behind her when she vacated the stage, and she intervened at Court only when Charles invited her opinion. This he evidently did, for example, in connection with the inadequate first plan for the Chelsea Hospital, which she revised wordlessly by laying strips of silk torn from her handkerchief on Christopher Wren's preliminary drawing.[19] That is the classic Philomela action, in which a silenced woman bides her time and finds her voice in indirect speech. All of that and much more may be evoked, therefore, by the simple mention of 'Nell', a name that many English-speaking conversationalists from all walks of life will be able to associate with the legendary actress, without the additional prompt of 'Gwyn'.

Thus did Samuel Pepys first note 'Nell' by name on the occasion of an unexpected star-sighting. He encountered her not as an actress taking a role for the King's company at the Drury Lane Theatre, her theatrical home, but as the lively person who happened to be seated next to him at a production in Lincoln's Inn Fields put on by the rival Duke's Company of players. On 3 April 1665, she attended *Mustapha, the son of Solyman the Magnificent* in the company of another King's Company actress, Rebecca Marshall. Their theatre-going coincided with that of King Charles II and his long-serving well-born paramour, Barbara Palmer (née Villiers), Lady Castlemaine. Pepys had little interest in what was acted on the stage that afternoon, Orrery's play having struck him as 'not good', but he was dazzled by the A-list celebrities seated around him: 'All the pleasure of the play was, the King and my Lady Castlemaine was there – and pretty witty Nell at the King's house, and the younger Marshall, sat next to us, which pleased me mightily.'[20] The presence of royalty and aristocracy excited the social-climbing Pepys, but he was most impressed by the proximity of the two actresses, emergent Covent Garden goddesses, especially the one whose familiar name he had already learned. It is as if the theatre challenged the church and Court as a place of social effervescence. The sacred monarch's ancient charisma, which was still imputed to his curative touch, could no longer work its magic directly as practical politics in the rising tide of republicanism; but its efficacy endured when it could be transferred surreptitiously to a more accessible object of worship – the stage beauty.

'Nell' might convince historians to take the idea of a 'Theatre Royal', which at the time the great actor Thomas Betterton called a 'mimic state',[21] more seriously, especially now, in light of what has come to pass for popular sovereignty in the absolute reign of the television personality. Betterton's allegory of the state and the stage is echoed in the political commentator Walter Bagehot's later theory of the theatricality that enables England's unwritten constitution to work its magic over its stage-struck subjects:

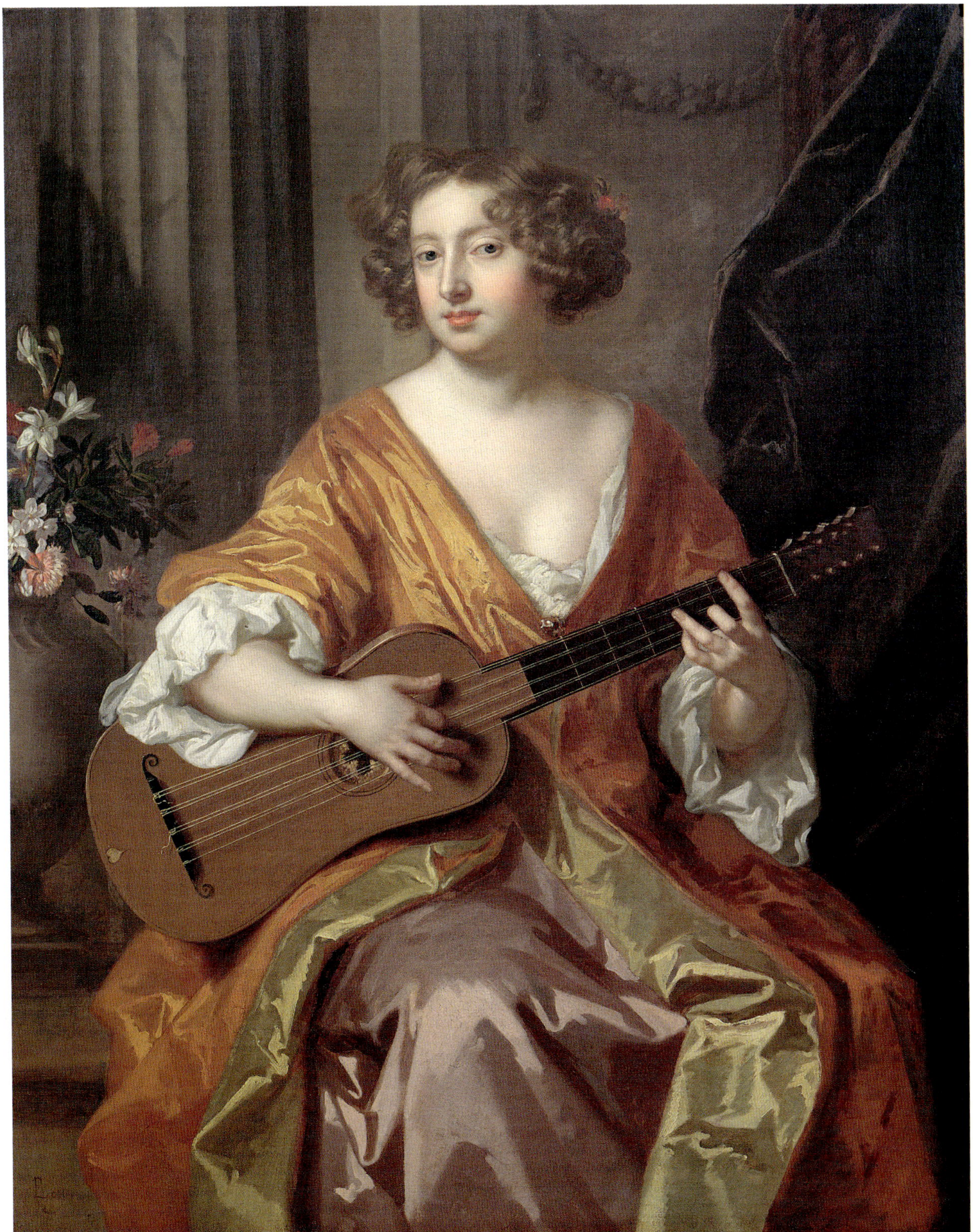

Fig.43

Mary ('Moll') Davis

Sir Peter Lely, *c.*1674

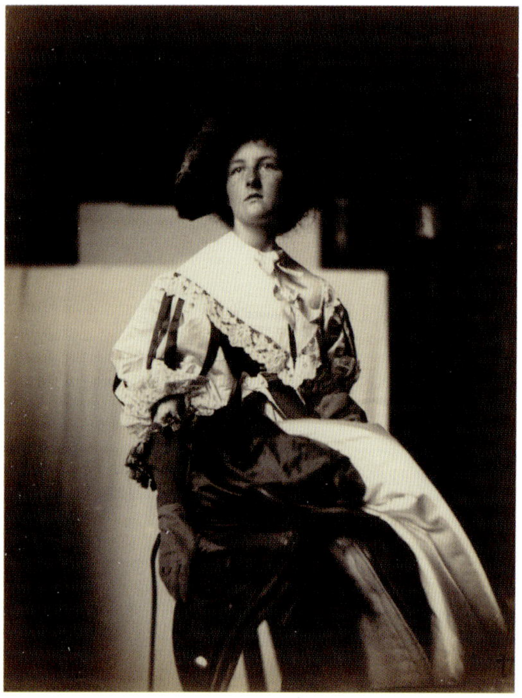

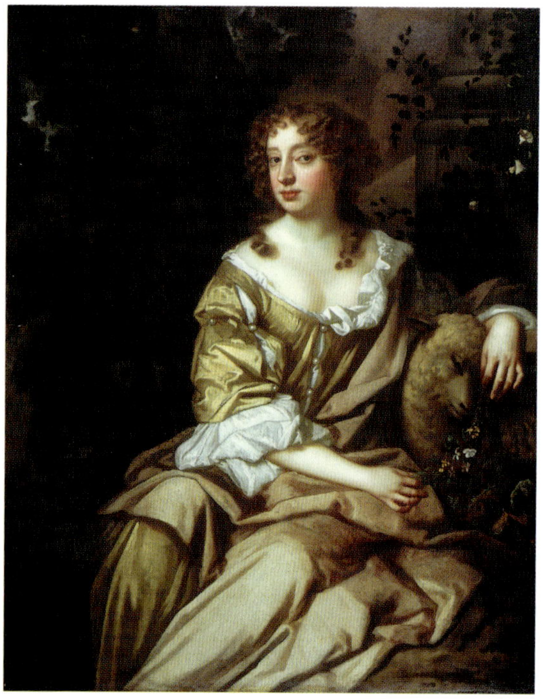

'In fact, the mass of English people yield a deference rather to something else than their rulers. They defer to what we may call the *theatrical show* of society.'[22] Under the conditions of global mass-mediation and celebrity culture, the English constitution continues to spread worldwide, like an oil slick. The charismatic power behind this throne, the force that 'Nell' demonstrably possessed, has been summed up by the word It. In its current usage, as a pronoun aspiring to the condition of noun, 'It' was coined by Elinor Glyn, a British expatriate in 1920s Hollywood, who dubbed silent-film actress Clara Bow the 'It Girl'.[23] 'It' is the power of embodying, apparently without effort, contradictory qualities simultaneously: strength *and* vulnerability, innocence and experience, and singularity and typicality among them. 'It' is based on the attractive power exerted by opposites, especially when they appear together in the same person.

Unsurprisingly, today examples of 'It' come readily to mind from the overlapping fields of politics, advertising and entertainment, but the Restoration stage pioneered the mix of all three, and Nell Gwyn was the 'It Girl' of her time. She radiated polarities, fascinating beholders by embracing contradictory qualities simultaneously – waif *and* countess, angel *and* whore, flesh *and* spirit. Hence the raptures experienced by Samuel Pepys at the revival of Dekker and Massinger's *The Virgin Martyr* in 1668, which paired up Rebecca Marshall and Nell Gwyn, the two Covent Garden goddesses he had ogled in civilian dress at the Duke's Theatre three years earlier. Now Marshall appeared as the saintly Dorothea and Gwyn as her guardian angel. This is the role she played in breeches for the first four acts, while the angel appears disguised as 'Angelo', a page-boy, before changing into her winged angel suit to descend from the heavens in full baroque splendor. Pepys describes his erotic response as a religious experience:

> With my wife and Deb to the King's House, to see Virgin Martyr, the first time it has been acted in a great while; and it is mighty pleasant; not that the play is worth much but it is finely Acted by Becke Marshall. But that which did please me beyond anything in the whole world was the wind-musique when the Angell comes down, which is so sweet that it ravished me; and endeed, in a word, did wrap up my soul so that it made me really sick, just as I have formerly been when in love with my wife; that neither then, nor all the evening going home and at home, I was able to think of anything but remained all night transported.[24]

The music-loving diarist's epiphany depends in part on the full panoply of stage technology and in even larger part on whatever tune the musicians played to cover the creaking winch that powered the angelic descent. The ethereal estrangement of the flesh-and-blood actress, however, also transported him. After another performance of *The Virgin Martyr*, Pepys went back-stage to the dressing rooms. Here, as he watched them change clothes, he found that Marshall's and Gwyn's painted faces and coarse language repelled him; but to work its magic, the contradictory allure of 'It' requires the perception of innocence and experience, blushing cheek and rouge.

As a cultural archetype, 'Nell' descends through history like the angel descending in *The Virgin Martyr*. She might come down just about anywhere (figs 44, 45, 46). Both Charles Dickens and Mark Twain, for instance, each a humorist with his finger on the democratising pulse of nineteenth-century popular culture, invoked Nell Gwyn. Revealingly, they both do so in books intended for a youthful readership. Dickens saw fit to include her story in *A Child's History of England* (1854), written for the better education of Victorian boys and girls. Partially exculpating 'Nelly',

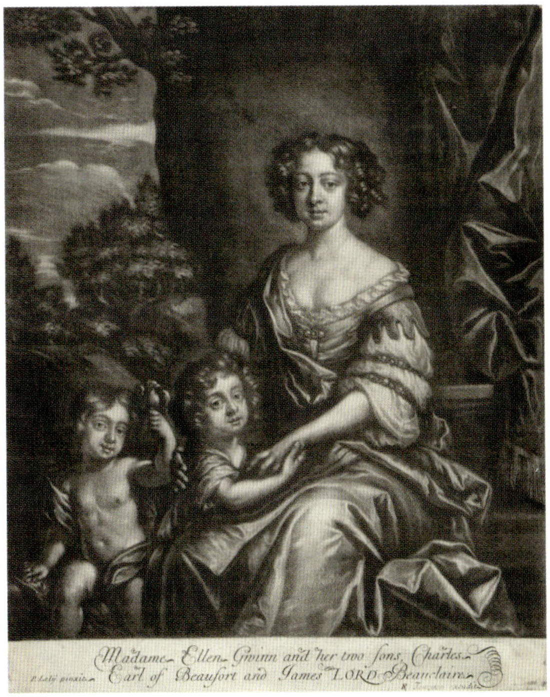

Fig.44 (opposite page, left)
'Nell Gwynne'
(Effie Gray James)
Rupert Potter, 1882–8

Fig.45 (opposite page, right)
Possibly Eleanor ('Nell') Gwyn
Studio of Sir Peter Lely, *c.*1675

Fig.46 (left)
James Beauclerk;
Charles Beauclerk,
1st Duke of St Albans;
Eleanor ('Nell') Gwyn
Richard Tompson, after
Sir Peter Lely, before 1693

Dickens separated out the truly 'bad' mistresses of Charles II, especially Lady Castlemaine, from the 'merry' ones. In the latter category, Nell Gwyn was joined by Moll Davis (fig.43), whose seductive portrait, seated with guitar, parallels the image of Nell Gwyn as royal muse and mistress. According to Dickens's story:

> Another merry lady named MOLL DAVIS, a dancer at the theatre, afterwards became [Castlemaine's] rival. So was NELL GWYN, first an orange girl and then an actress, who really had some good in her, and of whom the worst thing I know is, that she actually seems to have been fond of the King. The first DUKE OF ST ALBANS was this orange girl's child.[25]

Dickens wants his young readers to know where English kings and dukes are coming from, and he wants them, within reasonable limits, to root for the orange girl in her merry project.

Across the Atlantic, writing in *The Adventures of Huckleberry Finn* (1884), Mark Twain has Huck narrate the fine points of English history to Jim as they float down the Mississippi River on their raft. Huck struggles with dynastic chronology, 'all of them Saxon heptarchies that used to rip around so in old times and raise Cain', but he gets basically right the priapic hurly-burly of combining divine-right absolutism with serial polygamy:

> My you ought to have seen old Henry the Eighth when he was in bloom. He was a blossom. He used to marry a new wife every day, and chop off her head next morning. And he would do it just as indifferent as if he was ordering up eggs. 'Fetch up Nell Gwynn', he says. They fetch her up. Next morning, 'Chop off her head!' And they chop it off.[26]

Mark Twain counted on his readers immediately to recognise the anachronism in order to get the joke. He also expected them to recognise the humour of Huck's error in assigning conjugal status. He could be sure, nearly two centuries after her death, that they would not only know who Nell Gwyn was, but also who she wasn't.

The American author emphasises the vulnerability of the concubine's position at a debauched court, dependent on the whim of a tyrant. Dickens, a more reassuring storyteller, addresses this concern by looking ahead to the Whig ascendancy and constitutional monarchy of Bagehot's Victorian description. As a gentle reminder of the monarch's obligations to his or her subjects, the English novelist finishes off the chapter by quoting the famous last words popularly attributed Charles II on his deathbed, words that ended his reign but immortalised that of the Covent Garden goddess: 'Do not let poor Nelly starve.'[27]

DIVAS, DANCING
AND THE RAGE FOR MUSIC

by Gill Perry

DIVAS, DANCING
AND THE RAGE FOR MUSIC

In the spring of 1728 the runaway success of *The Beggar's Opera* catapulted Lavinia Fenton into the realm of celebrity stardom, and the production by the impresario John Rich ran for a remarkable sixty-three performances. Writers, pamphleteers and printmakers continually confused Fenton with the character of Polly Peachum. On 13 April the journal *The Craftsman* published a satirical ballad which mischievously claimed that 'pretty Polly' (Fenton) outshone the performances of some famous contemporary opera singers:

POLLY PEACHUM[1]

I Of all the Belles that tread the Stage,
There's none like pretty Polly,
And all the Musick of the Age,
Except her Voice is Folly.

II Compar'd with her, how flat appears
Cuzzoni or Faustina?
And when she sings, I shut my Ears
To warbling Senesino

V Some Prudes indeed, with envious Spight
Would blast her Reputation,
And tell us that to Ribands bright
She yields, upon Occasion

VI But these are all invented Lies
And vile outlandish Scandal,
Which from Italian Clubs arise
And Partizans of Handel

The Beggar's Opera belonged to a new genre of 'ballad opera' that satirised the pretentions and grand themes of Italian opera by using 'low-style' songs based on street ballads, which had wide popular appeal.[2] It is set in the criminal underworld of London, was full of satirical allusions to contemporary music and politics, and included sixty 'common tunes'. Ballad operas transformed musical theatre in Britain and Europe, and helped to create popular new roles for women.[3] Much of the dramatic action and the songs focused on their trials and tribulations, helping to place women at the centre of early celebrity culture. At the same time, this visibility made them vulnerable to feminine stereotypes.[4] Thus, Fenton's voice, which lacked the sophisticated training of the Italian soprano, was seen to express the supposedly 'natural' character of Polly Peachum.

The three Italian opera singers cited in the anonymous ballad are the sopranos Faustina Bordoni and Francesca Cuzzoni, and the 'warbling' castrato Francesco Bernadi 'Senesino' (fig.50), who had all been engaged in London in the 1720s by Handel's Royal Academy of Music, which had been founded in 1719. Bordoni and Cuzzoni were known as bitter rivals, and in Gay's opera the characters of Peachum and Lucy Locket, daughters of the fence and the jailor, were intended as satires on these two Italian divas.[5] And the 'natural' singing voice that characterised Peachum's role carried contradictory associations for an eighteenth-century audience. Untutored femininity was perceived by some to signify wanton or undignified behaviour. Moreover, ideas of coquetry and flirtation were often associated with the abilities to sing and dance that could be used to entice a male audience.[6]

As we saw in the Introduction, Peachum's role has been seen both as innocent and as promiscuous and manipulative, and a similar confusion surrounds accounts of Fenton's 'Reputation'. While ostensibly defending her against envious 'Prudes' and 'invented Lies', the ballad above sustains the ambiguity that has haunted Fenton's

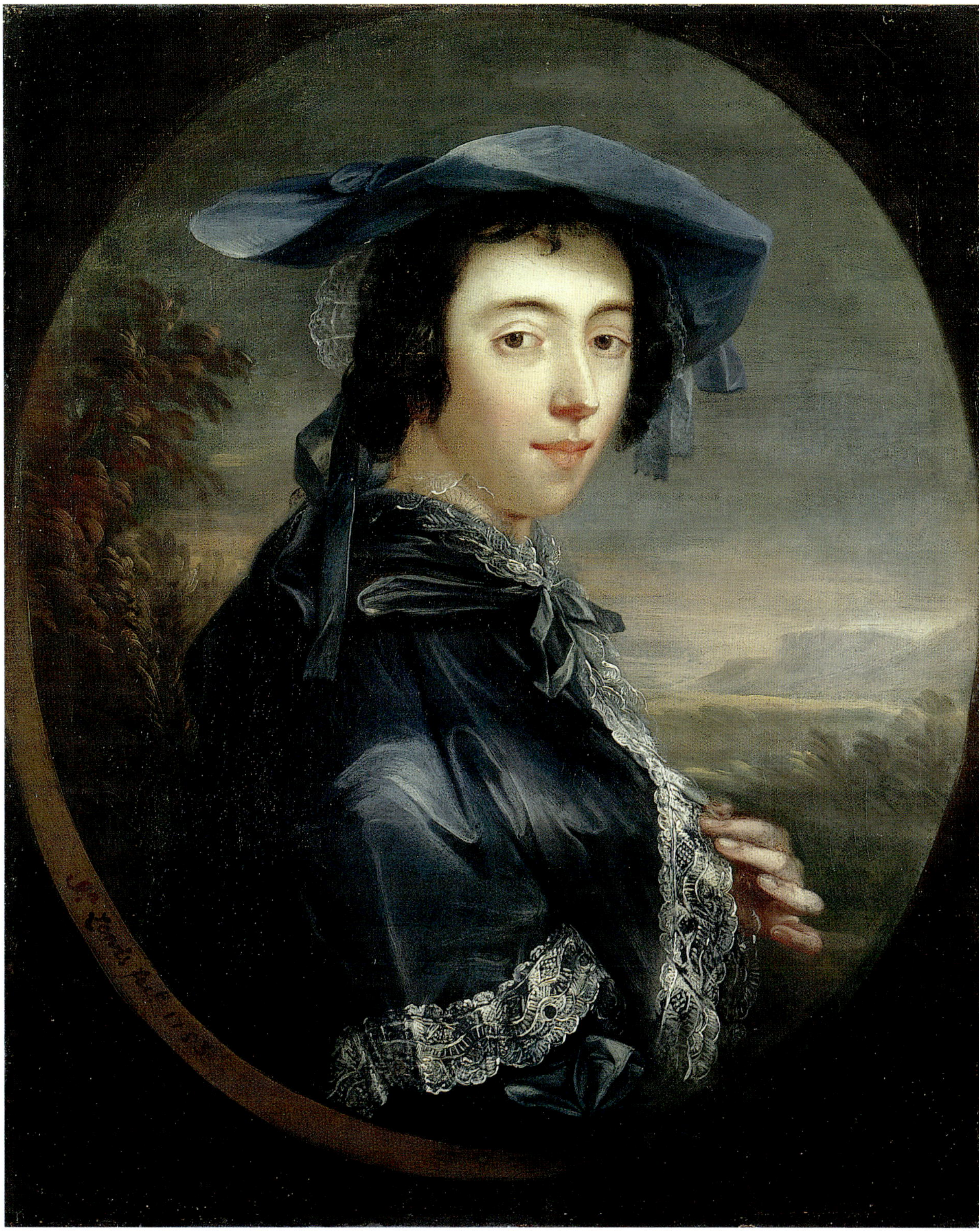

Fig.47

Margaret ('Peg') Woffington

John Lewis, 1753

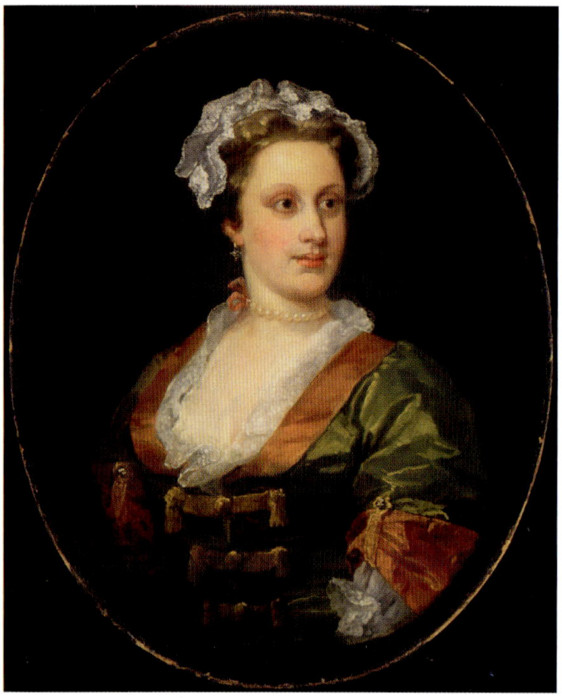

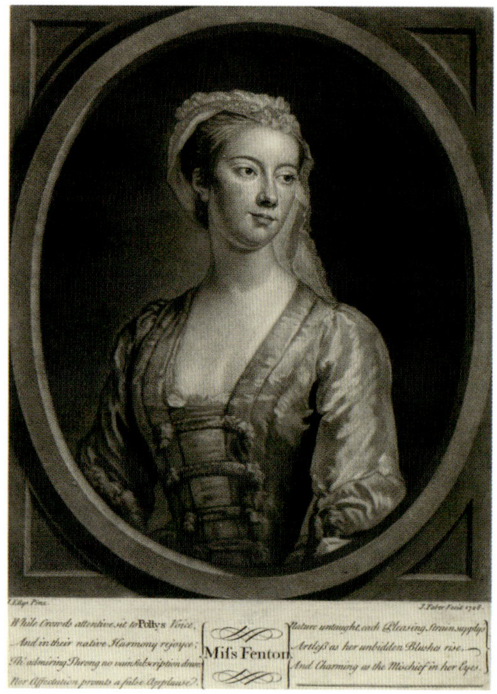

Fig.48 (above left)
Lavinia Fenton, later Duchess of Bolton
William Hogarth, *c.*1740–50

Fig.49 (above right)
Lavinia Fenton, later Duchess of Bolton
John Faber Jr, after John Ellys, 1728

Fig.50 (opposite page)
Gaetano Berenstadt; Francesca Cuzzoni; Francesco Bernardi ('Senesino') (detail)
Unknown artist, 18th century

life-story ever since. Many modern accounts continue to adopt the same salacious tone and sexual innuendo that have contributed to a pervasive rags-to-riches stereotype of the eighteenth-century actress (fig.48).[7]

Painting 'Pretty Polly'

After Fenton's wildly successful performance (according to Gay her popularity 'outstripped that of the play itself'), her life inspired a run of biographies, and her image as 'Polly' appeared on numerous prints and mass-produced objects, including fans, playing cards and porcelain.[8] John Ellys's portrait of 1728 was disseminated through a popular mezzotint printed with several lines of verse describing her 'native harmony' and 'pleasing strains' (fig.49). Musical talents could increase an actress's popular appeal. However, Fenton was also known as a singer of entr'actes and a dancer, and the range of her public performances, which involved exertions of both her voice and body, also caused continuing concerns about her sexual attractions. After settling with the third Duke of Bolton in 1728, she retired from the stage, and eventually married the Duke in 1751. But given her previous career, even this class mobility and retirement from public life could not ensure respectability. While her celebrity image was enhanced by her range of accomplishments, her moral status as a professional actress was less secure; hence the prurient tales that continue to be raked over by a more modern audience.

For eighteenth-century women, especially among the middle and upper classes, the social functions of music and dancing were fraught with tensions. While respectable women were encouraged to develop a range of accomplishments in music and dance, these were valued primarily in the private domestic sphere. At the same time, the boundaries between 'public' and 'private' spaces in the eighteenth-century theatrical world were often blurred.

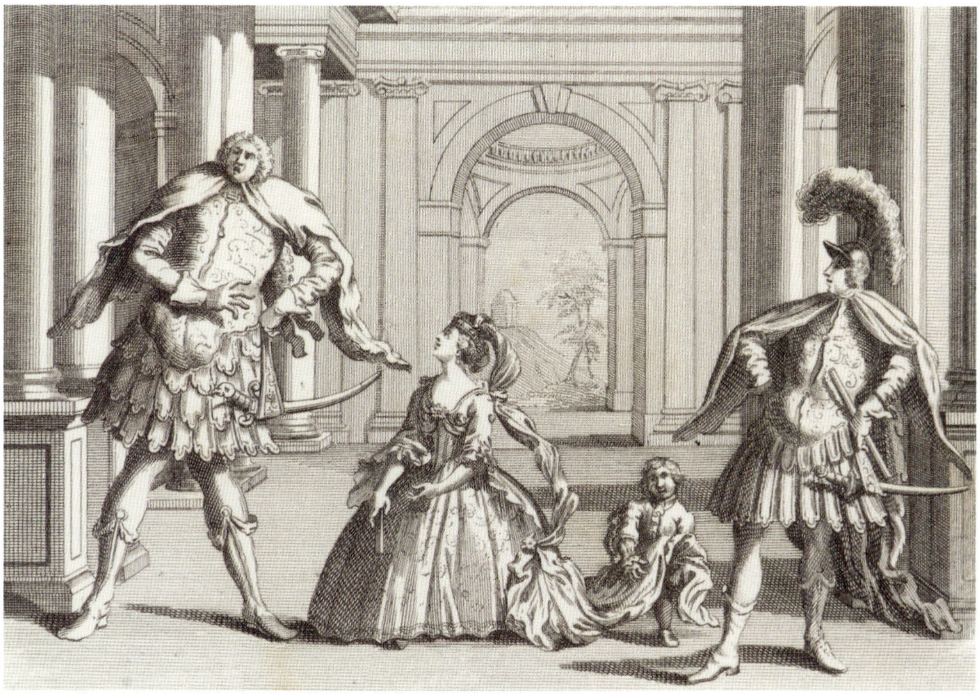

Performances in private homes merged easily into popular invitation-only concerts and balls with extended guest lists. Furthermore, the visibility of eighteenth-century actresses contributed to the instability of the boundaries between public and private. The literary scholar Felicity Nussbaum has argued that contemporary culture regarded the feminine as more accessible than the masculine, encouraging an imagined intimacy with actresses in performance. And the increased presence of women in the public sphere gave celebrity a 'feminine face'.[9] I suggest that the popularity of women in musical performance contributed to this 'feminine face', and to some of its uneasy contradictions.

Actresses, like their aristocratic patrons, were encouraged to acquire the skills of dancing and singing to develop graceful deportment and well-trained voices. But such skills could signify licentiousness as well as refinement. Without them, the actress could be seen as untrained, but the female performer who practised these activities for money in the commercial theatre, as opposed to pursuing an amateur pastime, was vulnerable to claims of overstepping the boundaries of acceptable (imagined) intimacy. Projecting and manipulating the voice and body on the public stage were seen as risky physical pursuits for many women, especially when associated with the bawdy plots of some comedies and comic operas. When dance was viewed as part of a vivid public spectacle, concerns were sometimes raised about how respectable women should use and display their bodies.

Throughout the century, the barriers between opera, musical comedy and 'straight' acting roles were less clearly defined than they are today, and famous actresses such as Peg Woffington (fig.47) and Dorothy Jordan were also known for their singing roles. By the second half of the century, the label 'musical performance' could embrace a wide range of genres, including the new ballad opera, comic opera, religious and Handelian oratorios, Italian opera and classical concerts. Opera, along with classical ballet, could claim the most refined historical pedigree. The ballad above claims that Fenton was maligned by slurs from the jealous supporters of Handel and opera in the 'Italian clubs', who felt threatened by a popular new musical genre. Handel's Academy was then the British centre of Italian opera, and employed expensive and captivating Italian singers such as Cuzzoni or Faustina. The unprecedented success of *The Beggar's Opera* may have contributed to the disbanding of his Academy in 1729, but in 1734 Handel responded to changing taste with his repertoire of successful oratorios in English, including the famous *Messiah* of 1741. These works, along with ballad operas, were seen to affirm the status of the nation's English-language arts, representing a growing British musical culture. In contrast with the Italian divas, Pretty Polly's untrained voice and simple delivery were seen to represent 'the putative British characteristics of rationality and lack of artifice'.[10] Thus, Fenton took on yet another important role, as a patriotic symbol of *British* femininity.

After Fenton had settled with the Duke of Bolton in 1728, her 'character' was embellished by painted portraits and their engraved copies, which merged traces of her history (as Polly) with her new social status. The painted portrait presents a frozen moment in time. However, the stage identities of actresses, singers and dancers are perceived in relation to performances through time, rather than a single moment. In the case of a dancer, of course, her bodily movement is a key aspect of her identity as a performer. The portrait therefore provides a timeless, composite construction that suggests the past life of the sitter, including her previous performances, as well as an indication of her present (or desired) identity and status. Portraiture enabled the actress-singer, perhaps with the person commissioning the work (often a lover or husband, if not the performer

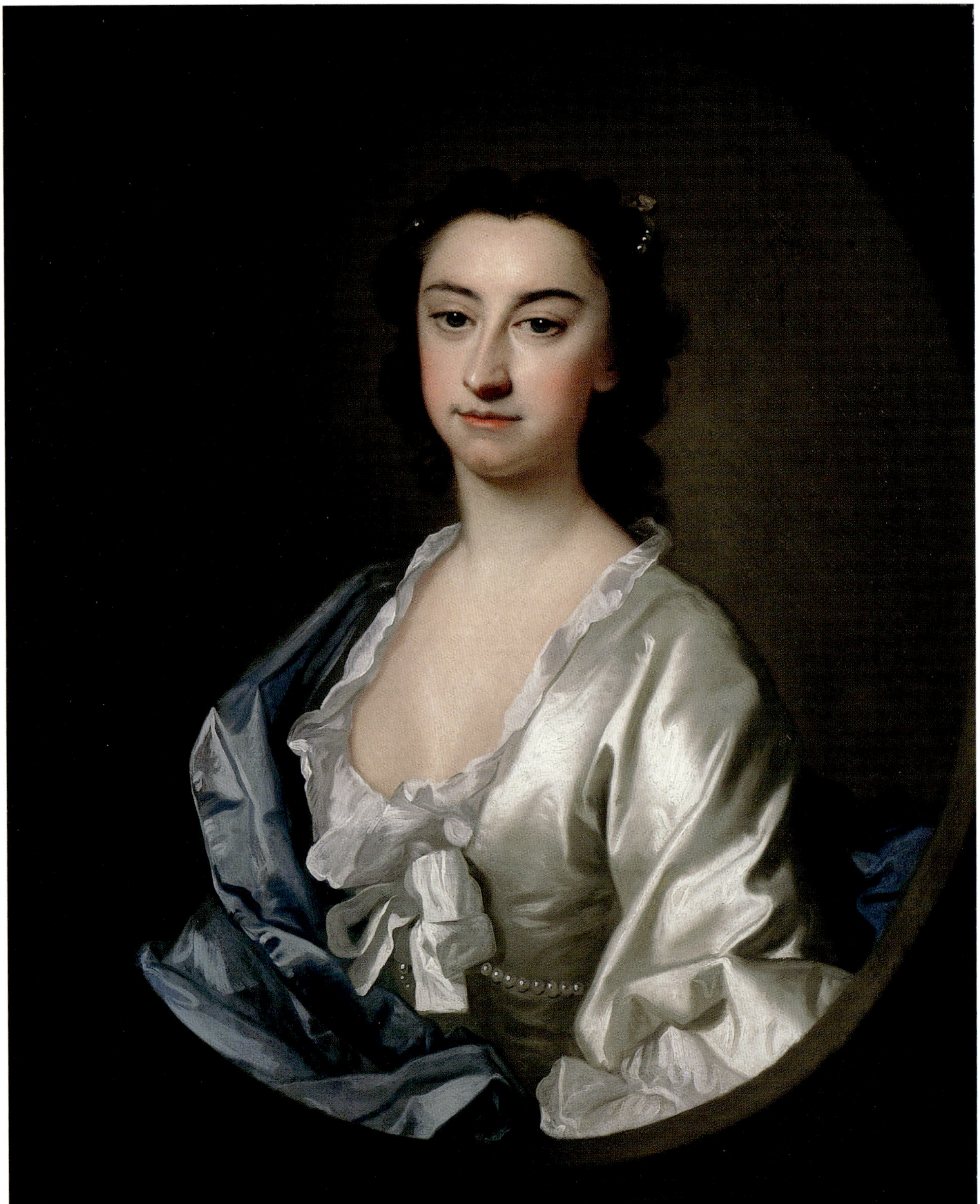

Fig.51

Susannah Cibber

Thomas Hudson, *c.*1749

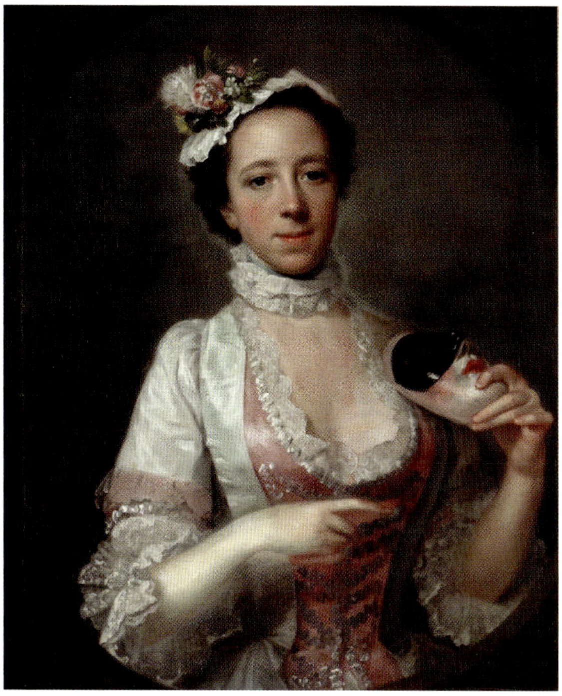

Fig.25

Lavinia Fenton

Possibly by George Knapton, *c.*1739

herself), to manage her social position and public image in collaboration with the artist. Such images also offer the viewer a feigned intimacy, providing traces and clues to who the sitter was or is. Dress, pose, jewellery, facial expression and props, such as drapery, song-sheets, masks and musical instruments, provide important clues and symbolic references. Mediated through the artist's skilful application of paint on canvas, these tactile, material objects offer the viewer traces of famous roles, class, professional achievements and feminine identity.

Thus, a portrait of circa 1739, possibly by George Knapton (fig.25), shows the Duchess dressed to kill, in a rich, white and pink silk robe with a tantalisingly laced and embroidered bodice, an indication of wealth, fashionable style and feminine sensuality.[11] Clothes could provide the visual emblems of rank, social status and desirable femininity, and the 'correct' arrangement of dress and accessories was closely monitored in women's magazines throughout the eighteenth century.[12] As less successful actresses often wore cast-off robes donated by wealthy patrons for stage performances, a portrait image that vividly declared their fashionable affluence could signify social and professional achievement. In this portrait, even Fenton's circular cap, prettily perched on one side of her head and decorated with flowers and laced pleats, was the height of fashion by the 1740s, and is positioned here to declare her style and status. English women were known for their use of caps and hats throughout the eighteenth century.[13] Caps provided a total hairdressing, a form of ornamentation that could both conceal and draw attention to the body. As accessories to the spectacle of the dress, they provided compact material signs of the 'glamour' now seen as part of celebrity.[14] When visible as part of the stage show, caps could also act as metonyms (or substitutes) for the actress herself – for her fashion sense, star status, and even coquettish tendencies, and were often copied by adoring fans. Later in the century the comic actress Frances Abington was known for her famous 'Abington Cap', frequently worn on stage and copied by milliners and followers of fashion from Dublin to London. Then as now, celebrity involved emulation, and caps and accessories were easier and cheaper to copy than more expensive dresses.[15]

Hogarth's scene from *The Beggar's Opera* (fig.52) shows Fenton dressed in a white laced satin robe and cap, which contrast vividly with the dark, shadowy surroundings of the prison, as she and Lucy Locket plead with their fathers for the life of the highwayman Macheath.[16] Here the whiteness of Polly's dress and its luxurious material presence suggest a natural feminine innocence, set against the criminality around her. Like many performances of the mid-eighteenth century, Rich's production was staged in modern dress, countering the overtly theatrical or quasi-historical costumes often used in Italian opera. Contemporary dress, selected by better established women players with a clothes allowance from the theatre, allowed the actress to shape her physical appearance on stage, to embellish and frame perceptions of her body and, more often than not, affirm her status as fashion icon. That body is seductively embellished in Knapton's portrait of 1739. The mask (a recurring motif in actress-portraits) in Fenton's left hand provides a reference to her previous career; and perhaps to her taste for masquerade and masked balls, popular leisure activities of the period that enabled women to exploit the freedom of theatrical disguise.[17] She also looks out directly at the viewer, as if about to smile, her finger pointing towards the mask, symbol of her past notoriety, emphasising the to-be-looked-at quality of such feminine portraiture. Her direct gaze invites an intimate exchange with an imagined spectator, albeit one distanced by her new respectability and her containment within a painted roundel within the frame.

Fig.52

The Beggar's Opera

William Hogarth, 1726–8

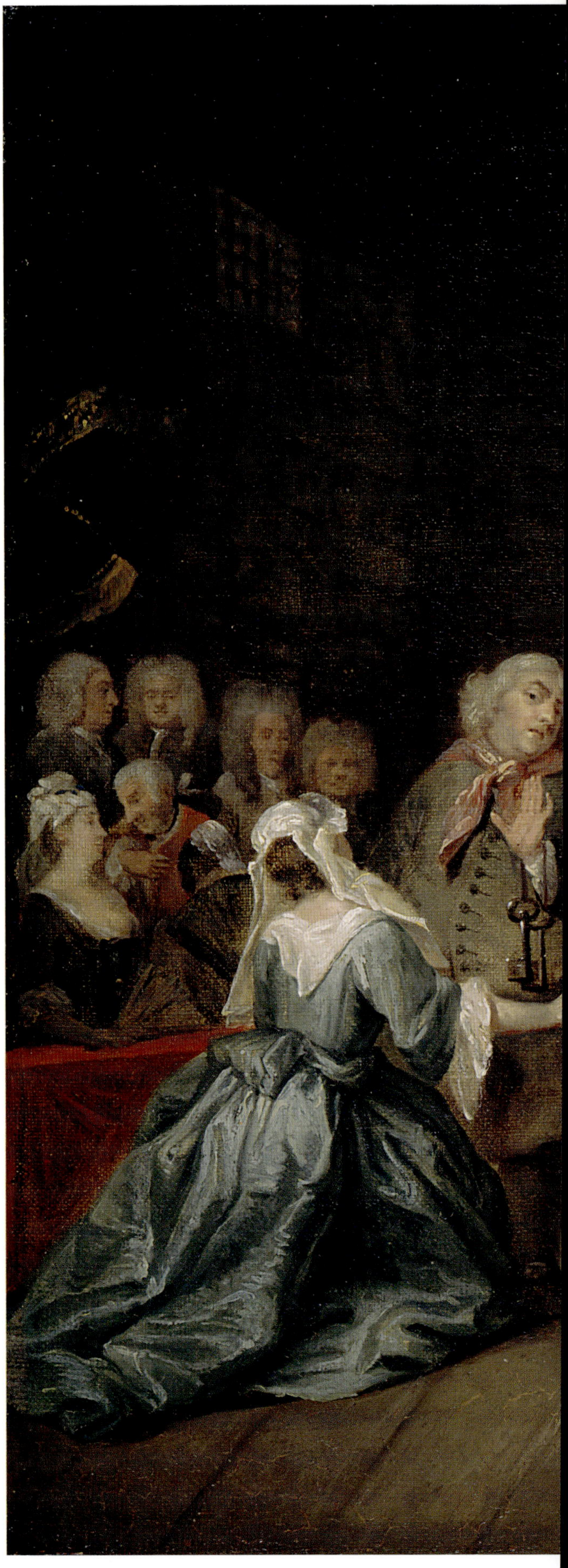

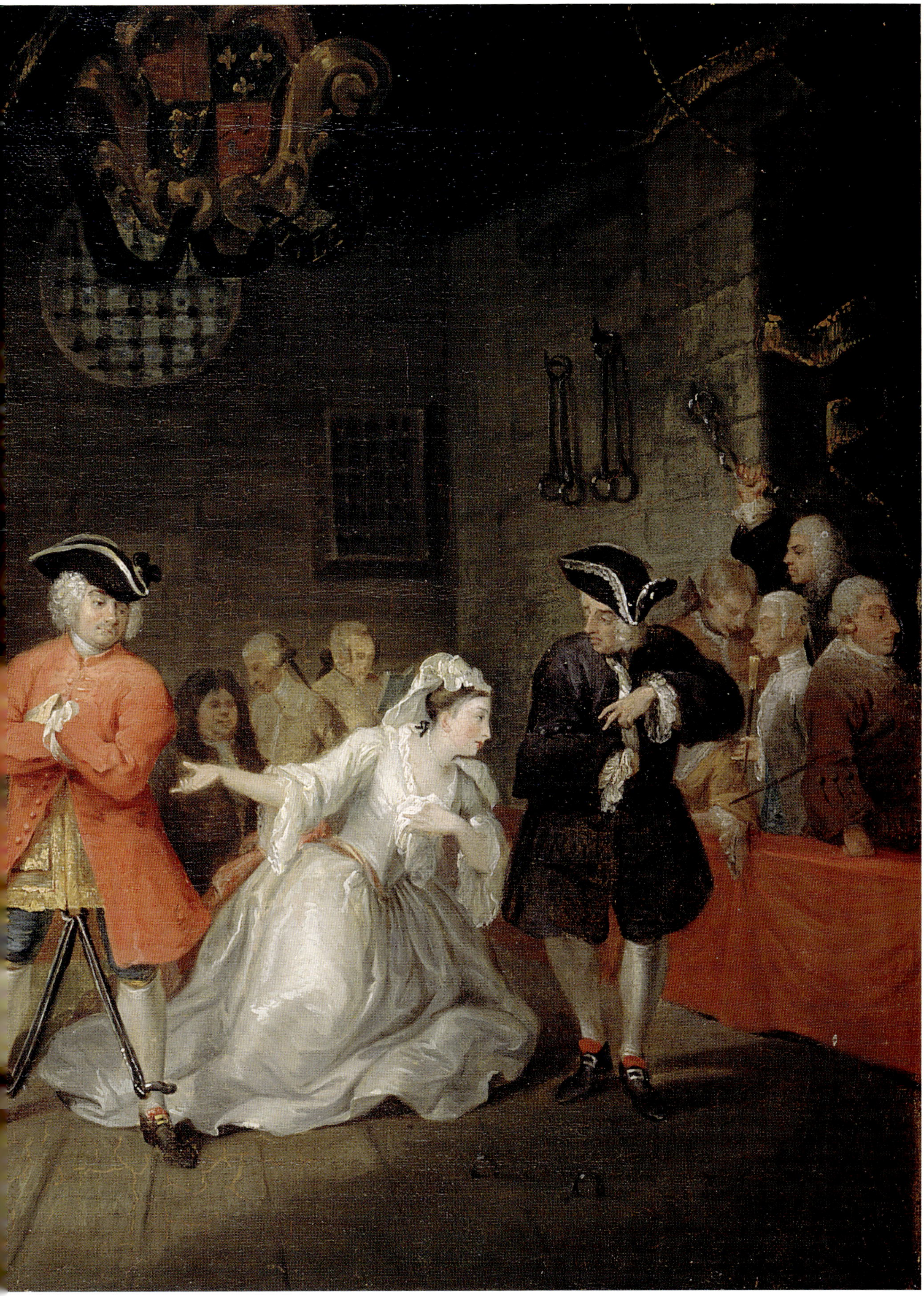

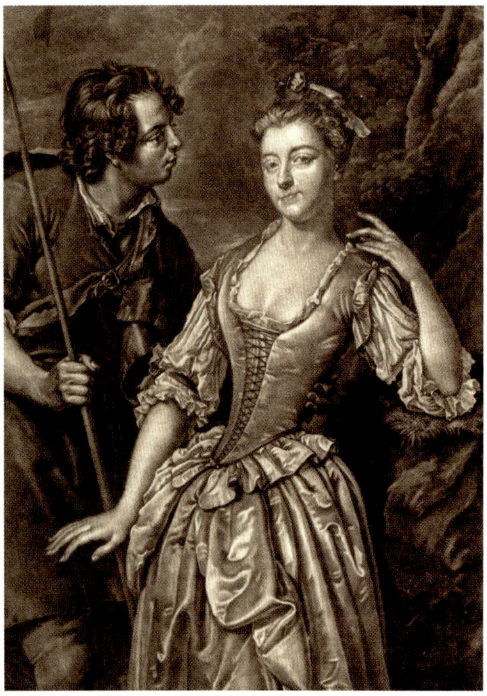

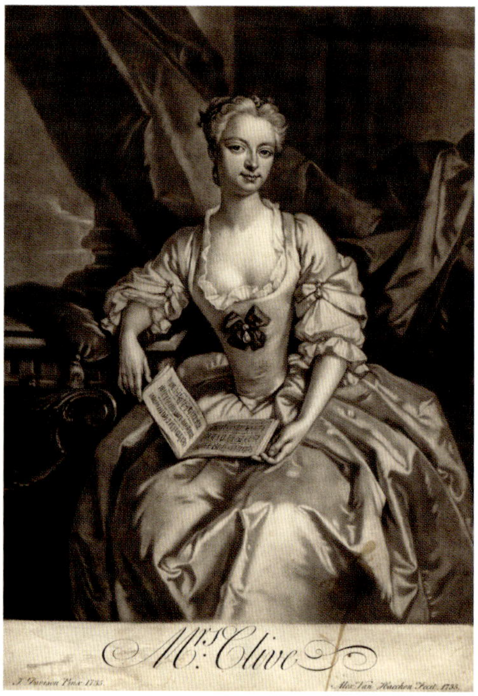

The viewer is invited to admire a complex character who appears to be both on and off the stage in the same image.

The role of Polly Peachum was much coveted by actress-singers in the period following Fenton's early retirement in 1728. Kitty Clive (1711–85) took over the part, making her debut in July 1732, and continued to play it until 1745, but not without some widely reported struggles and dramatic intrigues. In 1736 newspaper columnists were obsessed with the so-called 'Polly Row' when Clive's claim to the role was challenged by the actress-singer Susannah Cibber (fig.51), the new wife of Theophilus Cibber, then deputy manager of the Drury Lane theatre. Susannah Cibber had already established a reputation as a popular singer in Handel's Academy, and as a potential rival to Clive. After much pleading in the press by both sides, Clive managed to retain the role and enhance her star status.[18] Despite this familiar narrative of feminine rivalry exploited by the press, many of her biographies escaped the ubiquitous sexual innuendos that plagued most of her contemporaries, an achievement that has been attributed to her remarkable use of 'social leverage' and ability to manage and market her reputation.[19] The longevity of Clive's stage career from 1728 to 1769, her status as a founding member of Garrick's Drury Lane company in 1747, her multiple talents as actress, singer and playwright, all contributed to this skilfully negotiated (and evolving) public persona.

The music historian Berta Joncus has described Clive as 'perhaps the first female "pop star"' who won an early following through her performance of popular ballads.[20] This success was enhanced by the proliferation of visual imagery that linked her portrait image with her musical performances, especially when copies of commissioned portraits were disseminated through prints published with carefully chosen lines of verse. As with Fenton, Clive provides an early illustration of how the profusion of portrait imagery could be a powerful medium in the construction and marketing of celebrity myths. As her career developed, her repertoire was extended to include the later Handel compositions for which she was renowned.[21] In her early career she performed mostly in ballad operas, and was often represented in pastoral or shepherdess roles (fig.53), a common 'disguise' for feminine portraiture in the period.[22] It could signify a supposedly natural femininity or 'child of nature', an association that became increasingly desirable later in the century with the influence of the writings of Jean-Jacques Rousseau and the so-called cult of 'sensibility'. These early pastoral roles, along with that of Polly Peachum, were widely seen as evidence of Clive's early untrained voice, echoing perceptions of Fenton's 'natural' feminine talent and its flirtatious potential. Thus Clive's early portraits are often double portraits of a theatrical scene, for example with her amorous partner Damon, from Cibber's one-act opera *Damon and Phillida*, with whom she is engaged in a coy exchange.[23]

Later representations of Kitty Clive often show her in her famous parodic role as Mrs Riot, 'The Fine Lady' in Garrick's farcical play *Lethe* (fig.11), or as a dignified figure with her talents indicated by musical scores (fig.54). Davison's portrait of 1735 (fig.26) employs many of the conventions that framed noble sitters of the period, including a red draped curtain, a column and an arm resting decorously on a red velvet cushion.[24] Such rich, elegant drapery signified both artistic display (of the portrait) and the wealth and status of the sitter.[25] Clive's look engages with the viewer, yet this is a less flirtatious gaze than that of Fenton in Knapton's portrait. Clive appears relatively self-composed, and her tasteful white dress is less elaborately embroidered; the portrait signifies both sensuality and decorum, and professional achievement is reinforced by the open musical scores on her knee. In visual terms at least, Clive

Fig.53 (opposite page, left)
Catherine ('Kitty') Clive as Phillida in *Damon and Phillida*
John Faber Jr, after Peter van Bleeck, 1734

Fig.54 (opposite page, right)
Catherine ('Kitty') Clive
Alexander van Aken, after Jeremiah Davison, 1735

is distinguished from some of the ambiguous associations that haunted Fenton's 'Polly'.[26] Later portraits of Clive helped to present an image of accomplished, well-connected femininity. Upon her retirement in 1769 she moved into a house at Strawberry Hill, Twickenham, given to her by her close friend and neighbour Horace Walpole, and was well integrated into polite London society. Clive's remarkable visibility and her claims for feminine respectability, combined with her star status within a specifically British musical culture, added up to what a modern audience might describe as a 'national treasure'.

Divas, 'Divines' and Objects of Desire

Music was central to some of the most spectacular celebrity events in the mid- to late eighteenth-century social calendar.[27] The Licensing Act of 1737 (discussed in the Introduction) did not cover exclusively musical performances, and the Disorderly Houses Act of 1752 was an attempt to regulate a seemingly insatiable public appetite for musical events and fairs. The act stated that 'places of entertainment and houses used for music and dancing in London and Westminster' must obtain a licence.[28] Owners of theatres and public leisure spaces flocked to apply for music and dancing licences. Songs and musical scores were widely reproduced and disseminated, encouraging audience involvement and the cult of celebrity attached to their original performers. In mid-eighteenth-century London, ballad operas, musical comedies, pantomimes and concerts in public recreational spaces, such as Vauxhall Gardens and Ranelagh Gardens, had strong commercial appeal. In these 'pleasure gardens' actresses, actors, singers, aristocrats and royalty mingled with a mix of social classes, and a range of 'low' and 'high' music was performed, which directly influenced the repertoires of the main theatres. Both concerts and plays were staged at Ranelagh, where the glamorous actress-singer Sophia Baddeley gave some of her first performances (fig.55). By the end of the century some observers expressed concern that the nation was in the grip of a 'rage for music'.[29] Fears were rife that the popular taste for ballad and comic opera was causing a general dumbing-down of theatrical culture.

After a series of successful musical comedies in the 1760s, the Covent Garden Theatre was established as a centre of musical performance, usually lighter in style than the Italian opera performed regularly at the King's Theatre. This was London's main venue for opera and ballet in the late eighteenth century, a place where audiences could 'encounter a small part of Italy transported on to the south-west side of the Haymarket'.[30] The most famous opera singers were brought into London from an impressive continental circuit that included Rome, Naples, Milan, Florence, Venice, Lisbon, Paris, Vienna and St Petersburg, helping to create a transnational star system that echoed the international travels of the well-heeled British nobility and gentry. The expansion of British territories abroad encouraged such international contact, while also fuelling the national desire to define a British musical culture. In the early 1770s the Pantheon opened in Oxford Street as a lavish space for concerts, balls, masquerades, theatrical performances and exhibitions with both British and international appeal. This opulent site of entertainment was popular with women and became one of the most spectacular venues for Italian opera singers.[31]

Apart from Cuzzoni and Faustina earlier in the century, many of these international female stars who performed in London qualify for the gendered term 'diva'. Coined in the nineteenth century from the Italian *divina* or 'divine', it was originally used to describe great female opera singers, but its associations can be traced back to the eighteenth century.[32] The word signified the goddess-like character

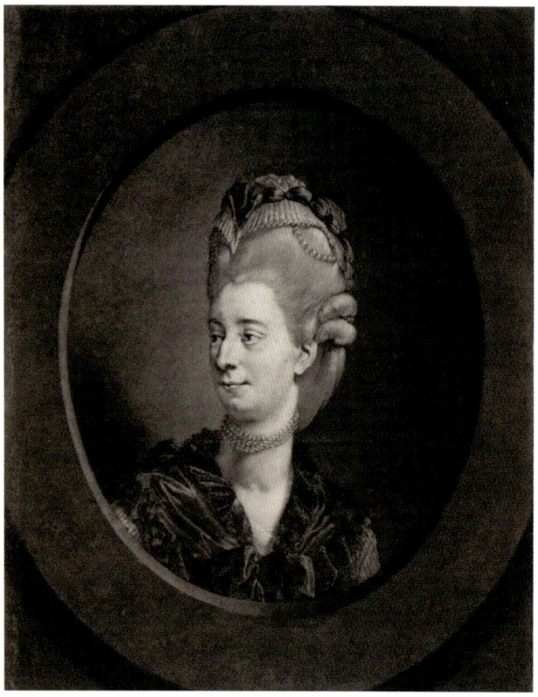

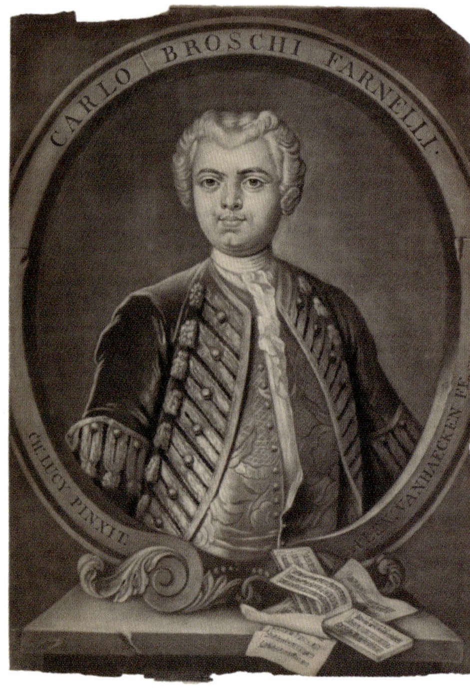

attributed to a soprano – or in some cases mezzo-soprano or contralto – with extraordinary musical virtuosity and a flair for the grandiose. Such singers could inspire emotive responses and obsessive admiration. In later usage the term has also come to signify a 'prima donna' who may be headstrong and difficult, exploiting her exceptional talents in other forms of theatrical display. More recently, the term has been expanded to describe singers of more popular forms of music, whose tempestuous lives or impassioned singing have inspired their admirers. Divas are fictional characters; like painted portraits they provide vivid reconstructions of dramatic, seductive, extravagant, ambitious or regal characters. Many aspects of the modern concept have their roots in eighteenth-century musical culture. It is often argued that the first operatic 'divines' were castrati who sang in soprano and alto registers and whose extraordinary florid voices, like those of the famous 'Senesino' or Farinelli (fig.56), were seen as ethereal or otherworldly.[33] As the undisputed stars of early opera, the castrati were celebrated but also abused, 'as half-men, capons … and monsters of vanity, extravagance and bad temper'.[34]

Apart from these vain and temperamental associations, the idea of the successful female singer or actress possessing extraordinary, goddess-like or 'divine' talents was also well established in earlier theatrical discourse. As Joseph Roach has vividly demonstrated in the preceding chapter, 'Nell' had already become a charismatic object of worship, comparable with the idolatry conferred on the monarch in the late seventeenth century. By the mid- to late eighteenth century, sobriquets such as 'the divine Siddons' and 'the divine Baddeley' had begun to pepper theatrical reviews and gossip columns.[35] A 'divine' could enthral her audience through both her voice and her acting abilities, as was demonstrated by Siddons's famously absorbing and majestic tragic roles (discussed on p.113), or the evocative performances of actress-singers such as Baddeley. Such female performers were seen to have a remarkable capacity to translate and communicate deep emotions, a quality often attributed to divas. And this representation of both the singer and the actress as 'divine' has been sustained and developed in theatre and film history of the last two centuries. From the 'divine Sarah' Bernhardt to the idolised 'divine Garbo' of the 1930s, or the 'divine Vanessa' (Redgrave) in the twenty-first century, the association has become common currency, perpetuated, refined and exploited by biographers, publishers and film directors.[36] A key concern of this book is the way in which such female idols have been constructed or mediated through visual imagery. 'Divinity' can be evoked – or undermined – by many painterly codes and portrait conventions.

A late eighteenth-century actress and mezzo-soprano who qualifies well for the retrospective designation 'divine diva' was Elizabeth Billington (1765–1818), a child prodigy who developed early talents as an actress, singer and composer of sonatas for violin and piano. Her capacity for self-promotion, essential to the stereotype of the modern diva, was established at an early age. She wrote while performing in Dublin in 1783 that she was fêted as a 'very pretty actress' and acclaimed as 'the greatest player in the world' on the pianoforte.[37] Once back on the London stage Billington won a reputation for her range as singer and her operatic performances were crowd-pullers. She famously commanded high fees and her success was consolidated through the commissioning of major portraits by Sir Joshua Reynolds, John Hoppner and George Romney, among others. Reynolds's work, titled *Portrait of a Celebrated Singer*, was displayed in the Royal Academy exhibition of 1790 (see fig.57). Eighteenth-century star-spotters would have easily identified the singer. And the association with St Cecilia, the patron saint of music, in this large-scale commission was an

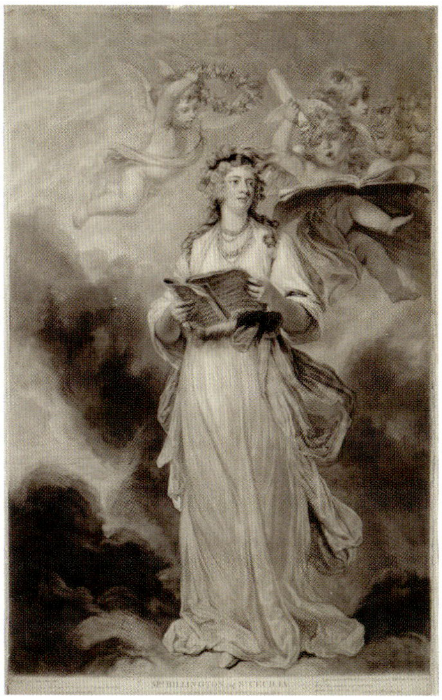

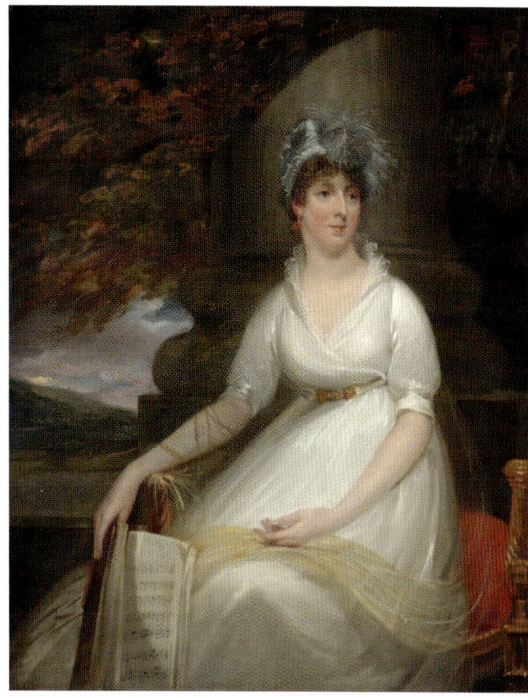

effective exercise in self-promotion, possibly chosen by the sitter herself. Reynolds rose to the challenge of endowing her with the trappings of divinity. Posed in pseudo-classical stage dress and monumentalised from below like a saint ascending to heaven, she is serenaded by cherubim. But such grandiose representations combined with her colourful private life (she was rumoured to have had affairs with many well-known figures), stunning commercial success and increasingly portly size also made her an easy target of popular satire.

Hoppner's three-quarter portrait (fig.36) presents a more earthly, self-composed figure, with the statutory musical score in her right hand. The white robe, gauze shawl and feathered hat may reference her stage dress, as parodied by Gillray, but transformed into 'everyday wear' for her painted portrait. The print reveals the hybrid nature of some women's stage costumes of the period, combining fashionable accessories with theatrical, pseudo-classical robes. Hoppner's more intimate portrait effectively deploys the delicately feathered blue hat as a signifier of the sitter's modishness and, perhaps, as a counter to the more majestic ambitions of the Reynolds. By the late eighteenth century white lace or satin, sometimes adorned with blue ribbons, had become a desirable combination for stylish feminine dress.[38] Billington's long career, musical diversity and much-trumpeted professional ambitions inspired a range of visual representations; a composite identity that ranged from sweet warbler (in her performance of 'Sweet Bird' in Handel's *L'allegro ed il penseroso*) to heavenly diva.

Gillray's *A Bravura Air* (fig.59), like other satirical images, portrays Billington with wide open mouth in full song, a pose rarely adopted in eighteenth-century high-art portraiture of women, for fear of presenting an unseemly image of feminine performance, despite the fact that the greatest divas were distinguished by their exceptional vocal

Fig.55 (opposite page, left)
Sophia Baddeley
Robert Laurie, after Johan Joseph Zoffany, 1772

Fig.56 (opposite page, right)
Carlo Broschi ('Farinelli')
Alexander van Aken, after Charles Lucy, 1735

Fig.57 (above left)
Elizabeth Billington
James Ward, after Sir Joshua Reynolds, 1803

Fig.36 (above right)
Elizabeth Billington
John Hoppner, *c.*1801

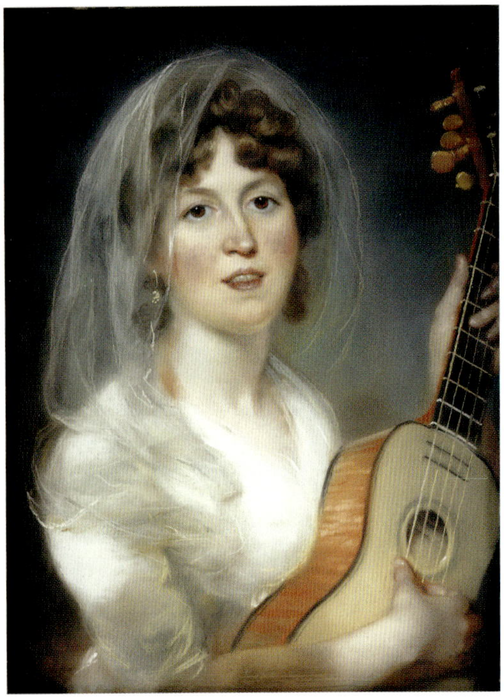

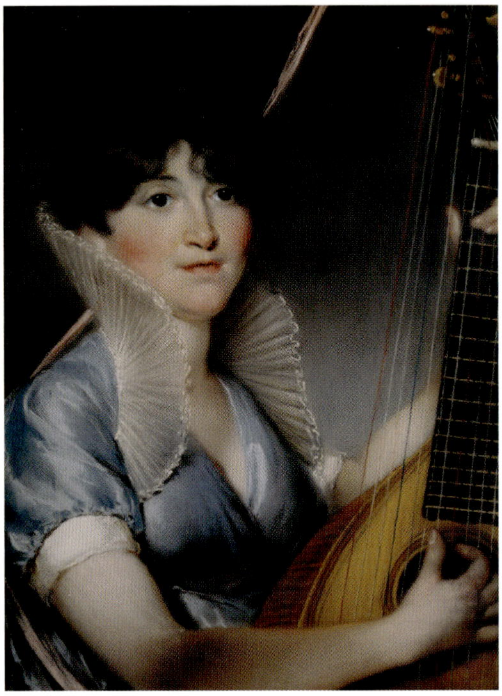

Fig.58 (above left)
Elizabeth Bannister
John Russell, 1799

Fig.35 (above right)
Dorothy Jordan
John Russell, 1801

Fig.59 (opposite)
Elizabeth Billington ('A Bravura Air')
James Gillray, 1801

skills. Yet to depict this unearthly, all-absorbing voice in a painted portrait, to represent the fully open mouth, could undermine desirable femininity and threaten established gendered oppositions. As the source of her extraordinary vocal power, the diva's mouth provided an ambiguous visual spectacle.[39] A wide open mouth could distort the feminine face and carry troubling sexual connotations.[40] Thus Reynolds's portrait depicts a slightly open mouth, full of promise yet appropriately contained for a divinity. More intimate portraits of women singers from the period, such as Dorothy Jordan (fig.35) or Elizabeth Bannister (fig.58) by the pastel artist John Russell, also avoid the full open mouth, although Bannister is shown singing with slightly parted lips. And both these portraits include musical instruments which their sitters had played on stage. Bannister plays the guitar, Jordan the theorbo, a seventeenth-century multi-stringed instrument. In eighteenth-century portraiture of both theatrical and upper-class sitters, women were more often represented with musical props than men, loading such instruments with gendered connotations. Social status and gender were indicated by both the uses and representations of these objects in commissioned portraits. While harpsichords, pianos, guitars and harps required seated performance and were deemed appropriate for private feminine use, violins – which require more vigorous movement of the upper body – were widely seen as suitable principally for men. Women were rarely represented playing the violin, a division of labour satirised by Gillray in his *Ars-musica* (fig.63).[41] The inclusion of a musical instrument in a painted portrait of a female performer could carry important symbolic functions. Its presence could affirm the gendered preferences, famous roles and iconic status of the singer, and also suggest her sexual desirability. Thus Russell's portrait of Jordan of 1801 presents the actress as a young-looking, rosy-cheeked and soft-skinned comedienne (she

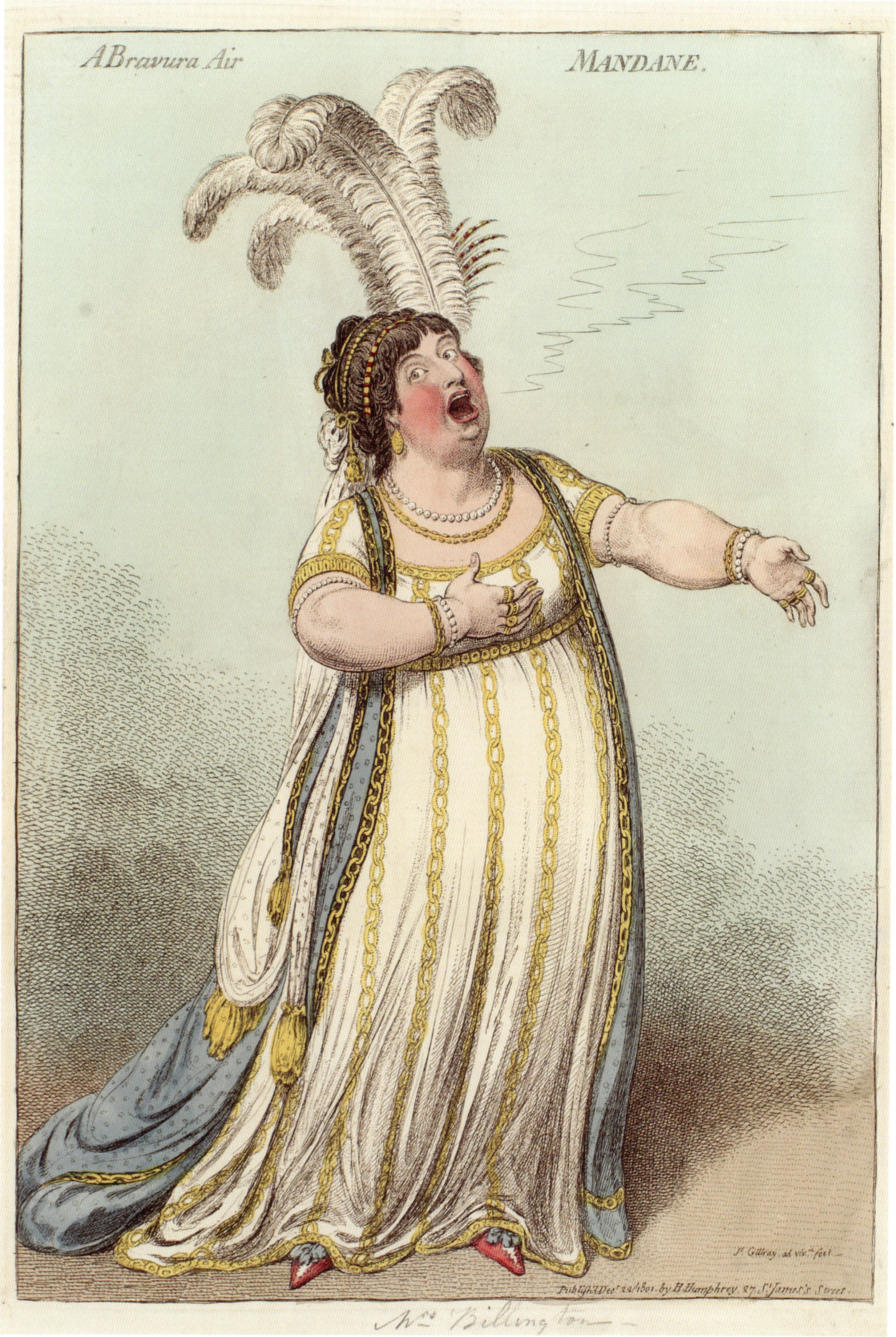
A Bravura Air
MANDANE.

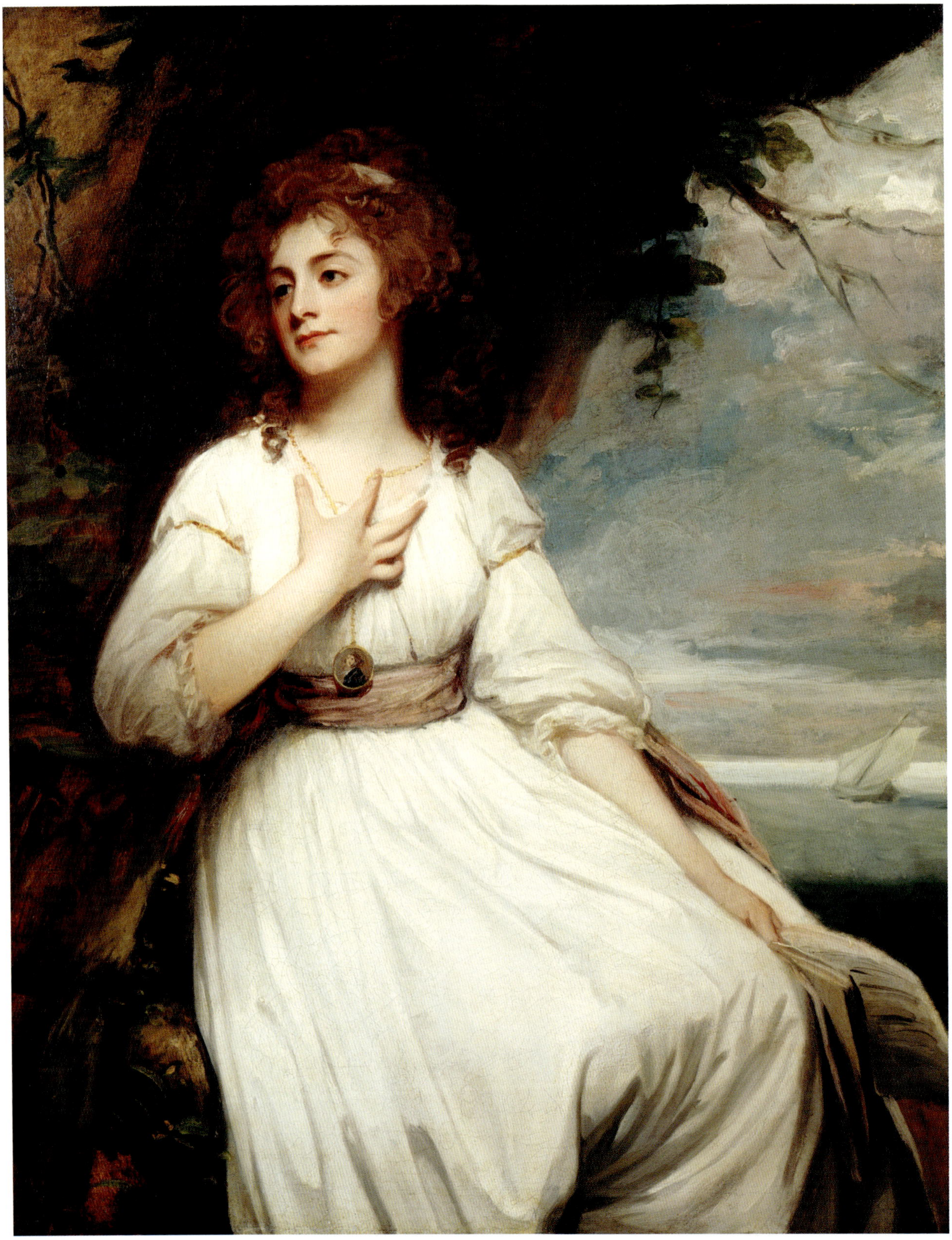

Fig.60

Anna Maria Crouch

George Romney, 1787

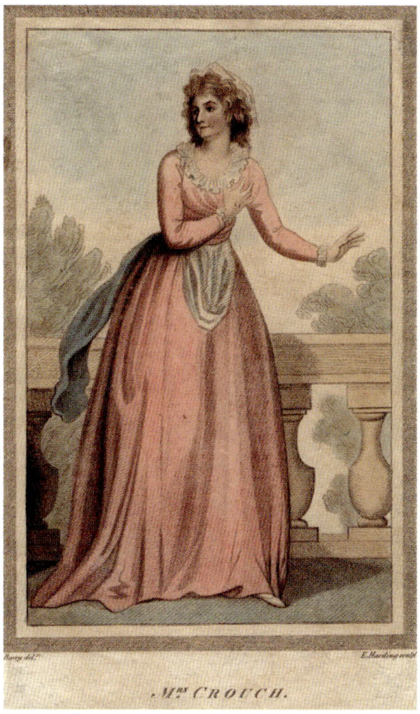

Fig.61 (left)
Anna Maria Crouch
Edward Harding, after James Barry, late 18th century

Fig.62 (following pages)
Marie Sallé Dancing
Nicolas de Larmessin, after Nicolas Lancret, *c.*1730–2

was in fact approaching forty). The artist was famous for his pastel technique of 'sweetening', using fingers to blend colours, creating the equivalent of a modern soft-focus lens. Such painterly techniques also contributed to the myth of Jordan as a 'natural' actress, fêted for her eponymous role as *The Child of Nature* in Elizabeth Inchbald's play of the same name.[42] Russell carefully crops his image, contributing to the emphasis on her 'sweetened' face and avoiding the dominance of the theorbo, a large instrument with a long neck, which became one of her famous stage props and evidence of her musical range. The cropped theorbo, like the guitar in the portrait of Bannister, becomes a part-object with multiple functions. Although only partly visible, its suggestive, rounded forms echo the curves and sensuality of the female singer's body, while also signifying her professional accomplishments.

Another pervasive myth of feminine theatricality was that of the jealous diva, and Billington was often seen as a direct rival to the soprano Anna Maria Crouch, who also combined popular roles as Polly Peachum with opera and acting. Crouch was glamorous and stylish. Her performances were as popular and her private life as colourful as those of Billington. As Lady Macbeth she reputedly impressed her followers in 'a fancy hat, powdered hair, rouge, point lace and linen enough to enchant the spectator',[43] reinforcing the power of the accessorised feminine performance to beguile an audience. Crouch also enhanced her celebrity status with commissioned portraits by Sir Thomas Lawrence, James Barry and George Romney (figs 60, 61). In Romney's portrait of 1787 Crouch is painted with hand on heart, clutching the chain of her naval lieutenant husband's miniature as he sails off in the background. She appears as if in character, holding her musical score in her left hand and leaning on a rock, a symbol of her constancy. For those in the know, the passions evoked by this portrait of feminine yearning had ironic overtones. In the same year, she became involved with the famous Irish tenor Michael Kelly, who apparently moved in with the Crouches before they separated in 1791. Romney has used allegory, pose, a natural setting and material clues to conflate the public and private identities of this celebrated soprano, constructing a mythical image of a late eighteenth-century 'woman of feeling'.

Dancer-Actresses and 'Impures'

During this period painted images of famous dancers in performance were rarely seen in public and private exhibitions, although dancing women can often be found in popular prints (fig.64).[44] This absence from high art reveals moral anxieties about displaying the female body in vigorous exertion, the difficulties of capturing movements through time in a single painted image, and the aesthetic and economic constraints of portrait conventions. The representation of a single dancer in performance was often best served by the full-length format, the most ambitious and expensive form of portrait commission. Cheaper and more popular head-and-shoulders commissions provide less scope for representing movement, and many surviving portraits of dancers are in this standard format, with no reference to their performance skills. And upper-class women sitters were usually only found performing graceful movement in full-length portraits when disguised as wood nymphs, goddesses, shepherdesses or bacchantes, which endowed the subject with mythological licence to jump, skip or dance.

Among the best-known early eighteenth-century portraits of professional dancers in performance are works by the French artist Nicolas Lancret, notably his paintings from the 1730s of the internationally renowned Marie-Anne Cupis Camargo and Marie Sallé (fig.62), which were

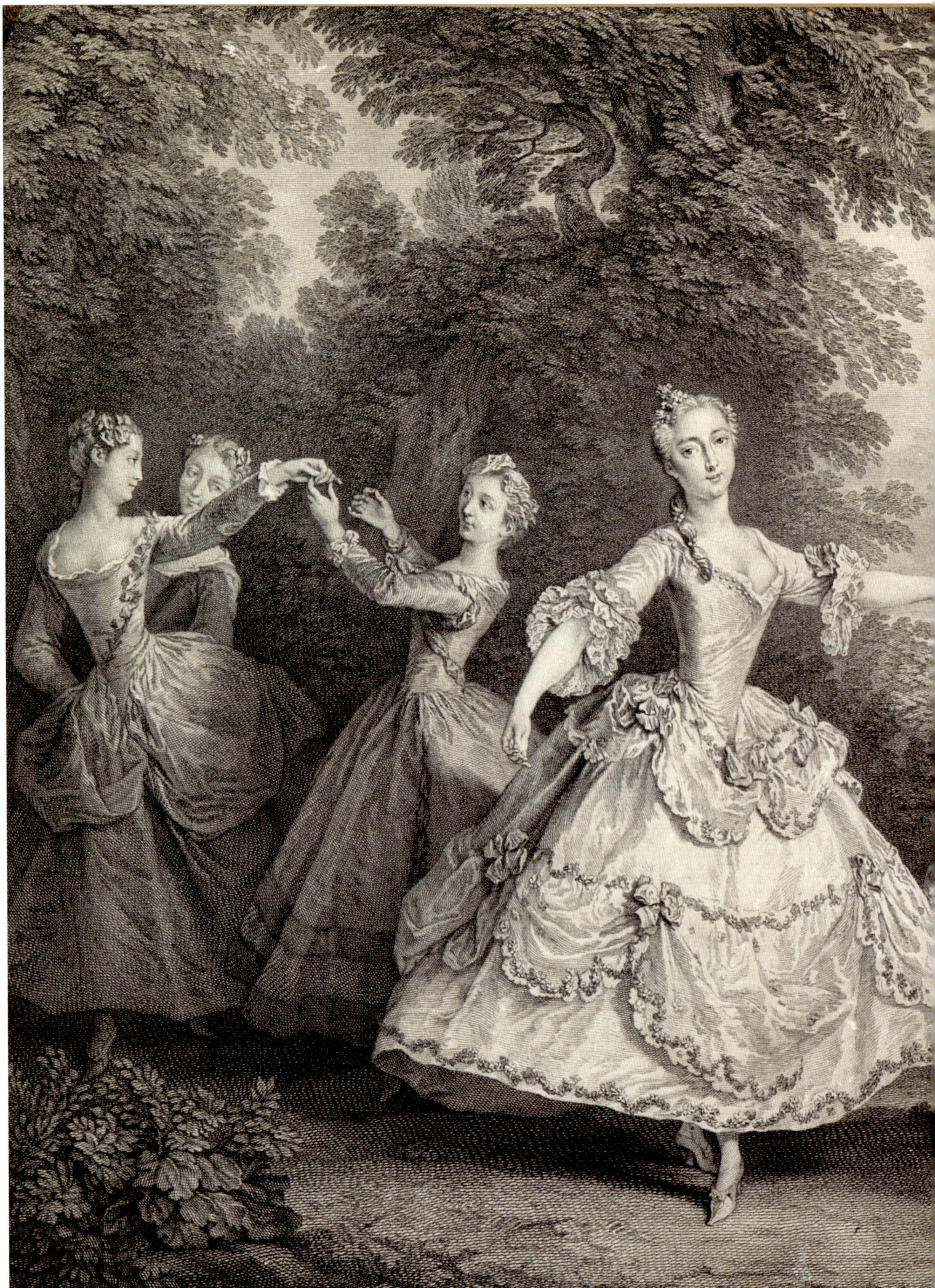

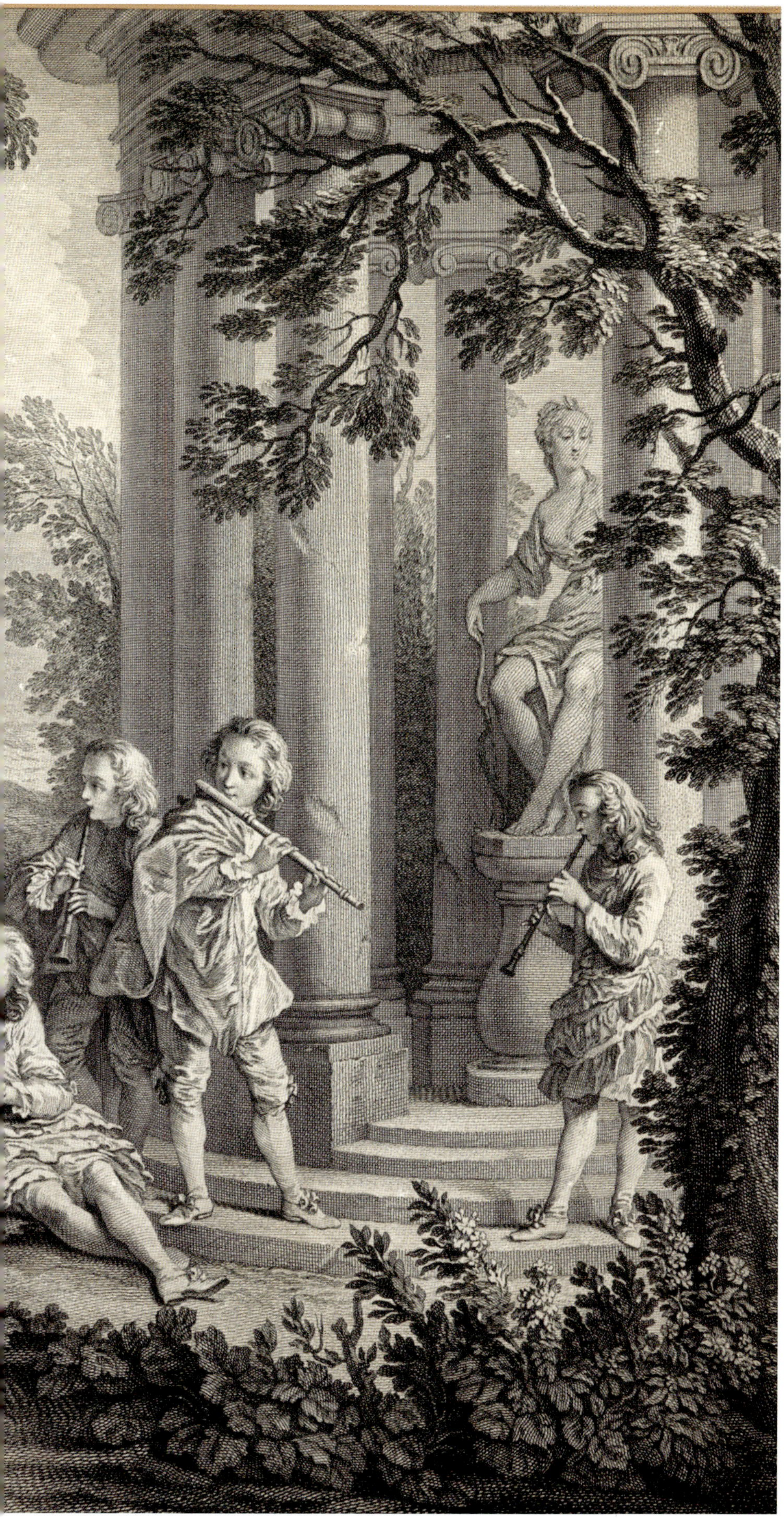

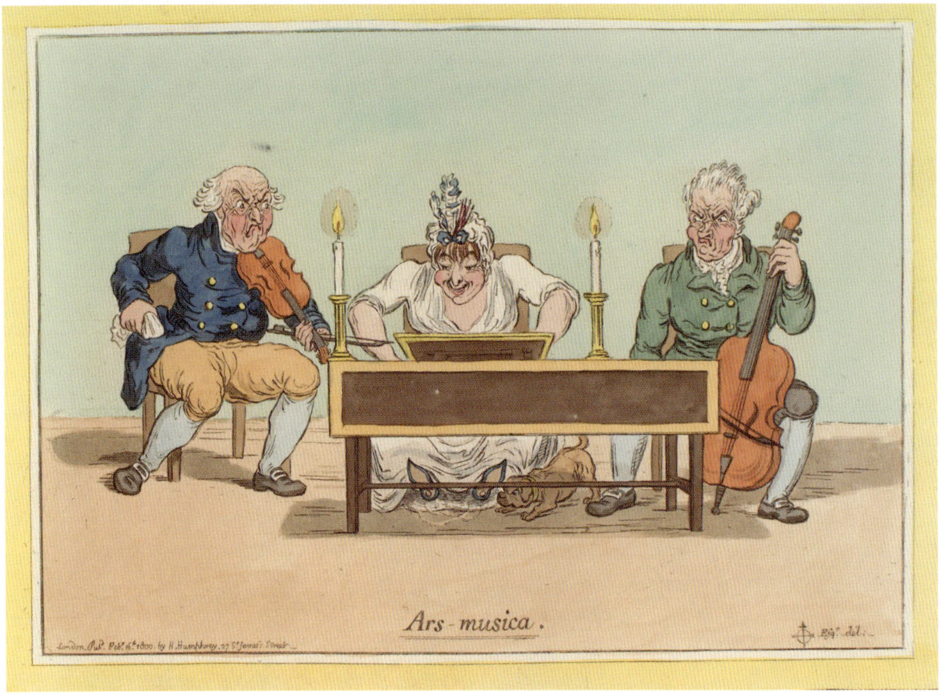

disseminated in Britain through printed copies and reflected the strong influence in Europe of the French tradition of *la belle danse*, originating in the Baroque era and patronised by the French court. Sallé followed an international itinerary and took London by storm, performing regularly at Lincoln's Inn Fields. Moreover, French dancing masters (usually male) dominated the teaching of dance and early ballet throughout the eighteenth century in Europe and Britain, and influential figures such as Jean-Georges Noverre and Gaeten and Auguste Vestris rose to pre-eminence later in the century, helping to establish ballet as an independent art form, rather than merely an adjunct of opera.

At the beginning of the century most London theatre companies included several women best described as dancer-actresses. An evening at the theatre usually included a main drama, an 'afterpiece' – often a dance – and entr'actes between the acts of the main play. Actresses were often expected to perform in each part of the programme. Hester Booth (née Santlow) was one such star performer whose repertoire included comic, Shakespearean and dance roles. Booth was closely identified with her popular entr'acte Harlequin solo that transformed a well-established *commedia dell'arte* character into a female dancer (Harlequine). In a striking portrait by John Ellys (fig.24),[45] she wears a feminine adaptation of the male Harlequin outfit, comprising a stunning jacket and skirt of purple, blue, red and yellow triangular patches, and a jaunty version of the Harlequin's hat. The portrait shows her performing specific dance movements more often represented in engravings, which have been identified with her famous Harlequin solo. Movement is largely represented in the upper body, as the dancer's legs are politely covered with her floor-length skirt (which would probably have been un-hooped to allow movement), rather than the shorter skirts usually worn in performance. These revealed their footwork and seductively exposed the ankles (see also fig.62).[46] Framed by the familiar draped curtain and stately column, the dramatic physicality of the dance is transformed into a frozen image of decorous femininity in a fabulous costume. She appears to be turning to the right, with her right arm and fingers gracefully resting on her hat, and her left hand clasping her slapstick, probably following a notated Harlequin dance.[47] One aspect of this portrait sits uneasily with this static image of decorous movement: the long locks of her auburn hair blow out in horizontal bands, suggesting a more vigorous, centripetal movement as she turns. Booth is reported to have used her hair, a powerful symbol of her femininity, as part of the spectacle of this vigorous dance. According to a later account, 'in the very ecstasy of her dance, Santlow contrived to loosen her clustering auburn hair, and letting it fall … danced on, the locks flying in the air'.[48] Despite established conventions for representing the passions in art, the ecstasy of the dance was not easily translated into the language of early eighteenth-century feminine portraiture.[49] Yet it is Booth's 'clustering' hair that appears to dance and flow in this portrait, standing metonymically for the movement of her whole body. Ellys's portrait therefore provides subtle indicators of both graceful feminine movement and the physical exertions of dance; as such, it is an image that encapsulates the social and aesthetic contradictions confronted by dancer-actresses and also their portraitists.

Later in the century one of England's most successful painters of theatrical portraits, John Hoppner (1758–1810), also rose to the challenge of depicting actresses in movement. Hoppner was distinguished by his flattering images of sitters in fashionable costumes and accessories of rich, tactile fabrics which pronounced the well-heeled glamour of his clients. Apart from his many royal and aristocratic commissions, his theatrical clients included

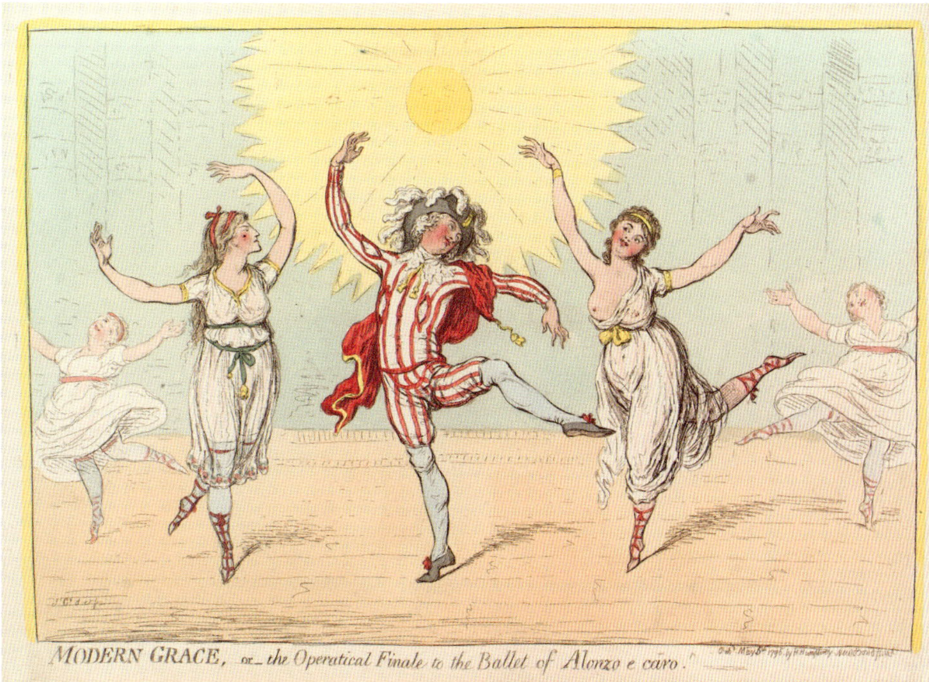

Mary Robinson, Dorothy Jordan, Elizabeth Inchbald, Elizabeth Billington and the dancer Mlle Hilligsberg.[50] In 1786 he exhibited at the Royal Academy an ambitious full-length portrait of his friend Dorothy Jordan as the Comic Muse (Thalia), when she was living with the Duke of Clarence (with whom she had a twenty-year relationship, and ten children, but never married). The portrait (fig.65) shows a sweet-faced Jordan turning her body dramatically towards the viewer, as if performing a demanding dance movement. Meanwhile, Euphrosyne, the Grace of Good Humour, repulses a lecherous satyr. Although Hoppner had used a mythological disguise to licence this physical movement, Jordan's strangely twisted body was, I suggest, too close to the contortions of an unfeminine dance movement, and provoked some hostile reviews. Her body did not match with the 'accepted ideas of Thalia', and she was described as a 'dwarfish muse'. Such negative criticisms were easily associated with salacious speculations about the actress's sexual availability.[51] Allegorical or mythological disguises could not guarantee the elevation or dignity of their sitters, especially if the physical demeanour of the actress appeared overtly sensual or involved odd or vigorous movement.

However, of his portrait of *Mlle Hilligsberg* (fig.66), Hoppner allegedly claimed he had painted 'the best thing I ever did'.[52] Hilligsberg is shown with dainty dancing feet and ankles clearly visible and framed by rich red drapes (possibly a stage curtain), with a tambourine on a table beside her. Another woman who commanded high fees, Hilligsberg was one of the leading dancers at the King's Theatre and was renowned for her light and graceful style.[53] In comparison with Jordan's strangely twisted body, her demeanour appears both graceful and restrained. Her hair is motionless and her arms barely raised as she engages the viewer's look. Unlike some other famous dancers whose

Fig.63 (opposite page)
'Ars-musica'
James Gillray, 1800

Fig.64 (above)
'Modern grace, – or – the Operatical Finale to the Ballet of Alonzo e Caro' (Rose Didelot; Charles Louis Didelot; Mme Parisot)
James Gillray, 1796

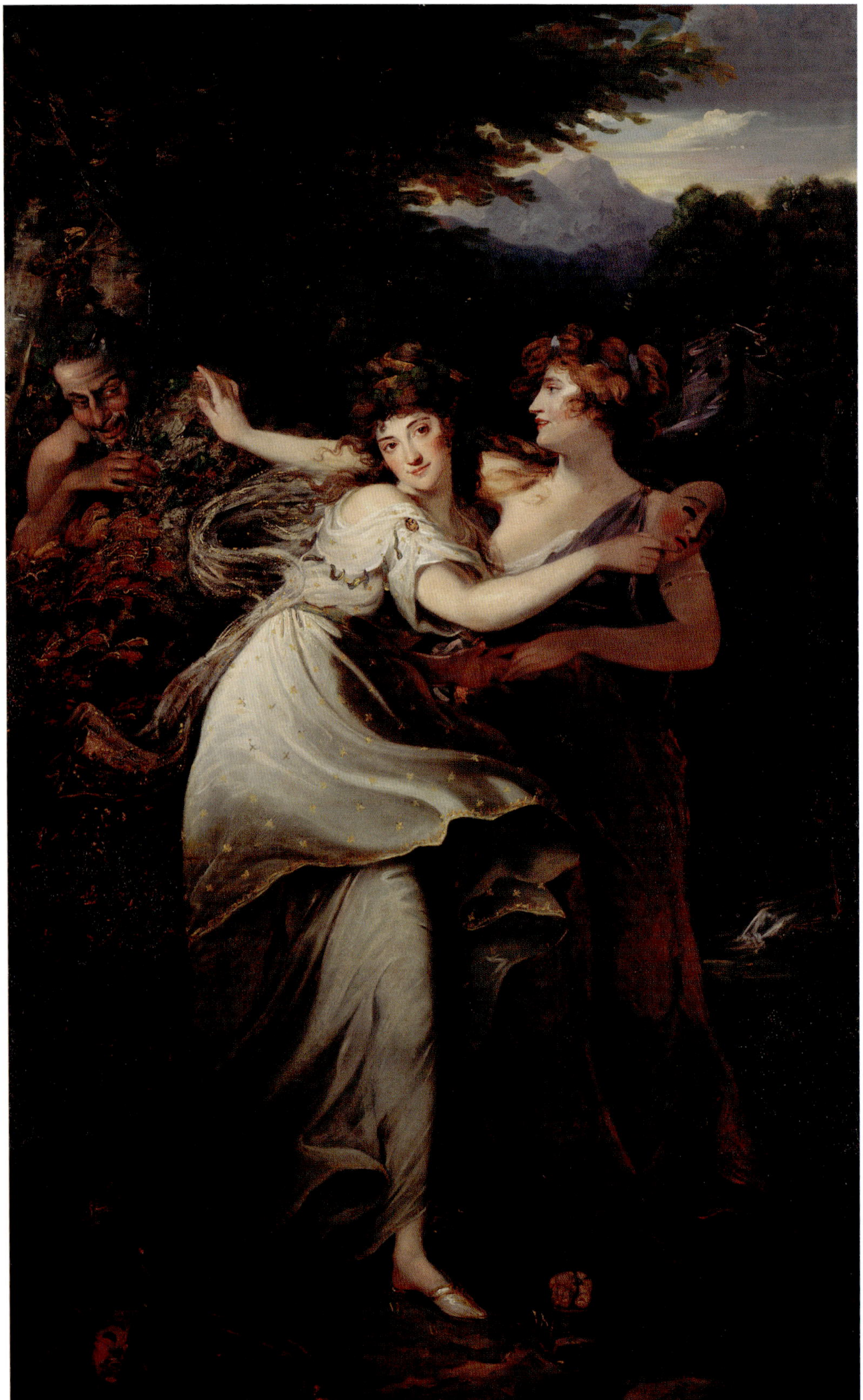

Fig.65

Dorothy Jordan as the Comic Muse

John Hoppner, 1786

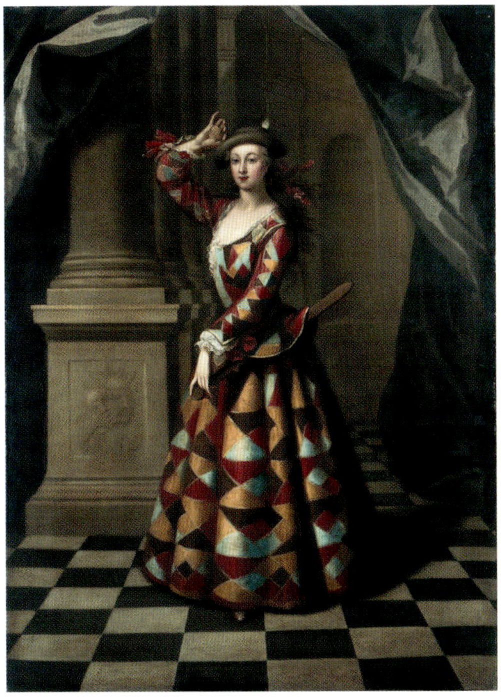

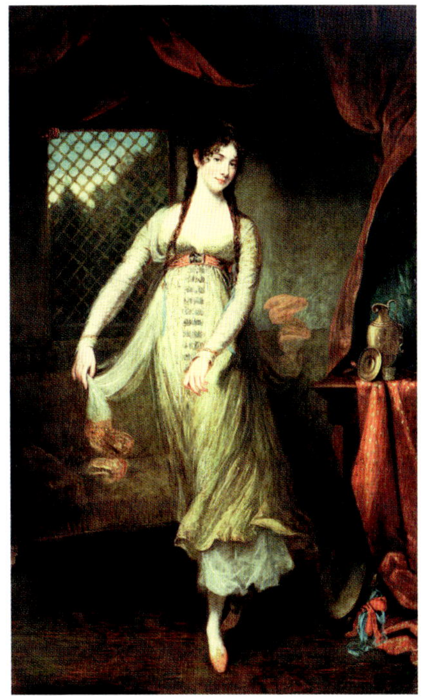

Fig.24 (above left)
Hester Booth
John Ellys, *c.*1722–5

Fig.66 (above right)
Mlle Hilligsberg
John Hoppner, *c.*1781

potentially dangerous sexuality was often signalled by reviewers, Hilligsberg's performances gave rise to a myth of 'chaste' dancing.[54] After her death in France in 1804 the *Gentleman's Magazine* noted that 'her style of dancing was chaste and simple, and her execution light and elegant'.[55] Hilligsberg's genteel style of movement was seen then to correct the unseemly physicality of some women's dance, to convey a quality of elegant, sexual restraint.

Despite this apparently 'chaste' performance, sexual innuendo and fears of their loose morals haunted reviews of both the performances and portraits of many women dancers throughout the century: they were seen by some newspapers to belong to 'the highest order of the impures'.[56] For some, retirement following marriage was the only respectable option, as demonstrated by the Austrian-born dancer Eva-Maria Veigel, sometimes known by her stage name Violette, who left the stage when she married David Garrick. Although early paintings of Veigel in performance are rare, there are several later double portraits with Garrick, in which she appears as a model of respectable femininity, assisting with, or admiring his creative productions (figs 67, 68). In Reynolds's portrait of 1772–3, her previous professional identity is politely ignored. Veigel is represented in terms of her marital status, her fabled beauty and exquisite taste in dress. In this context, her gorgeous, richly embroidered white dress denotes her husband's financial and social success, and dominates the foreground of the portrait, in which Garrick appears to be seeking her approval after a play-reading. Such forms of double portraiture were unthinkable outside marriage, and reflected the star status of the partnership.[57]

Although she was fêted for the elegance and refinement of her dancing, Giovanna Baccelli (see fig.30), another international star of the Paris Opera and the King's Theatre in the 1780s, could not escape prurient gossip, despite her

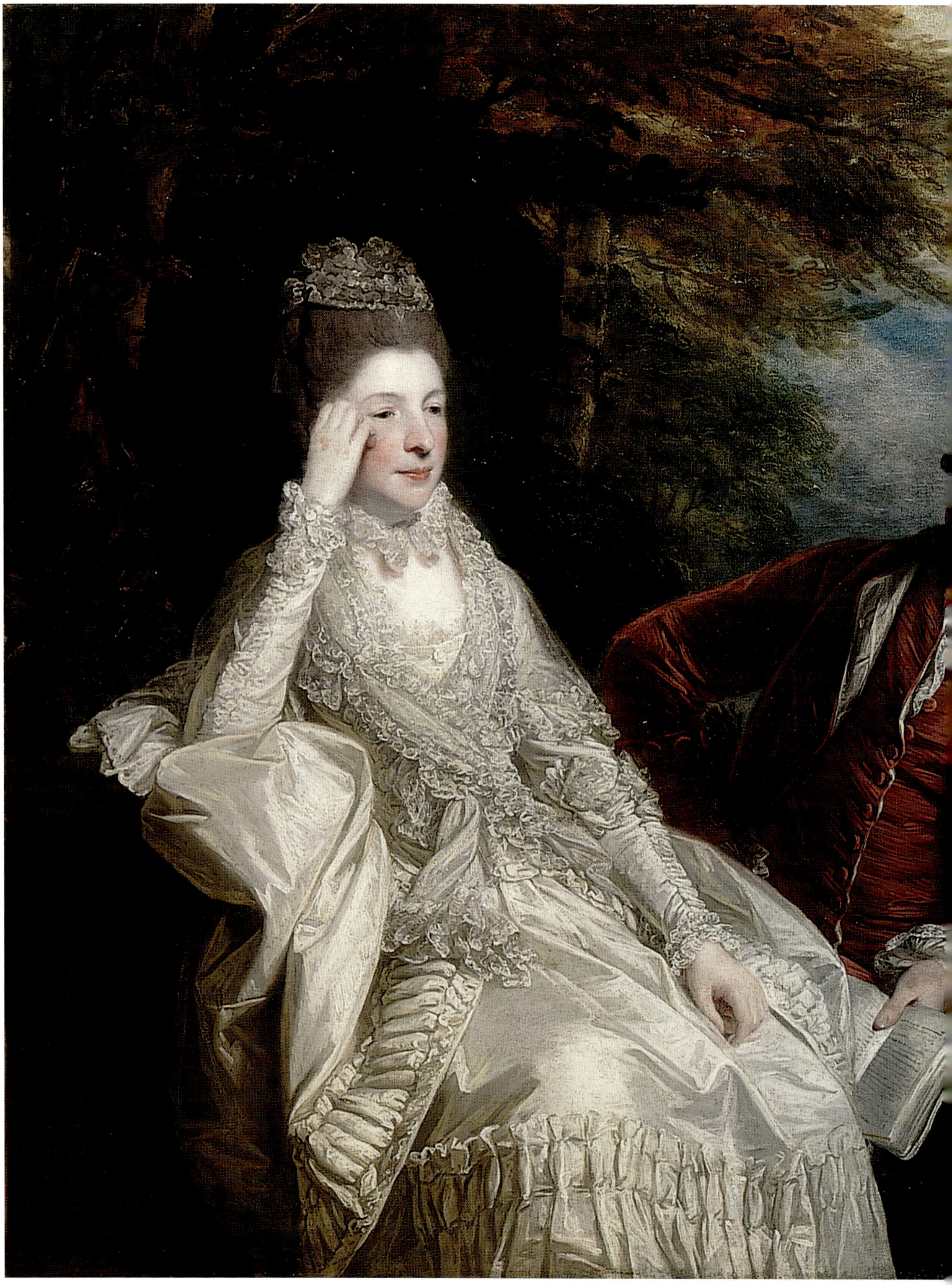

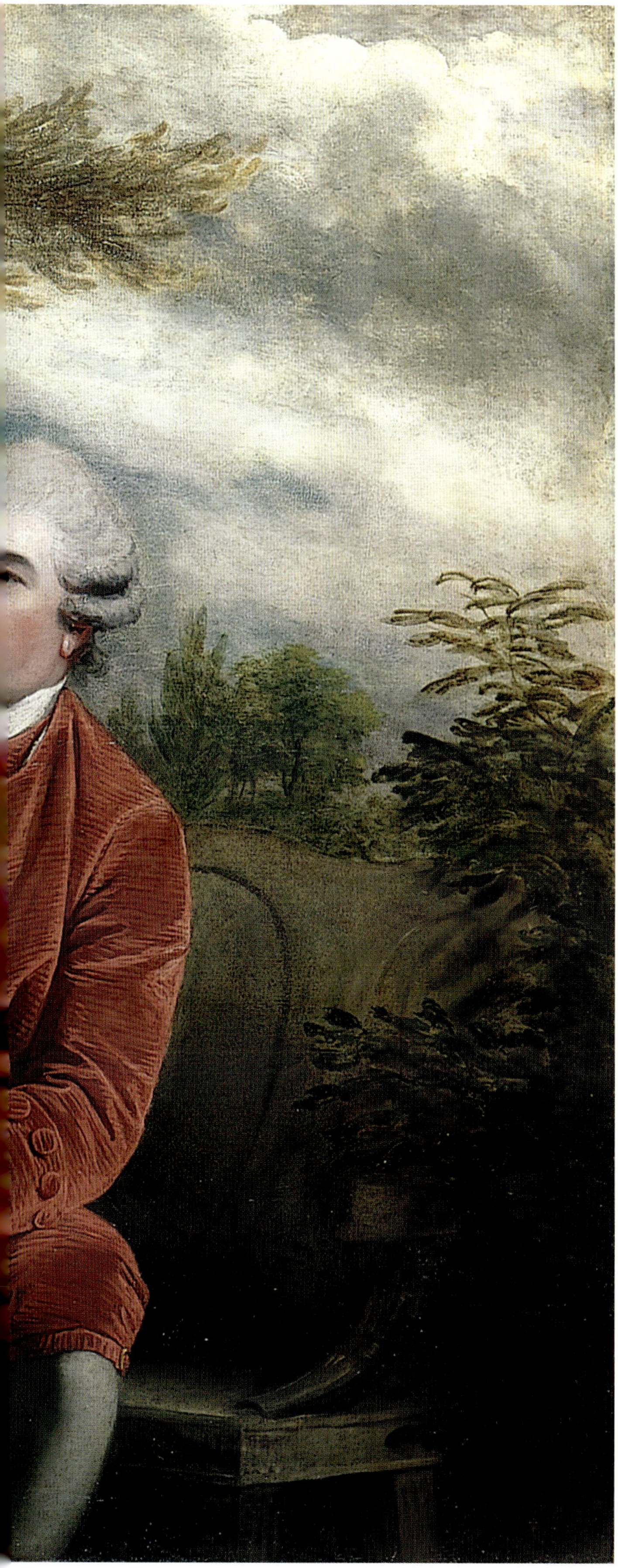

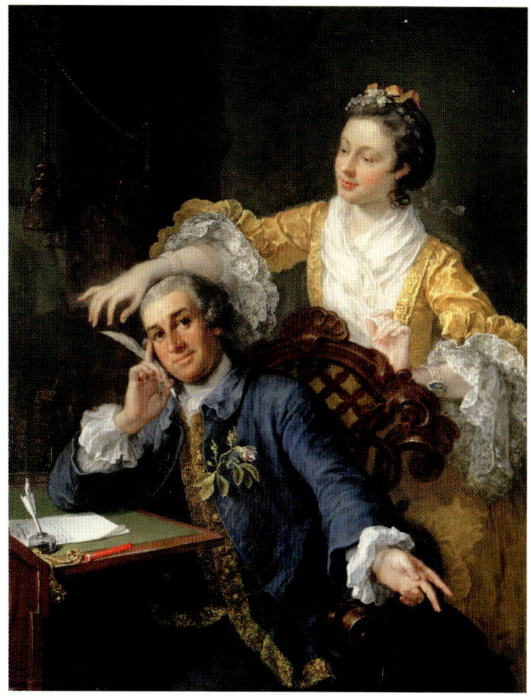

Fig.67 (left)

David and Eva-Maria Garrick

Sir Joshua Reynolds, 1772–3

Fig.68 (above)

David Garrick and his Wife, Eva-Maria

William Hogarth, 1757

Fig.30 (following page, left)

Giovanna Baccelli

Thomas Gainsborough, exhib. 1782

Fig.69 (following page, right)

Mary Robinson – Perdita

Thomas Gainsborough, 1781

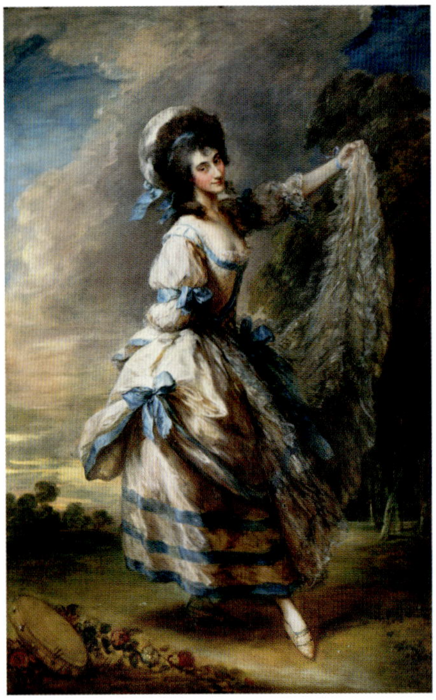

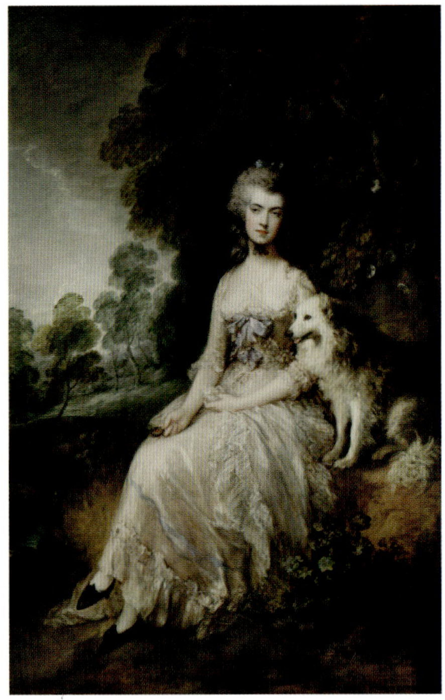

ten-year relationship with John Frederick Sackville, 3rd Duke of Dorset, whom she accompanied to Paris when he was appointed British Ambassador in 1783. Although they never married, he commissioned portraits of Baccelli by Reynolds, Gainsborough and Ozias Humphry, and publicly exhibited at the Royal Academy. This remarkable public visibility, and the engraved copies of portraits that circulated after her famous performances (fig.124), contributed to Baccelli's status as 'the Object of so much Admiration'.[58]

Gainsborough was a keen supporter of the King's Theatre, and the commission may have been initiated by Baccelli herself. He painted her in character in the ballet *Les amans surpris*, directed by Jean-Georges Noverre at the King's Theatre in 1781–2. In the portrait the 'toe-poised' Baccelli has both feet firmly on the ground, and Gainsborough may have loosely followed the choreography and costume of the ballet, perhaps aided by Baccelli herself.[59] We saw in the Introduction that this portrait was described as 'paint-painted' by one reviewer, referring to the artificiality of her heavy stage make-up. At the same time, Gainsborough avoided the representation of a theatrical set; he placed his dancer in nature, in front of scudding clouds. Movement here is less corporeal than painterly, suggested as much by the artist's characteristic light and rapid brush-strokes as by any physical movement. Baccelli shared this landscape setting with several of Gainsborough's other famous theatrical clients, including Mary Robinson (fig.69) and the singer Elizabeth Linley (fig.70). The artist removed these women from the troubling associations of the public stage and reframed their reputations as 'children of nature', with dignified, wistful expressions.

Linley was a popular singer, seen by some to be between 'a woman and an angel', who also left the stage when she married Richard Brinsley Sheridan in 1773.[60] Sheridan's belief that his status as a gentleman would be compromised if his wife continued to sing in public inspired lively debates within theatrical and intellectual circles. Such debates pivoted around the moral precariousness of public performance for women. Gainsborough's portrait represents Linley as a 'woman of feeling' sensitive to her landscape setting. Her affinity with these natural surroundings was even seen by the critic Bate Dudley to be directly linked to her married retirement. He claimed that Gainsborough had captured a 'characteristic expression', and that her depiction under 'a romantic tree, and the accompanying objects are descriptive of retirement'.[61]

However, in Gainsborough's portrait of the unmarried Baccelli, the clues are more equivocal. Although her dance pose, dress and stage make-up evoke her feminine masquerade, her 'natural' background conjures up the more elevated context of a rural estate. As one observer wrote of the dancer in 1789, in then fashionable franglais, 'Nature and Art have both joined to make her the Demi-caractère … Elle vous dites mille choses.'[62] Painting actress-singers, divas and dancer-actresses presented the eighteenth-century portraitist with many challenges. Artistic convention required that their enthralling voices or sprightly dance movements were translated into composite images, rich in symbolic reference and tantalising visual clues of their 'divine' status. Thus, Ellys's *Hester Booth* and Gainsborough's *Giovanna Baccelli* were themselves complex, painted performances, celebrity images that embodied the contradictions inherent in their famous roles. Such idolised women were represented in paint as both public and private, both on and off stage. They were carefully *re*staged – as somewhere between masquerade and 'natural' femininity, between art and nature.

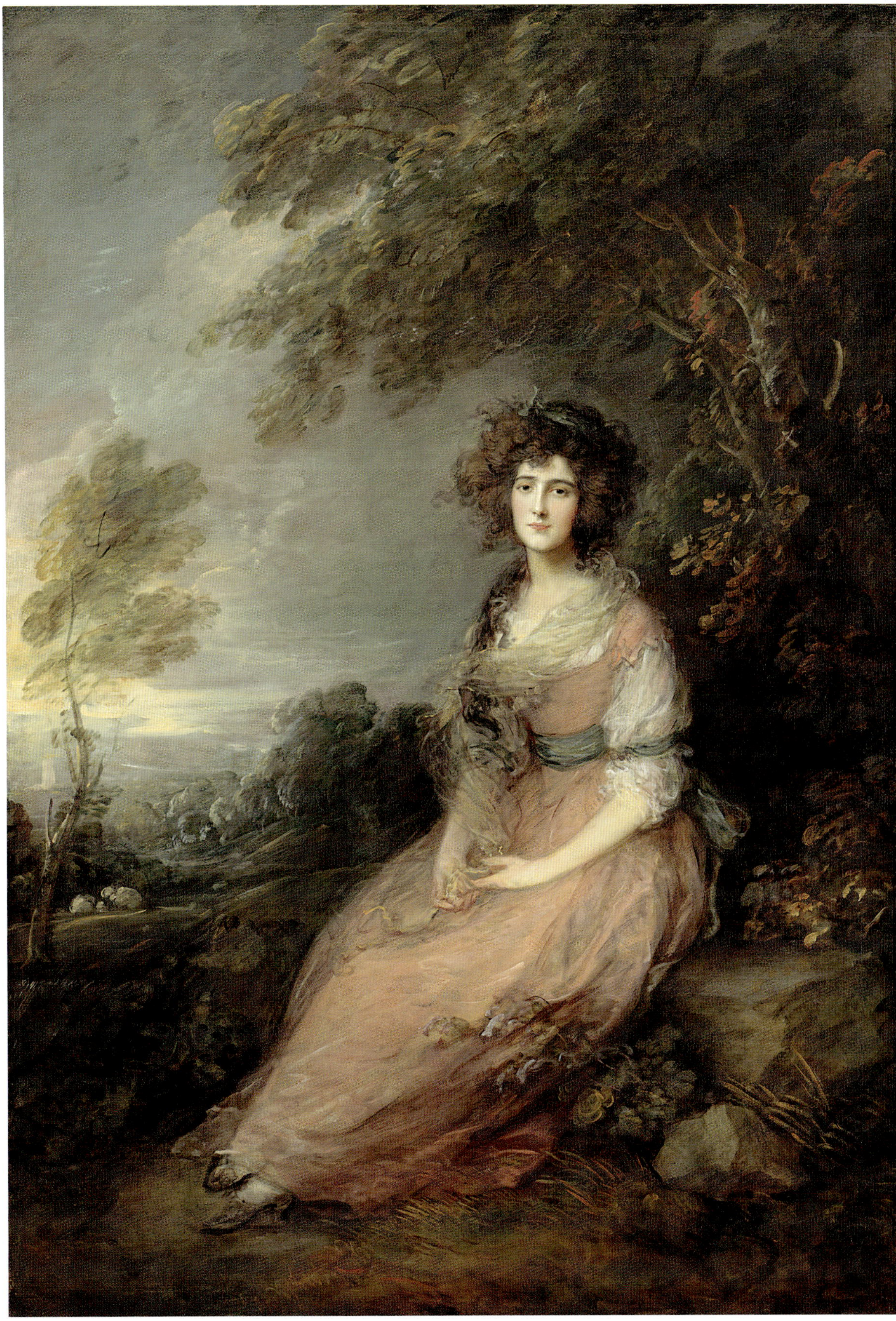

Fig.70

Elizabeth Linley

(Elizabeth Ann Sheridan)

Thomas Gainsborough, *c.*1785–7

BEAUTY, AGEING
AND THE BODY POLITIC

by Shearer West

BEAUTY, AGEING
AND THE BODY POLITIC

For as long as there have been actresses on the stage, audiences have scrutinised their bodies. Commenting on the beauty, shape and age of women who are in the public eye also has a long history, underpinned by questions of whether it is seemly for 'ugly', old or corpulent women to parade themselves on the boards. Controversies about the dearth of good roles for mature women in television, film and theatre are hardly new, but the realities of an ageing Western population have brought these questions sharply into focus.[1] In the second half of the eighteenth century, actresses' bodies also received renewed attention, but for different reasons. From mid-century, a proliferation of theatrical criticism in the public press complemented the plethora of actresses' portraits exhibited at the newly founded Royal Academy, and a growing consumer demand for popular prints, which flooded print shops with images of favourite performers, such as Sarah Siddons, Frances Abington, Elizabeth Farren and Dorothy Jordan.

Observing Actresses' Bodies

Furthermore, until the 1790s, when both Covent Garden and Drury Lane were rebuilt as larger theatres, audiences were in intimate proximity to the performers and could observe them closely. The consequences of this constellation of circumstances were that 'the person', or body, of the actress became an ever more frequent subject of public comment. It is perhaps no surprise that the beauty, shape and age of actresses dominated these narratives, and often descriptions of actresses' bodies became a barely disguised means of articulating desire.[2] However, it is instructive to observe not only what audiences found engaging about actresses' bodies, but why they responded in the way they did.

There was a consistently expressed opinion about what a beautiful actress should look like, and this was tied up with an idealism that favoured symmetry of facial and bodily features, accompanied by a harmonious voice and the judgement to understand how the role should be performed.[3] Thus a performer should not only have 'a well-formed person, a graceful deportment, a well-turned face, a just disposition of features', but they should also have 'improved the art of his whole person, by a habititude and intercourse with gentlemen'.[4] Women were judged by similar standards. Although such phrases could seem merely formulaic, the most favoured actresses were those who were perceived to have the full package of physical, vocal and intellectual beauties. Sarah Siddons, in the early stages of her career, was perceived to be just such a paragon, and both criticism and portraiture helped seal this reputation for perfection (fig.72). When Siddons first made a name for herself in London in 1782, a contemporary critic lingered over her beauty: 'There never, perhaps, was a better stage figure than that of Mrs Siddons. Her height is above the middle size, but not at all inclined to the *em-bon-point*. There is, notwithstanding, nothing sharp or angular in the frame; there is sufficient muscle to bestow a roundness upon the limbs … The symmetry of her person is exact and captivating.'[5] This perception was strongly reinforced by Sir Joshua Reynolds's stunning portrait *Sarah Siddons as the Tragic Muse* (see fig.73), exhibited at the Royal Academy in 1784, and still acknowledged by Sir Thomas Lawrence nearly forty years later as 'the finest female portrait in the world'.[6] Reynolds chose to idealise Siddons by placing her on a throne, flanked by Aristotle's Pity and Fear, draped with a generalised dress, posed like one of Michelangelo's Sistine Chapel Sibyls and making a grand gesture that was distinctive enough to spark a range of anecdotes about its origin. In addition to appreciation of her symmetric form, reviews of Siddons's acting tended to focus as much on her prodigious range of facial expressions,

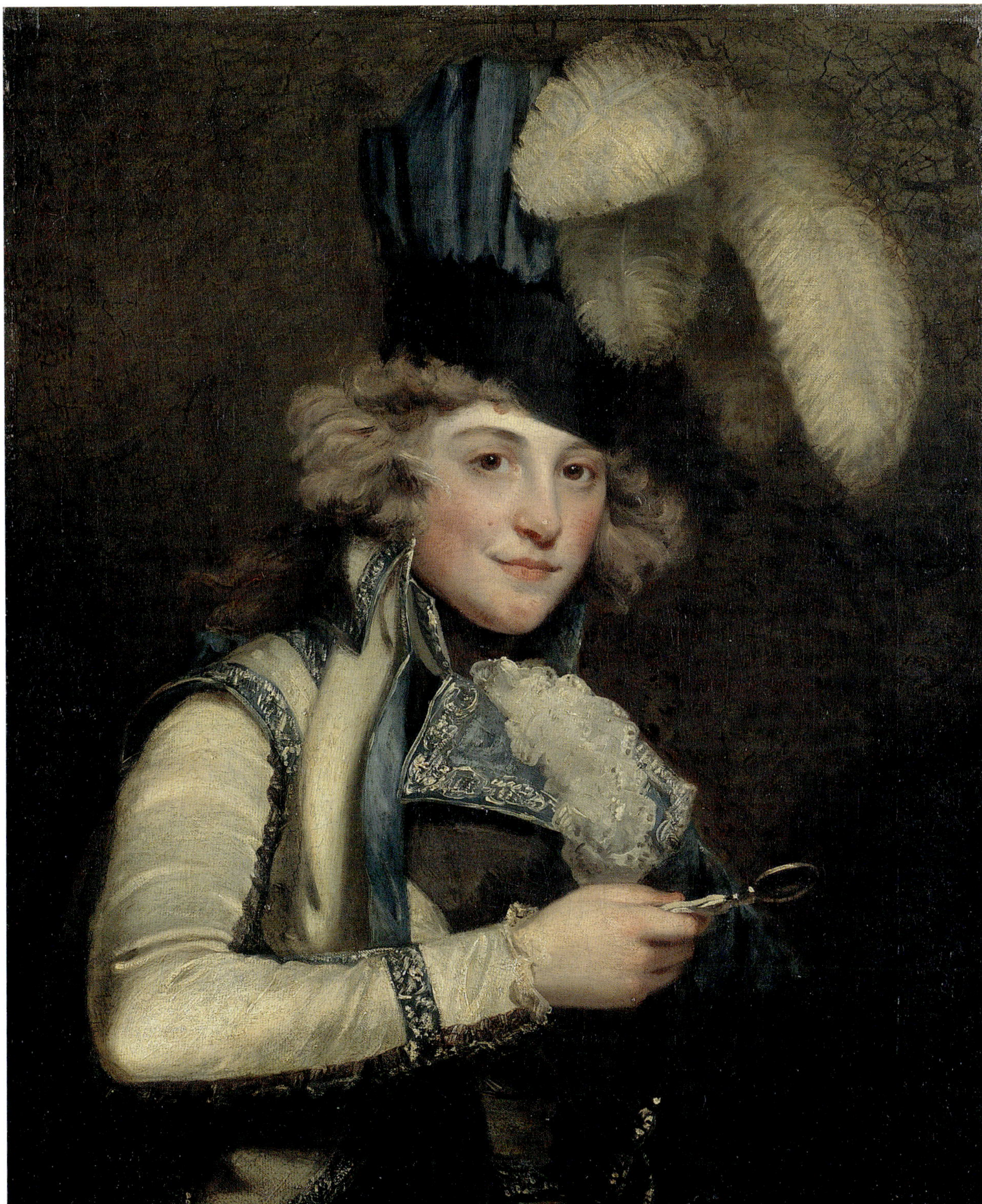

Fig.71

Dorothy Jordan as Hypolita in
She Would and She Would Not
John Hoppner, exhib. 1791

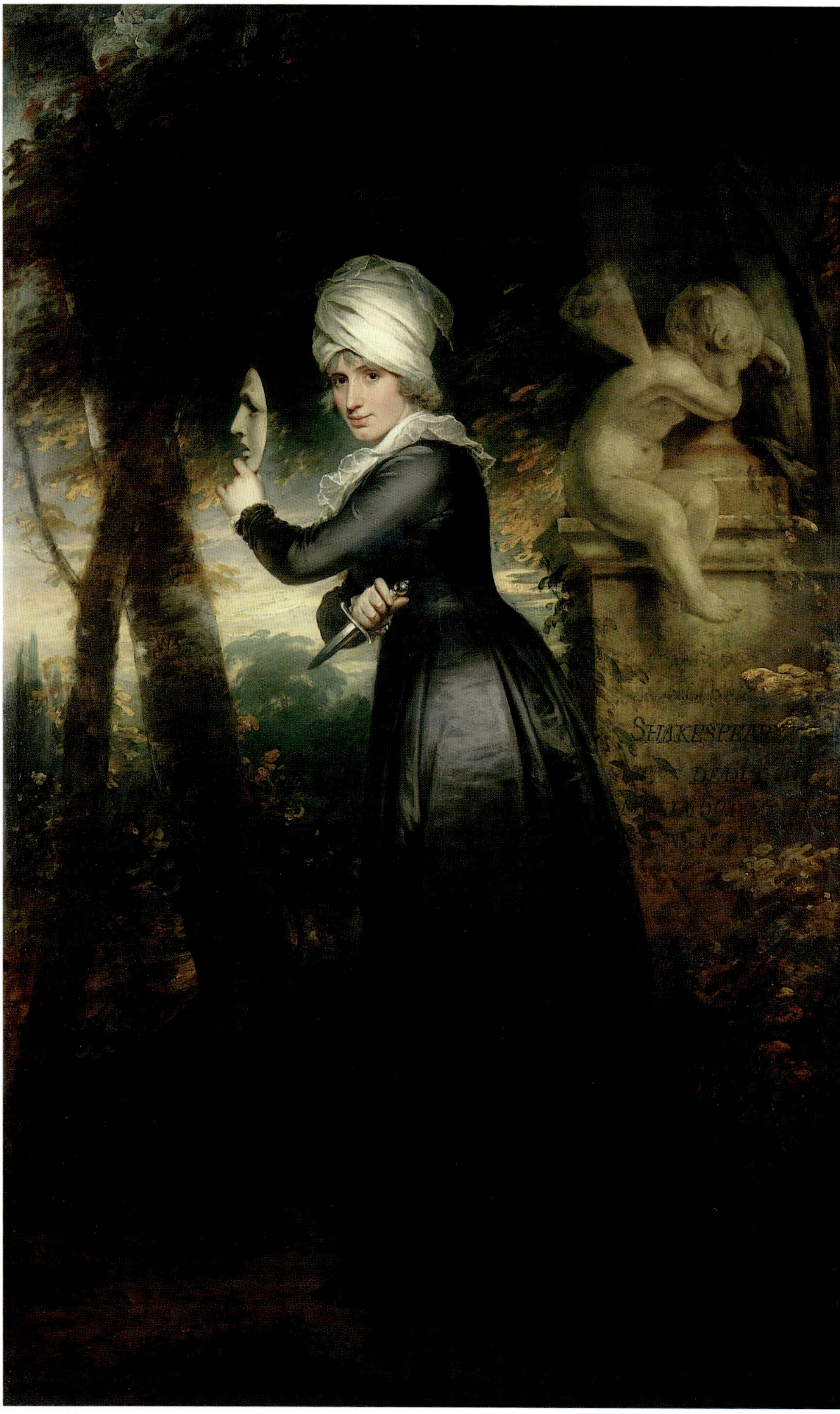
SHAKESPEAR

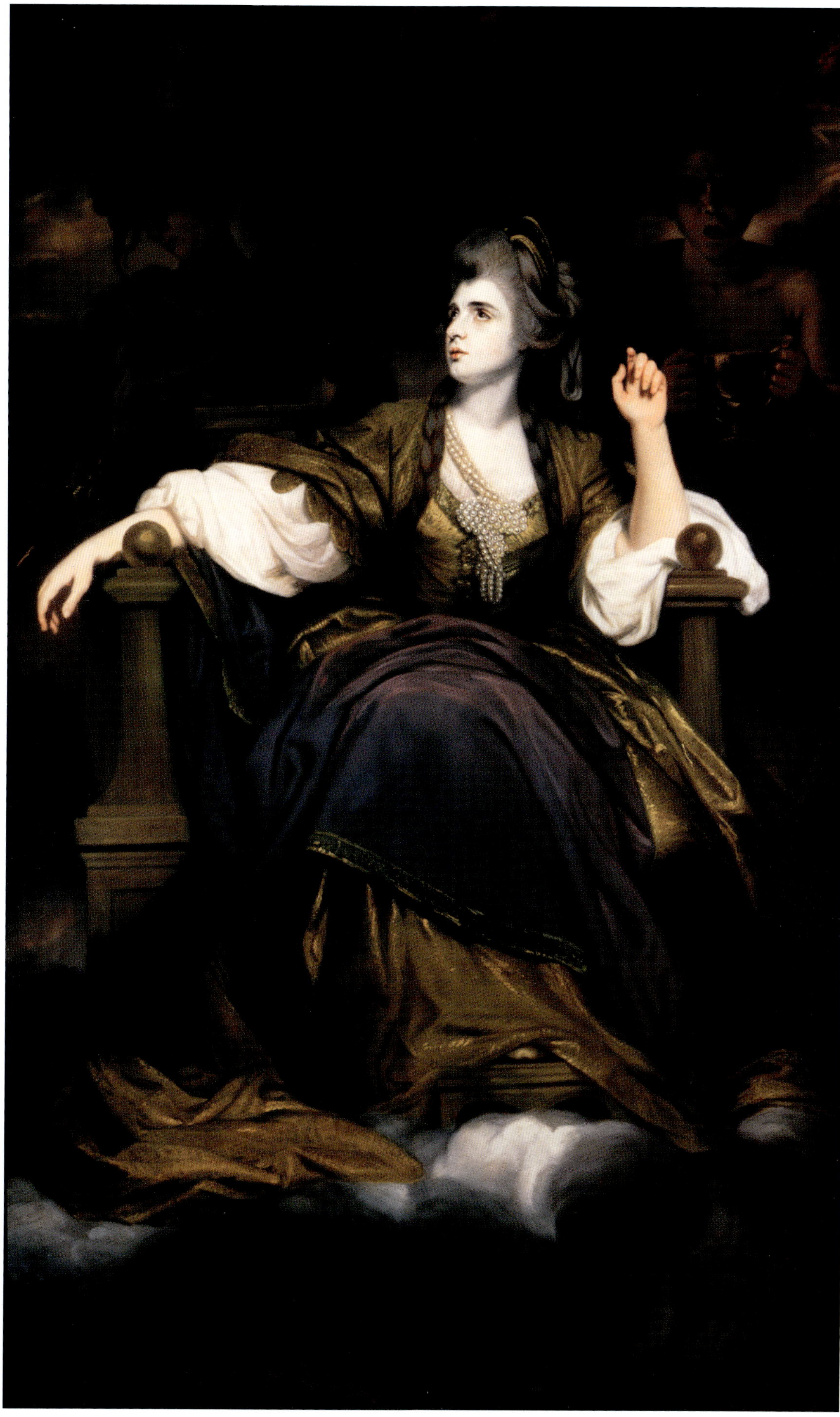

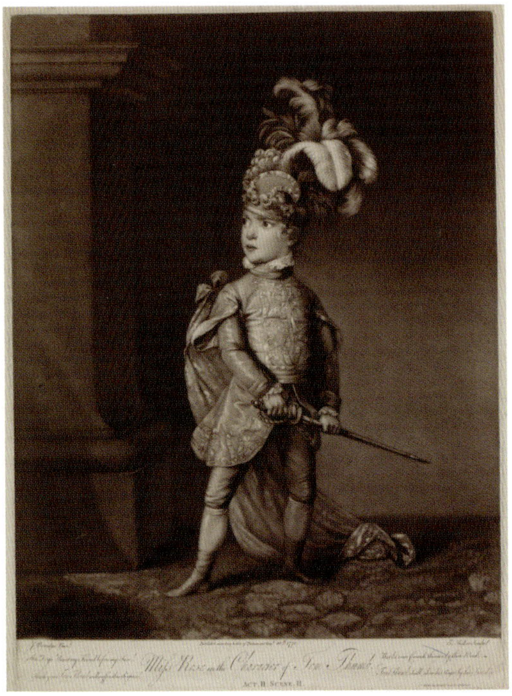

Fig.72 (previous page, left)

Sarah Siddons with the Emblems of Tragedy

Sir William Beechey, 1793

Fig.73 (previous page, right)

Sarah Siddons as the Tragic Muse

Studio of Sir Joshua Reynolds, 1784

Fig.74 (right)

Miss Rose in the Character of Tom Thumb

Edward Fisher, after John Berridge, 1770

and the intellectual approach she took to character development. With its allusions to classical drama and Italian art, Reynolds's grandiloquent portrait associates Siddons with the finest examples of creative expression of the past.

However, not all representations of actresses' beauty were dominated by such high-minded notions of classical symmetry and intellectual merit. As one observer pointed out of the actress Elizabeth Hartley, 'This Lady is … the finest figure on the London stage: therefore it is not to be wondered, a lady endued with such requisites for this profession, should gain great applause, had she absolutely little or no merit.'[7] The beauty of actresses was often conflated euphemistically with their desirability, and numerous references to 'embonpoint' (plumpness) in the critical literature became a cipher for the size of the actress's breasts and buttocks. This became particularly explicit when actresses cross-dressed in 'breeches' parts (fig.74). Audiences responded eagerly to the opportunity to see their favourite actresses wearing clothes that clung to their legs and upper body; as the theatrical biographer James Boaden put it, 'the attraction after all is purely feminine, and the display of female, not male perfections. Did the lady really look like a man, the coarse *androgynous* would be hooted from the stage.'[8]

Critical literature could naturally be much more explicit than portraiture, and Dorothy Jordan – who was famous for her cross-dressing roles – was frequently in the spotlight (figs 71, 75). Jordan, whose 'bosom concealed everything but its own charms',[9] was admired for her voluptuous body shape. However, in one rare portrait of her in a cross-dressing role, as Viola in Shakespeare's *Twelfth Night*, John Hoppner swathes her body in the finely crafted uniform of Duke Orsino's page-boy. Hoppner appears more interested in her yearning demeanour and hunched gesture of obeisance as she declares her love for Orsino, and this emphasis draws attention away from her body and towards her expressive profile.

Indeed, artists – even in satirical prints – paid less notice to the breasts of the actresses than critics did. While Boaden archly refers to the unnatural quality of the 'upper *half*' of Abington's figure – implying that she used synthetic means to enhance her breast size – portraits of Abington mask or undermine this observation. Thomas Hickey's portrait of Abington as Lady Bab Lardoon (fig.76), like Hoppner's portrait of Jordan as Viola, attends more to the garlanded fashionable dress of the actress than to her body.[10] Likewise, Reynolds's portrait *Frances Abington as Miss Prue in Love for Love* (fig.28) occludes Abington's body behind the chair on which she leans. Nevertheless, both portraits allude to the actress's beauty and desirability – the former through the lush natural setting where Lady Bab is plucking a posy to present to an admirer outside the picture, and the latter through what many felt to be Miss Prue's suggestive gesture with her thumb touching her lip.[11] And the satirical print of Abington, performing as Scrub in Farquhar's *The Beaux' Stratagem* (fig.77), obscures the actress's body in a shapeless sack of male servant attire. Scrub was not a breeches part but normally a male role, and Abington was criticised for playing it, not least because her audiences felt that her fifty-year-old body was no longer in an appropriate state for the revealing nature of breeches roles.[12] Her sensitivity to this can also be seen in Siddons's decision to play Rosalind, in Shakespeare's *As You Like It*, in a hybrid male/female dress that covered her body but bemused her audiences, who found it 'the most unaccountable we ever witnessed upon the stage. It was not that of either man or woman. Her Hussar boots with a gardener's apron and petticoat behind, gave her a most equivocal appearance.'[13]

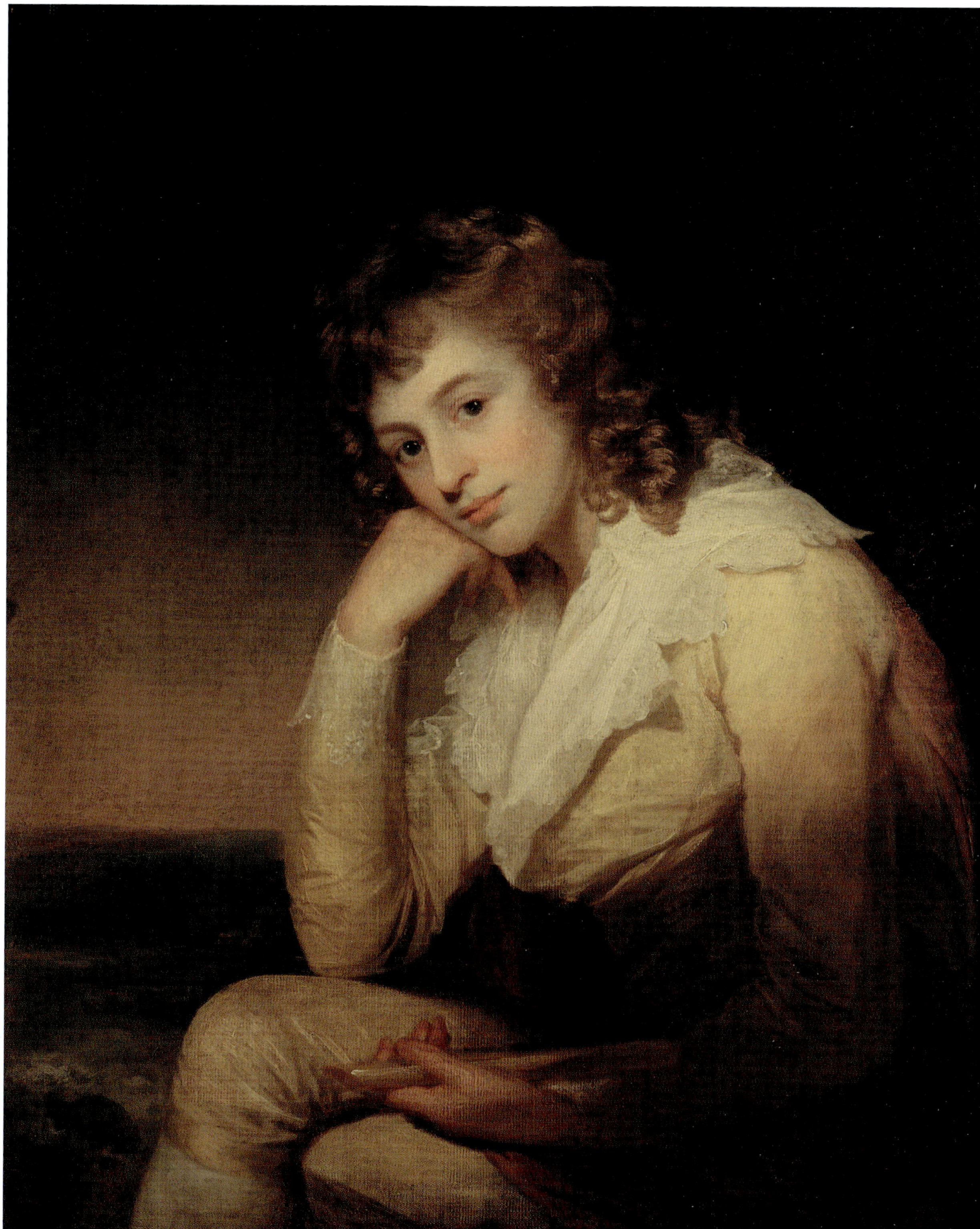

Fig.75

Dorothy Jordan as Rosalind in *As You Like It*

Sir William Beechey, 1787

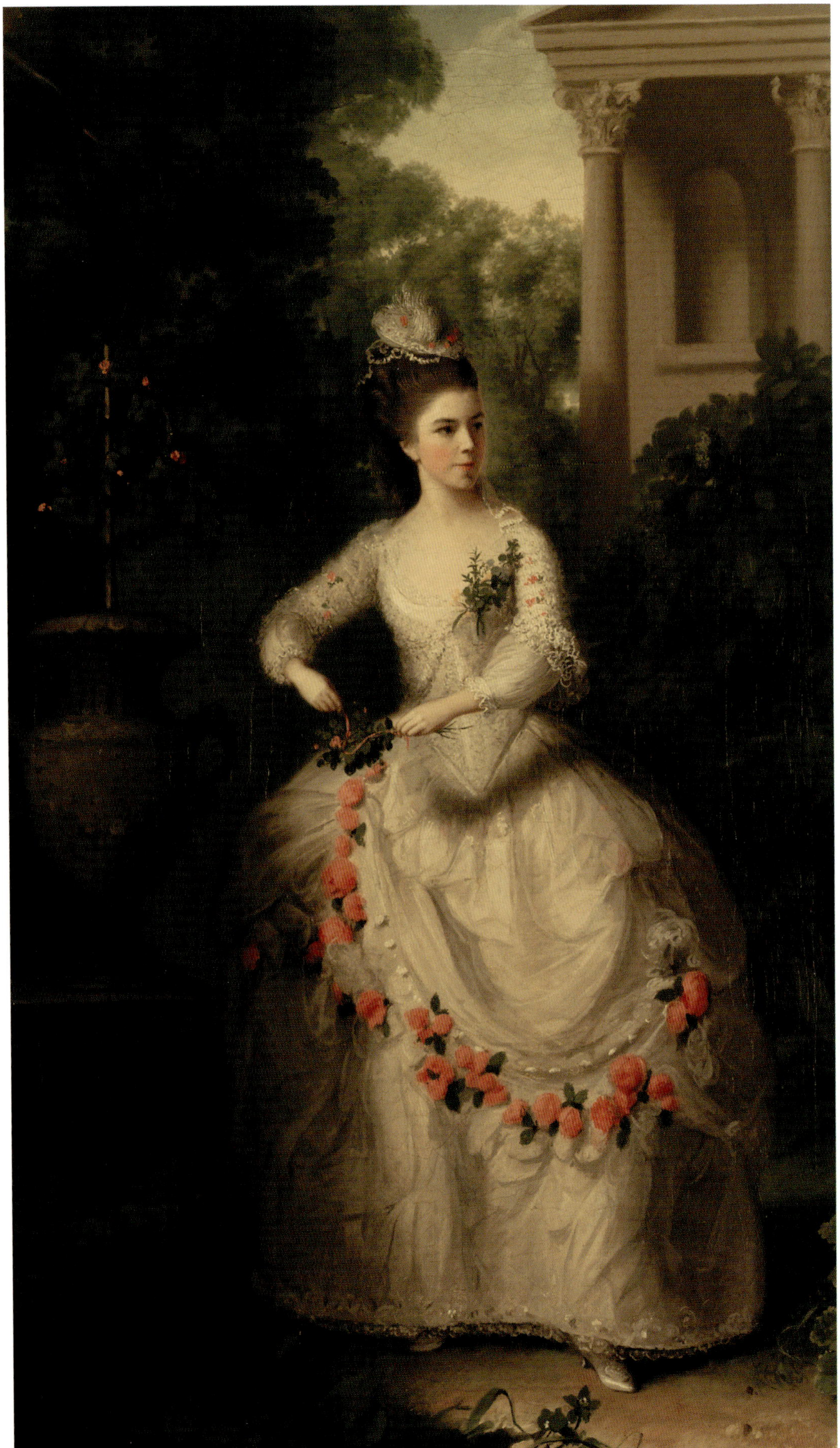

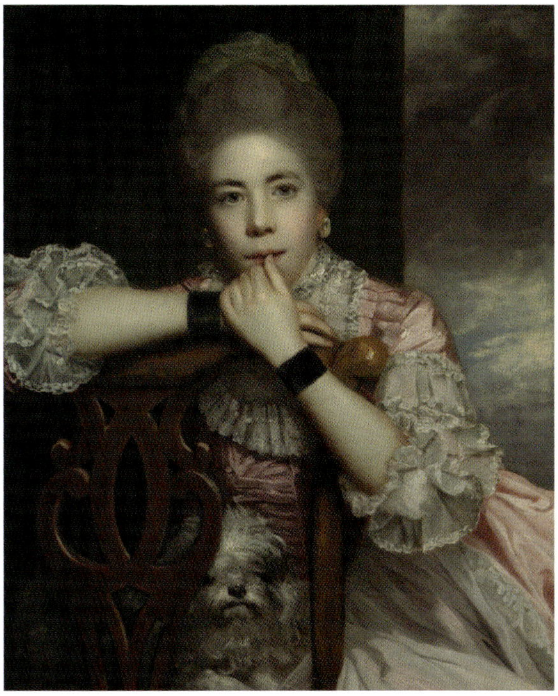

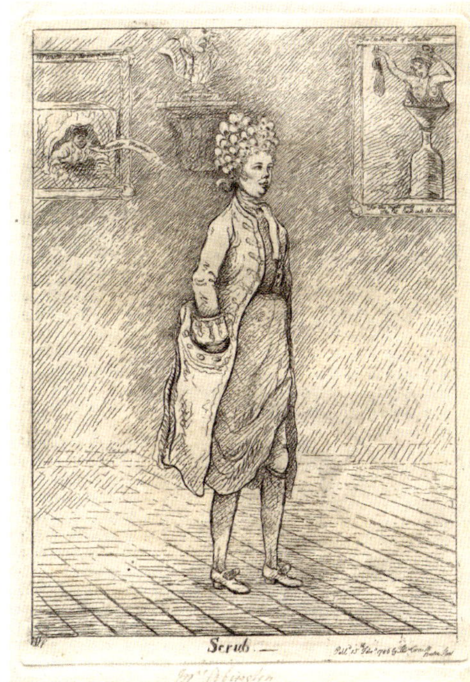

It is worth noting that when men dressed up as women on the stage, commentary focused on the burlesque quality of the dressing-up itself, rather than the body. Well before the 'pantomime dame' became the stock of British theatre, the idea of men in women's dress was seen to be absurd, rather than alluring. This is captured in representations of male actors performing in female dress, such as Zoffany's portrait of Garrick as Sir John Brute in Vanbrugh's *Provok'd Wife* of 1777 (fig.78), or the many portraits and popular prints of Henry Angelo performing as the aged Methodist inebriate, Mrs Cole (fig.79), in Samuel Foote's controversial farce, *The Minor* (1760).

Although the shape of actresses' bodies became a focus of critical attention and a conundrum for portraitists, the discourse was not always about desirability. The expectation of symmetry meant that critics would very quickly pounce upon an actress who was felt to be either too fat or too thin, whether or not these body types were appropriate to the role being performed. A pamphlet published in 1782, for example, accused a number of actresses of excessive weight: 'all the vocal and comic ladies, of each house, have grown out of all reasonable compass.'[14] Despite the fact that corpulence could reinforce the character of comic types, even successful actresses such as Jane Pope, renowned for her comic roles in the 1760s and 1770s, could be condemned for her 'bulky and unweildy [sic]' figure.[15] Many noted that Siddons became larger as she grew older, but the strength of her reputation meant that critics were somewhat more polite about her increasing girth, claiming that her 'matronly' or 'statuesque' form gave her a certain authority in tragic roles such as Queen Katherine in Shakespeare's *Henry VIII*. Sir Thomas Lawrence's portrait of Siddons of 1804 (fig.32), attempts to express visually the statuesque quality of her increasing bulk, by representing the actress as imposing and distant, statue-like in her stillness.

Fig.76 (opposite page)
Frances Abington as Lady Bab Lardoon in *The Maid of Oaks*
Thomas Hickey, 1775

Fig.28 (above left)
Frances Abington as Miss Prue in *Love for Love*
Sir Joshua Reynolds, 1771

Fig.77 (above right)
Frances Abington as Scrub in *The Beaux' Stratagem*
After James Sayers, 1786

Fig.78

David Garrick in *The Provok'd Wife*

Johan Joseph Zoffany, 1763

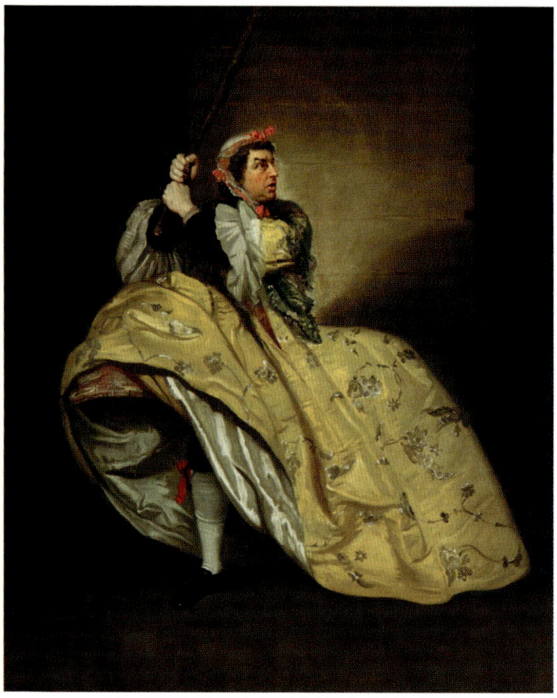

The frequent pregnancies of actresses, who often had to perform until just before their confinement in order to ensure a steady income, also elicited much comment. Siddons herself first came to David Garrick's attention in 1775, when he sent a scout, Henry Bate, to observe her performance in Worcester and determine whether she was fit for the London stage. Bate reported back positively on Siddons, but noted that she was pregnant. Garrick's reply showed his concern that a pregnant actress would not gain public approbation: 'Your account of the *big belly* alarms me – when shall we be in shapes again?'[16] While Siddons was condemned for performing in her final trimester such roles as Lady Macbeth, Jordan caused public and critical frustration for 'her nearly annual confinement,' and the actress Henrietta Smith was scoffed at for playing the role of virgins while heavily and visibly pregnant.[17]

Thin bodies could receive as much attention as fat ones, however. Elizabeth Farren was one such actress whose thinness was the subject of regular public attention. Charles James Fox, who had a reputation for his salacious eye, was allegedly 'disgusted' at seeing Farren in a breeches role, reportedly exclaiming, 'D–n it, she has no prominence either before or behind – all is in a straight line from head to foot.'[18] As a more delicate critic observed, 'were it [Farren's body] a little more embonpoint, it would be one of the finest the theatre can boast.'[19]

That Farren was self-conscious about her lean body can be evidenced by her reaction to Sir Thomas Lawrence's portrait of her which was exhibited at the Royal Academy in 1790 and then purchased by her lover, the Earl of Derby (fig.83). Unlike the portraits of Jordan and Abington already discussed, Lawrence was overt in representing the svelte body shape for which Farren was known. Despite the fact that Farren is draped in voluminous and distractingly elaborate outdoor garments, her slight frame is apparent underneath all that cloaking. Several years after the portrait was exhibited, Farren wrote to Lawrence asking him to alter it: 'One says it is so thin in the figure, that you might blow it away – another that it looks broke off in the middle; in short, you must make it a little *fatter*, at all events, diminish the *bend* you are so attached to.'[20]

Age and Ageing

Discussions of beauty, corpulence, pregnancy and thinness were overshadowed by critical attention to an actress's age.[21] There was a strongly held view that certain roles, such as comic country girls and tragic heroines like Juliet or Belvidera in Thomas Otway's *Venice Preserv'd*, required a youthful actress to perform them; whereas other roles – tragic queens or matrons such as Hermione in *The Winter's Tale* – could benefit from a more mature actress. In the late eighteenth century, attitudes to age and ageing, as Susannah Ottaway has argued, were strongly tied up with anxieties about 'dependent poverty', and actresses, whose livelihood relied on their ability to continue working, would of necessity continue to play familiar roles beyond what was felt to be an appropriate age.[22] A German visitor to England noted with dismay that Dorothy Jordan was still performing the adolescent Miss Lucy in Bernard Mandeville's *The Virgin Unmask'd* when she was well past a credible age to play this perky *ingénue* (fig.80). What this visitor saw was 'a lady upwards of forty, with prodigious *embonpoint*' playing 'a raw country girl of sixteen; so puerile, as to appear playing with her doll.'

Siddons was also accused of playing inappropriately young characters on a number of occasions, as she continued to revive the roles of her youth when she was well into her sixties. The waning of vitality that accompanied the onset of the menopause could be more problematic for women than genuine old age. Certainly, for actresses,

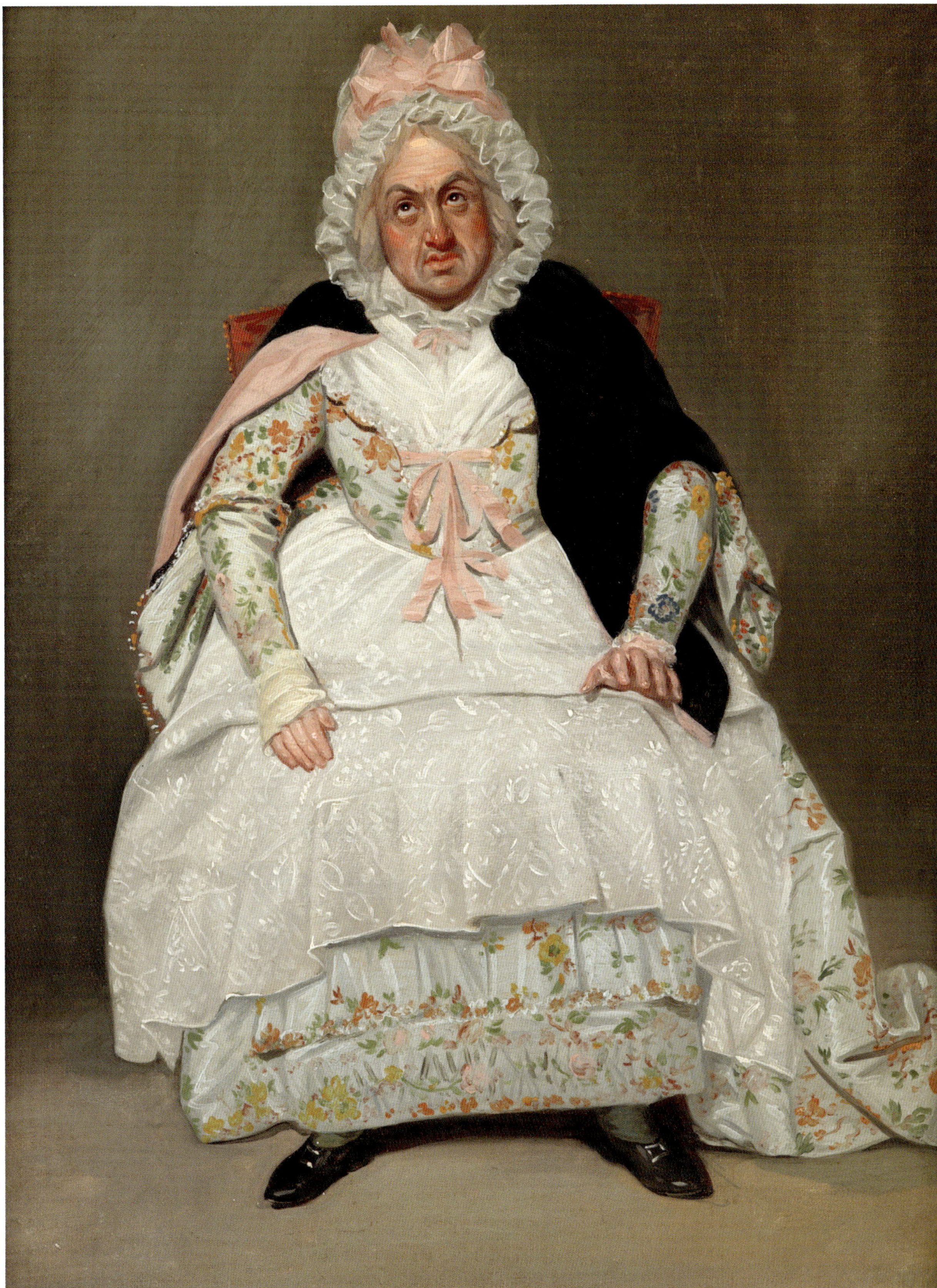

Fig.79

Henry de Angelo as Mrs Cole in *The Minor*

Samuel de Wilde, *c.*1792

Fig.80 (right)
Dorothy Jordan as Lucy in *The Virgin Unmask'd*
Unknown artist, 1787

Fig.81 (opposite page, left)
Sarah Siddons, said to be Mrs Haller in *The Stranger*
Sir Thomas Lawrence, *c.*1796–8

Fig.32 (opposite page, right)
Sarah Siddons
Sir Thomas Lawrence, 1804

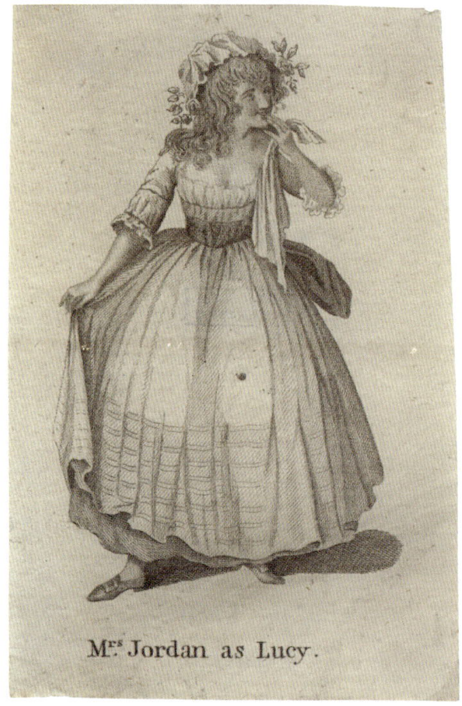

there was a deep anxiety about the loss of a livelihood that depended on youthful beauty. There are very few portraits of older actresses from this period, but Siddons is one who was still represented when she was past middle age. When Lawrence painted a half-length of Siddons for the Royal Academy exhibition of 1797 (fig.81), he deliberately restored the youth of the forty-two-year-old mother of five by effectively air-brushing her portrait to evoke a youthful state. 'Anthony Pasquin's' criticism of this work was blunt in its assessment, and contrasted a menopausal Siddons to Lawrence's sensitive evocation of a young woman in love:

> It is no more like her than Hebe is similar to Bellona. We have here youth, flexibility of features, and an attempt at the formation of beauty, to denote a lady who is proverbially so stern of her countenance that it approaches to savageness – so determined in the outline of her visage, that it requires the delusion of the scene to render it soft and agreeable, and who is so far from being young, that her climacteric will be no more.[24]

Pasquin's remarks are typical of the kind of easy misogyny that characterised many responses to ageing actresses, but actors were also subject to accusations of impropriety when they chose roles that were felt to be too young for them. Few ageing actresses were subjected to the kind of vitriol that was poured upon Charles Macklin when he first played Macbeth in 1773 as a septuagenarian. While the disapprobation was apparently fuelled by a small group of conspirators, the commentary permeated the daily papers. Critics condemned his 'treacherous memory ... imperfect utterance, a person neither elegant, nor full of dignity', and even his admiring biographer, William Cooke, admitted that 'the audience saw a clumsy old man, who looked more like a Scotch Piper than a General and Prince of the Blood'.[25]

Thus neither actors nor actresses were immune from this sort of scrutiny and the tendency to scoff at the impropriety of old actors. However, a more ambivalent attitude to ageing performers also emerged, growing more from anxiety than contempt. The diary of the inveterate theatre-goer, Henry Crabb Robinson, is full of shuddering references to the loss of youth in famous actresses. When he met Frances Abington in 1811, he marvelled that she had once been the darling of the town: 'Besides being an old woman which of necessity takes from most of the charms of youth she bears the marks of having always been very plain. Her snub nose, at which she laughed herself, is however not so bad as her lips, on which there seem to hang excrescences of flesh', and he opined in the same year that Siddons's 'advancing age is really a cause of pain to me'.[26]

Ageing actors could thus bring home sharply to fans the fact of their own mortality. Charles Lamb's essay on 'old actors' looks back nostalgically to the theatrical heyday of his youth, but he regards an old playbill with a lump in his throat, and seems to feel almost physical pain at seeing the ageing comic actor James William Dodd walking through Gray's Inn lost in sombre thought: 'There is something strange as well as sad in seeing actors ... subject to and suffering the common lot.'[27] Even the snide Pasquin could offer a melancholy reflection on human mortality when, in his *Children of Thespis*, he describes the once lusty Sophia Baddeley 'stretch'd on her bier', her body 'emaciate' and 'squalid'.[28]

The intimations of mortality are most poignantly represented in a portrait of Siddons painted by Henry Perronet Briggs the year before she died (fig.82). Here the seventy-five-year-old actress is seated, as she was when Reynolds represented her as the Tragic Muse, but instead of classicising drapery, she is enveloped in matronly black and an old lady's bonnet, and instead of exuding confident

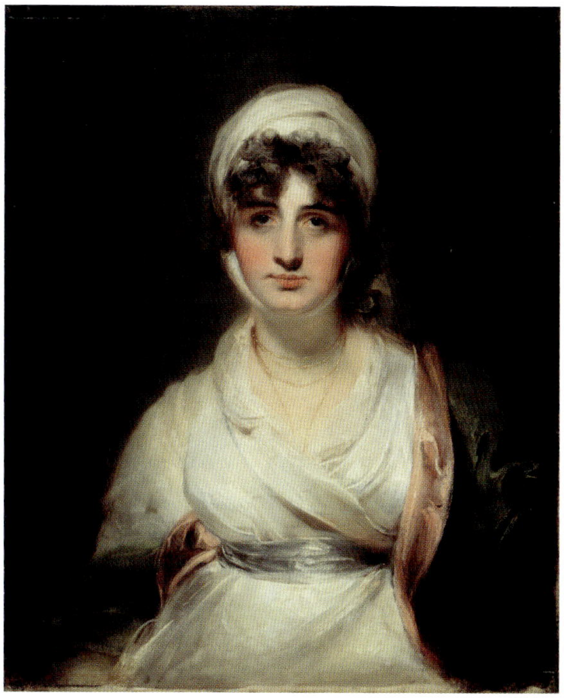

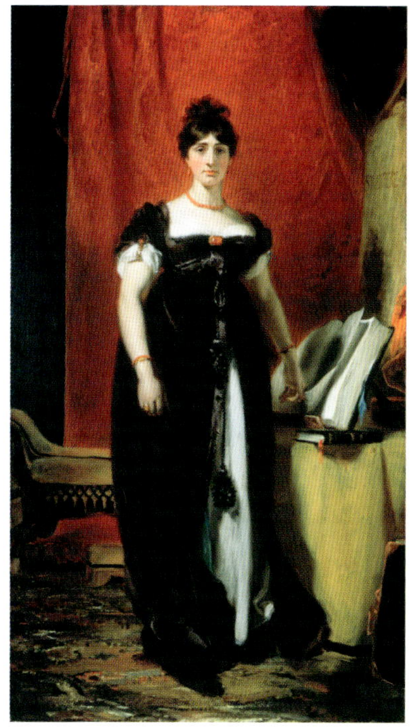

authority, she looks frail and confused, with strongly marked, even masculine, features. The portrait offers a somewhat cruel contrast between the superannuated Siddons and her vital young niece, Fanny Kemble, who had already taken the Siddons family's fame into a new generation. Nevertheless, the portrait is a moving tribute to a legendary actress and a reminder to her audiences of their own eventual decay and death.

This reflective underpinning of what might otherwise seem to be rather uncompromising attitudes to the age of actresses leads me to suggest that there were other reasons – apart from salaciousness and prejudice – that led viewers and critics to scrutinise actresses' bodies and find them wanting in some way. Underlying many of the comments on the age, shape and beauty of actresses was a strong sense of visual decorum – the idea that the real bodies should somehow match the imaginary characters they represented. So pregnant women should not play virgins, old women should not play young ones, and spry adolescent girls should not be portrayed by women whose bulkiness made them lumber awkwardly across the stage. While the reputation of actresses improved over the course of the eighteenth century, there remained a broad suspicion of a profession where women could, metaphorically speaking, change their shape from one night to the next; when a performer 'who, in one part of the night represents an old woman bowed down with age, with wrinkled brow and hollowed eyes, in another part of the night represents a young stripling in all the bloom of youth.'[29] Earlier in the century, some arguments were made that countered this obsession with visual propriety. The writer Charles Churchill made a valiant attempt in 1760 to defend the profession of acting as one that relied more on the genius of the actor than on their physical shape, and his famous pronouncement deserves quoting in full:

In comedy – 'Nay there,' cries critic, 'hold.
Pritchard's for comedy too fat and old.
Who can, with patience, bear the grey coquette,
Or force a laugh with over-grown Juliet?
Her speech, look, action, humour, are all just.
But then, her age and figure give disgust.'

Are foibles then, and graces of the mind,
In real life, to size or age confin'd?
Do spirits slow, and is good breeding plac'd
In any set circumference of waist?
As we grow old, doth affectation cease,
Or give not age and vigour to caprice?
...
FIGURE, I own, at first, may give offence,
And harshly strike the eye's too curious sense;
But when the perfections of the mind break forth
Humour's chaste sallies, Judgment's solid worth:
When the pure genuine flame, by nature taught,
Springs into sense, and ev'ry action's Thought;
Before such merit, all objections fly;
Pritchard's genteel, and Garrick's six feet high.[30]

In Churchill's view, the fact that Garrick was short and Pritchard fat was irrelevant – he felt that the power of their performances, based on judgement and understanding, should make audiences disregard their actual physical attributes.

Visual Art and the Power of Criticism

Such an idealistic view of acting was not to prevail, as visual qualities became increasingly privileged in representations and discussions of the actor's art. There were many reasons for this. Firstly, theatrical criticism changed. Theatre critics in the first half of the century focused largely on how actors

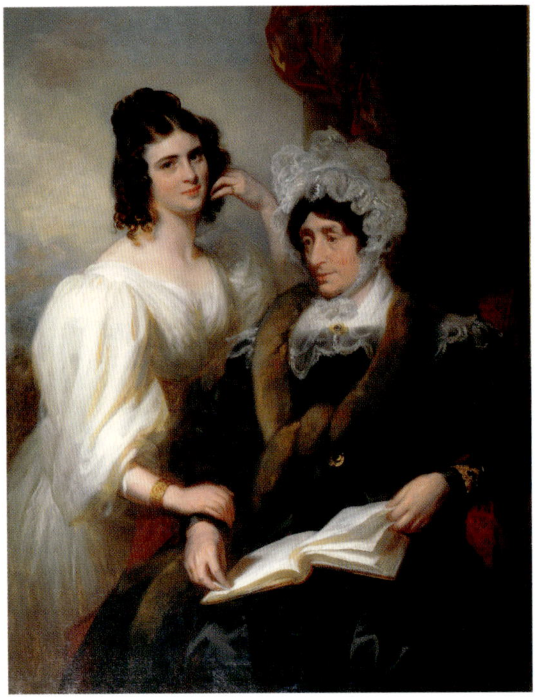

Fig.82 (left)

Fanny Kemble and her Aunt, Sarah Siddons

Henry Perronet Briggs, *c.*1830–1

Fig.83 (opposite page)

Elizabeth Farren, later Countess of Derby

Sir Thomas Lawrence, 1790

interpreted their part, and they expressed themselves by recourse to rules of dramatic criticism, many of which dated back to Aristotle.[31] Later critics – perhaps hampered by the need to feed an ever-hungry daily press – relied more on their natural observation, rather than the formulas of ancient dramatic criticism. So while critics before the mid-century might concentrate on the unities of action or the characteristics of tragedy versus those of comedy, later critics would report what they saw with their own eyes from the pit. Increasingly therefore, critics abandoned a solid theoretical framework for their remarks and relied instead of observing details of the performance itself.[32] Secondly, the increasing prevalence of visual art in exhibitions and print shops, and the popularisation of art criticism, led theatrical and artistic criticism to cross-fertilise. The German aesthetician Gotthold Ephraim Lessing, whose work was known in England, was particularly forceful about the problems of ugliness in visual art. Lessing felt that 'disgust' was not something confined to foul smells or nasty tastes:

> A liver spot in the face, a hare-lip, a flattened nose with prominent nostrils, an entire want of eyebrows, are uglinesses which are repugnant neither to the smell nor taste nor touch, yet it is certain that there is a sensation experienced at them which approaches more closely to disgust than any which is produced by other deformities of the body, such as a crooked foot or a high shoulder.[33]

Art critics who agreed with Lessing's view felt repelled by visual representations of old age; as one wrote, 'What turns the stomach, when we see it in nature, will have the same effect, when we see it represented in painting.'[34] The idea of 'nausea' arising from disgusting visual images also permeates writing which refers to actresses' bodies. When Garrick was asked by the King to revive his partnership with Hannah Pritchard (now fifty-seven years old) in *The Jealous Wife*, he wrote in a letter '[I] have not play'd Oakly these three Years – Sick – Sick – Sick – & Mrs. Pd will make me Sicker – great Bubbies, Noddling head, & no teeth – O Sick – Sick – Spew.'[35] Through the kinds of ideas that Lessing advocated, the visual was ideally confined to beautiful objects, and those that were not could elicit a visceral reaction like that expressed by Garrick.

The combination of aesthetic disgust, notions of decorum, and a burgeoning visual culture in the later eighteenth century became coupled with sexual desire, anxieties about ageing and the prurient interest of theatre audiences in a generation of celebrity actresses. These circumstances brought the bodies of actresses into sharp critical focus, and created new challenges for the portraitists who represented them.

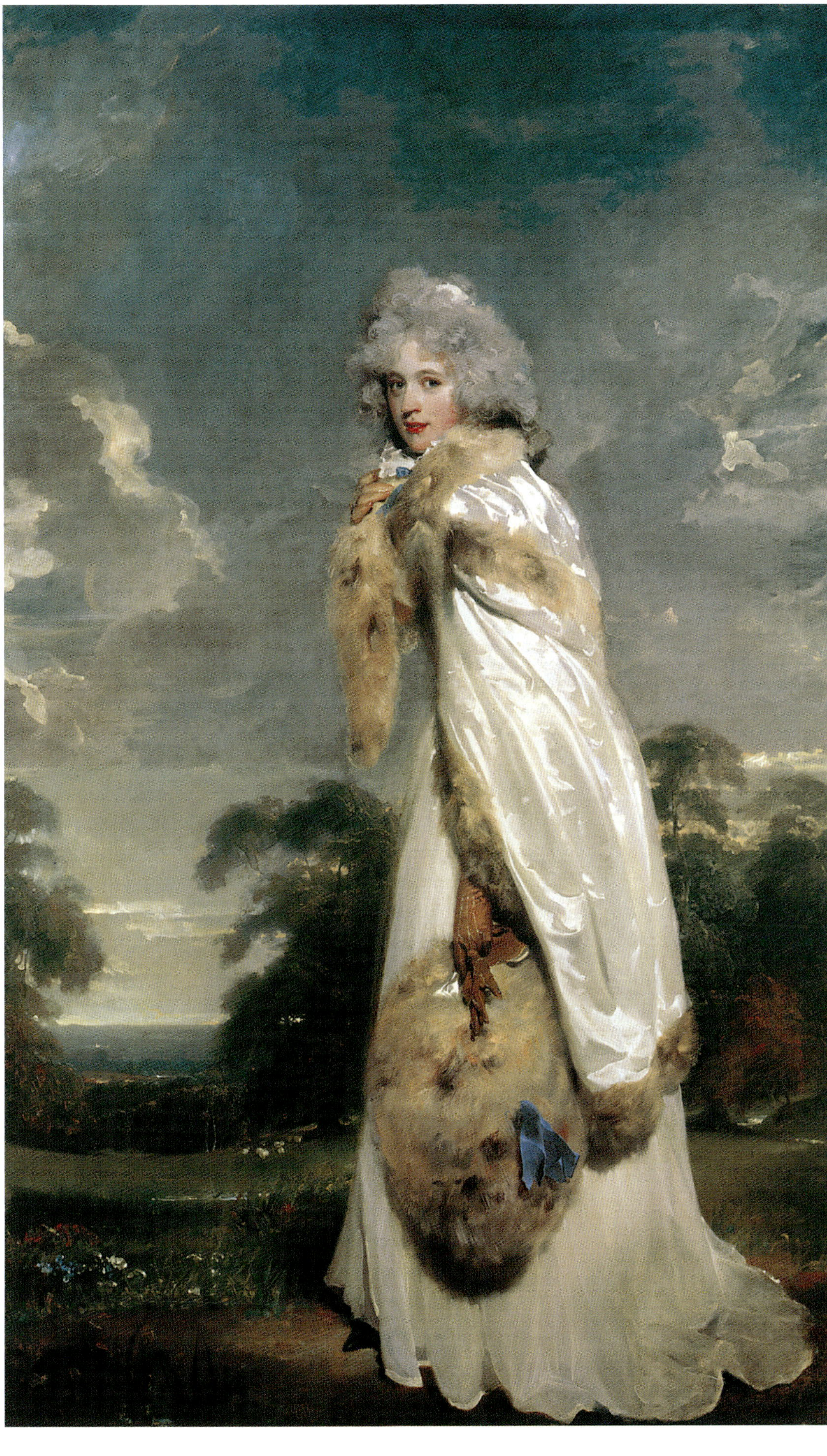

STAR SYSTEMS
THEN AND NOW

by Gill Perry

STAR SYSTEMS
THEN AND NOW

On 19 April 1787 a parliamentary debate on the national budget was postponed to allow some of its members to attend the opening night of the Richmond House Theatricals. These were exclusive private performances hosted by the Duke of Richmond in 1787–8, and the first night was performed to – and by – a dazzling array of well-known figures from the realms of aristocracy, politics and the theatre. The business of national politics was deemed less pressing than attendance at this stellar celebrity event. The audience included the Prince of Wales, the Duke and Duchess of Cumberland, Richard and Elizabeth Ann Sheridan, David and Eva-Maria Garrick, John Philip Kemble and the political enemies William Pitt and Charles James Fox. The actress Elizabeth Farren (fig.85), then mistress of the Earl of Derby (whom she later married in 1797, shortly after the death of his first wife), was employed to oversee these theatricals, and Derby played the male lead, Lovemore, in the opening performance of Arthur Murphy's comedy *The Way To Keep Him*.[1] Farren's relationship with Derby had enabled her social mobility. The growing taste for 'country house' theatricals in Georgian society, held in specially built private theatres on many of the grandest estates, including Blenheim Palace, Ampthill Park and Wynnstay in Denbighshire, encouraged porous boundaries between theatrical and upper-class circles.[2] Both social groups were seduced by the intensification of celebrity produced by their combined talents, social status and visibility.

The World as a Stage

Not surprisingly, the vogue for amateur dramatics or 'spouting' also caught the attention of the wider public and the national press.[3] A few decades earlier, Henry Fielding had opened Book Seven of *Tom Jones* (published in 1749) with an account of his protagonist's exploits in London and 'A Comparison Between the World and the Stage' in which he noted that this comparison 'hath been carried so far ... that some words proper to the theatre, and which were metaphorically applied to the world, are now indiscriminately and literally spoken of both.'[4] Fielding was reworking a well-established theatrical cliché – that the boundaries between stage and reality have become blurred – to comment on a society that seemed to be seduced by performance, hypocrisy and spectacle in 'this great theatre of nature'.[5] The taste for theatrical spectacle was much in evidence in mid- to late eighteenth-century cultural life, and the opening of the Richmond House theatricals, prioritised over political business and dominated by fashionable display, provided ongoing evidence of Fielding's earlier observation.

The theatre at Richmond House was an adapted room with a capacity of 150 and a select group were invited to supper with the Duke after the opening performance, reinforcing the seductive exclusivity of the event. According to a report in *The General Evening Post*, women were 'requested to come without hats, bonnets and feathers', to avoid blocking the view.[6] The guests' elaborate dresses, along with details of the invitation and dramatis personae, were avidly noted in the press and gossip columns, anticipating the magazine paparazzi and voyeuristic reports of modern celebrity culture, replete with inane details of the parties of the rich and famous. In the *General Evening Post* the relatively long column inches of 'Theatrical Intelligence from Richmond House' sat cheek by jowl with more serious, but short, reports on, for example, the election of Scottish peers and anxieties about commerce with France. Despite the huge historical gulf that separates this 'news' from our media-dominated culture in the twenty-first century, it is tempting to draw parallels with contemporary concerns that our obsession with celebrity can distract us from more serious forms of political news and events and act as 'a form of escape from pressing issues of the day'.[7]

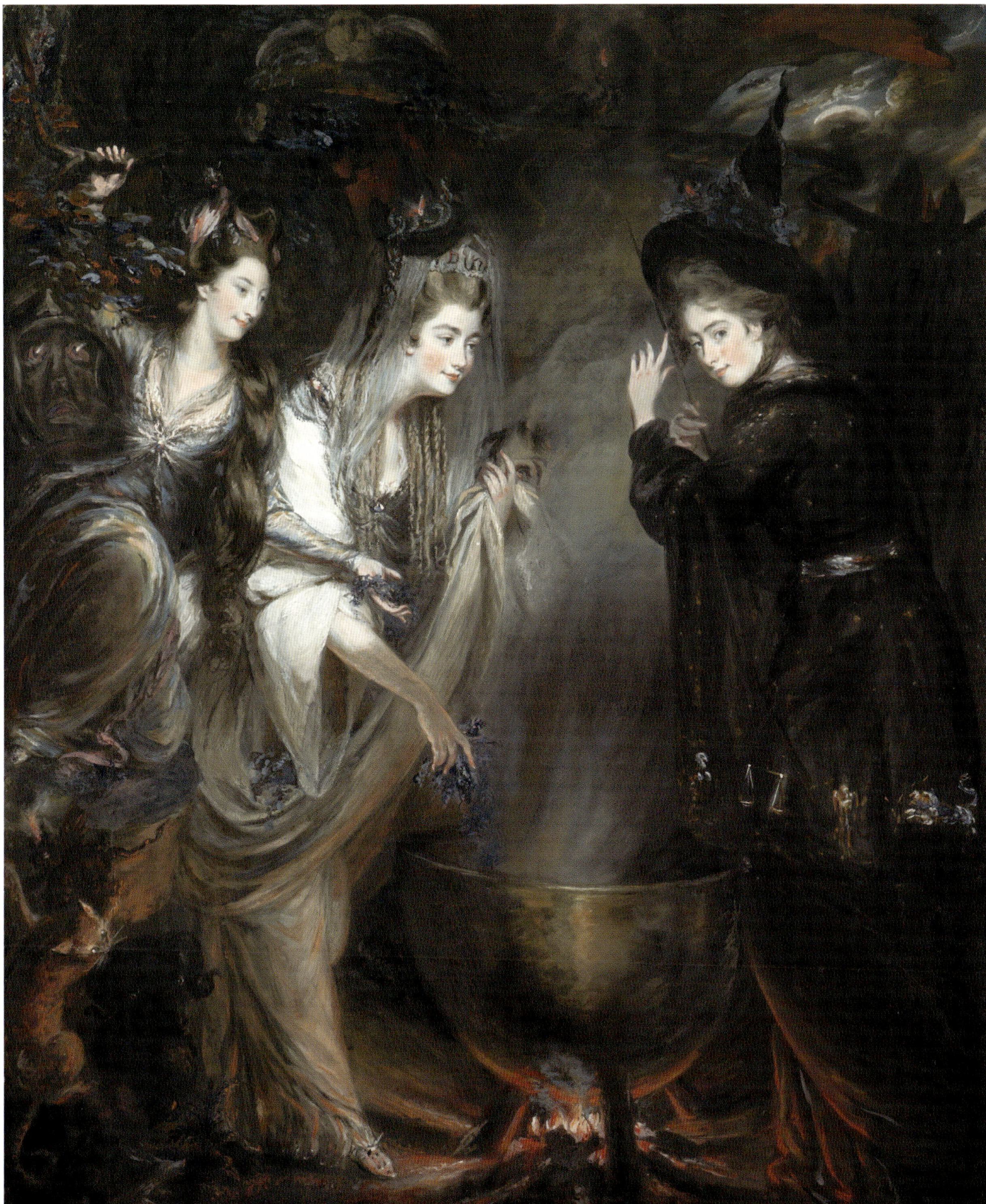

Fig.84

The Three Witches from *Macbeth* (Elizabeth, Viscountess Melbourne; Georgiana, Duchess of Devonshire; Anne Seymour Damer)

Daniel Gardner, 1775

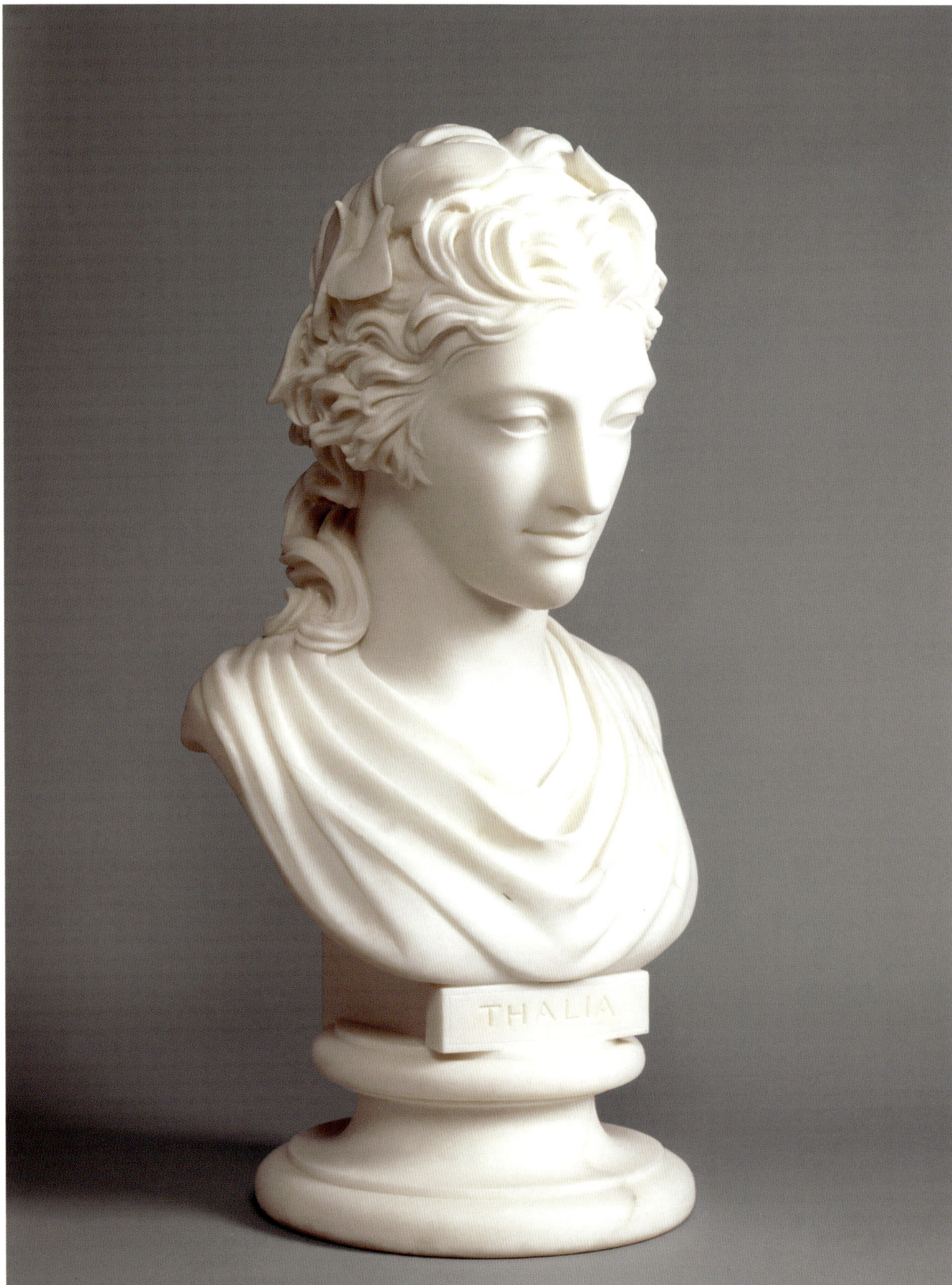

Fig.85

Elizabeth Farren as Thalia

Anne Seymour Damer, *c.*1788

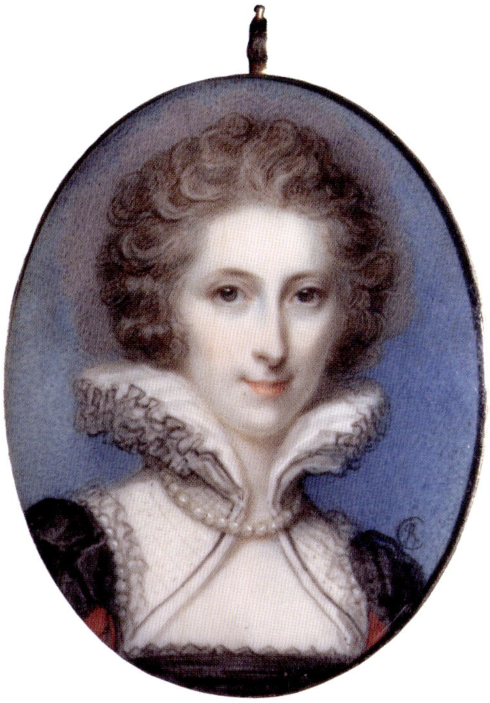

Fig.86 (left)
Anne Seymour Damer
Richard Cosway, 1785

Fig.87 (following pages)
Dilettanti-theatricals: – or – a Peep at the Green Room
James Gillray, 1803

Notwithstanding these issues of escapism, there is little doubt that the visibility of glamorous, well-connected women in the management, performance and audience for eighteenth-century private theatricals contributed to the lively press interest. Apart from Farren, the Richmond House theatricals were supported by Anne Seymour Damer (fig.86), who – unusually for a woman – pursued a successful career as a sculptor (her bust of her friend Farren was among Damer's best-known works). Damer was a 'bluestocking' known for her love of amateur dramatics and played the female lead, Mrs Lovemore, on the opening night at Richmond House. Her play-acting is the subject of a group portrait of 1775 by Daniel Gardner, *The Three Witches* (fig.84), in which three prominent noblewomen who shared a passion for Whig politics and the performing arts are represented as the three witches from *Macbeth*. Apart from Damer, these bewitching women are Georgiana, Duchess of Devonshire and Elizabeth, Viscountess Melbourne, shown dancing in fashionable dress around an unlikely cauldron which, according to the diarist Mary Coke, was made of 'roses and carnations'; Coke commented, 'I dare say their charmes [are] more irresistible than all the magick of the Witches.'[9]

The increasing vogue for private theatricals and the exhibitionism of well-connected actors manqués was vulnerable to some biting graphic satire, such as Gillray's *Dilettanti Theatricals* (fig.87). It also attracted the disapproval of some moral commentators, who feared an assault on class boundaries and respectable femininity. Thomas Gisborne's *An Enquiry into the Duties of the Female Sex* (1797) warned against the 'recent custom of acting plays in private theatres, fitted up by individuals of fortune', claiming that it encourages vanity and 'is almost certain to prove, in its effects, injurious to the female performers'.[10] The 'pressing social issue of the day' is expressed here in relation to gender. Once again, it was the dangers of *feminine* display on stage which encapsulated so many cultural and social anxieties.

Within the world of the professional theatre, this vogue for private theatricals was easily mocked. Issac Jackman satirised the craze in his popular farce *All the World's a Stage* (1777), which featured an amateur performance of *The Beggar's Opera* directed by Sir Gilbert Pumpkin, a country squire whose house has been completely taken over by theatricals (fig.91). This comic play-within-a-play reminds us that these activities could venture a little too close to home for some members of the theatrical establishment. In 1802 Colonel Granville set up the short-lived Pic Nic Society, made up of notoriously stage-struck aristocrats such as the well-proportioned Lady Buckinghamshire. The group held performances in the Tottenham Street Concert Rooms, seen as a bid for professional status. Gillray lampooned their run-in with the professionals in his *Blowing up the Pic Nic's* of 1802 (fig.88). Sheridan, dressed as Harlequin and brandishing his quill, leads an attack on the Pic Nics performing *Tom Thumb*, with an exaggeratedly *décolletée* Lady Buckinghamshire centre-stage. A crowd of angry thespians follows Sheridan, including Sarah Siddons as Lady Macbeth, Elizabeth Billington with mouth wide open in full song, and Charles Kemble as Hamlet, while the ghost of Garrick (who died in 1779) rises from beneath the boards.

The aristocratic desire to tread the boards was seen by some foreign commentators as evidence of social degeneration, of a 'poor beleaguered English nobility' reduced to vain and extravagant pursuits.[11] Fielding's confusion of the world and the stage took on both literal and metaphorical meanings for these observers of British social culture, and has some uneasy echoes in our own obsessions with celebrity.

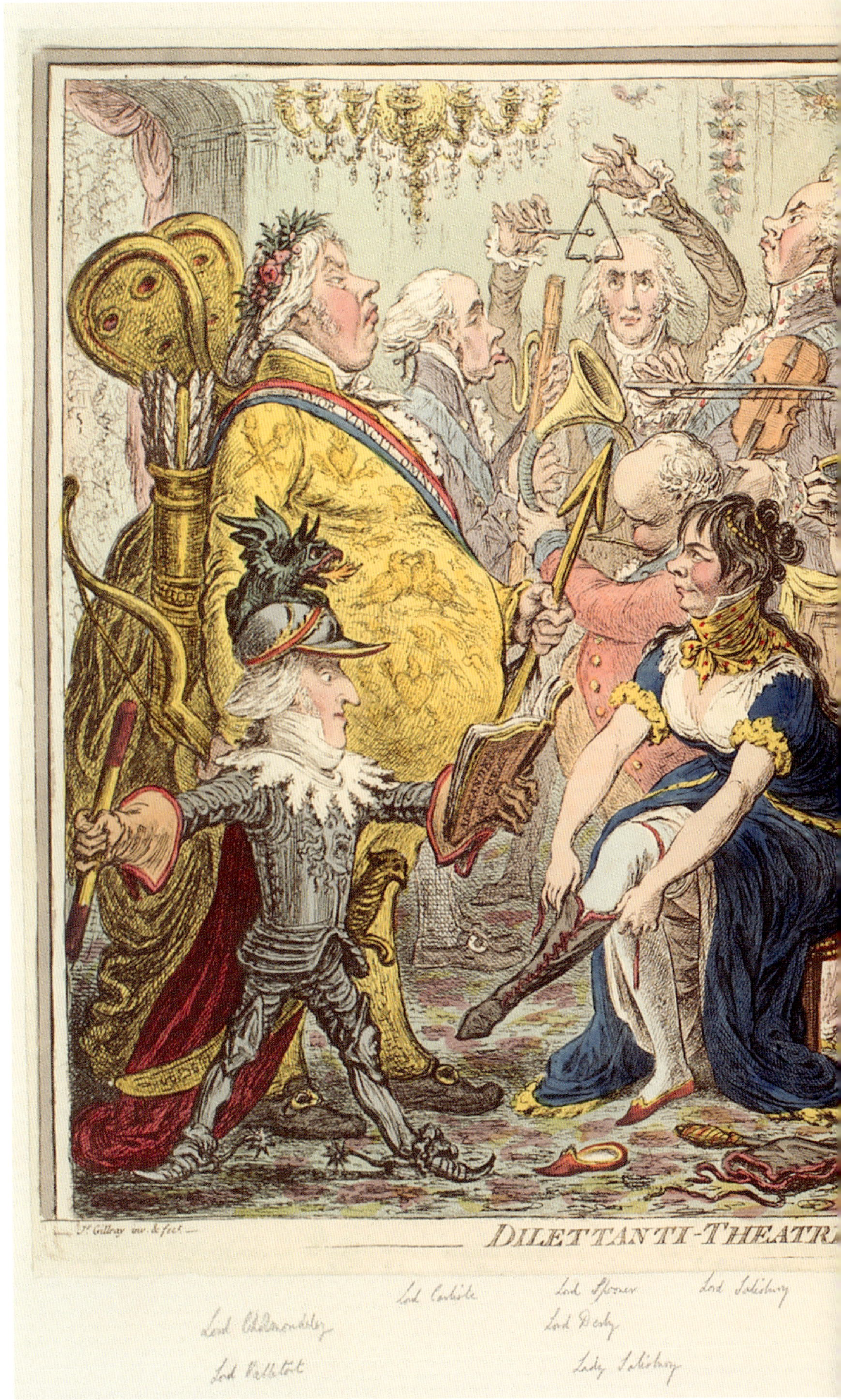
Js. Gillray inv. & fect.
Lord Cholmondeley
Lord Carlisle
Lord Spencer
Lord Salisbury
Lord Derby
Lord Valletort
Lady Salisbury

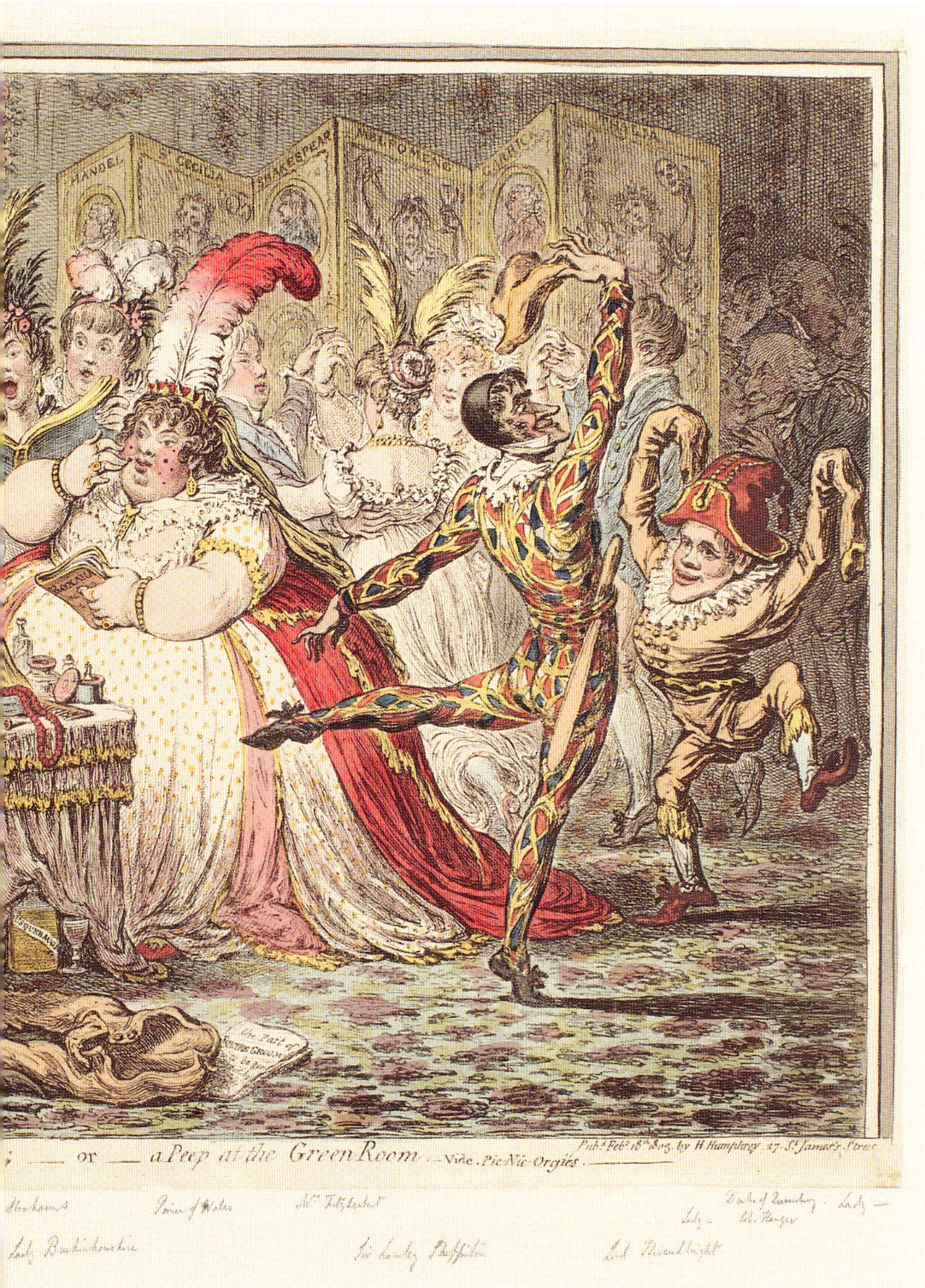
HANDEL
SHAKESPEAR
— or — a Peep at the Green Room. — Vide. Pic-Nic-Orgies
Pubd. Feby. 18th. 1803. by H. Humphrey 27 St. James's Street

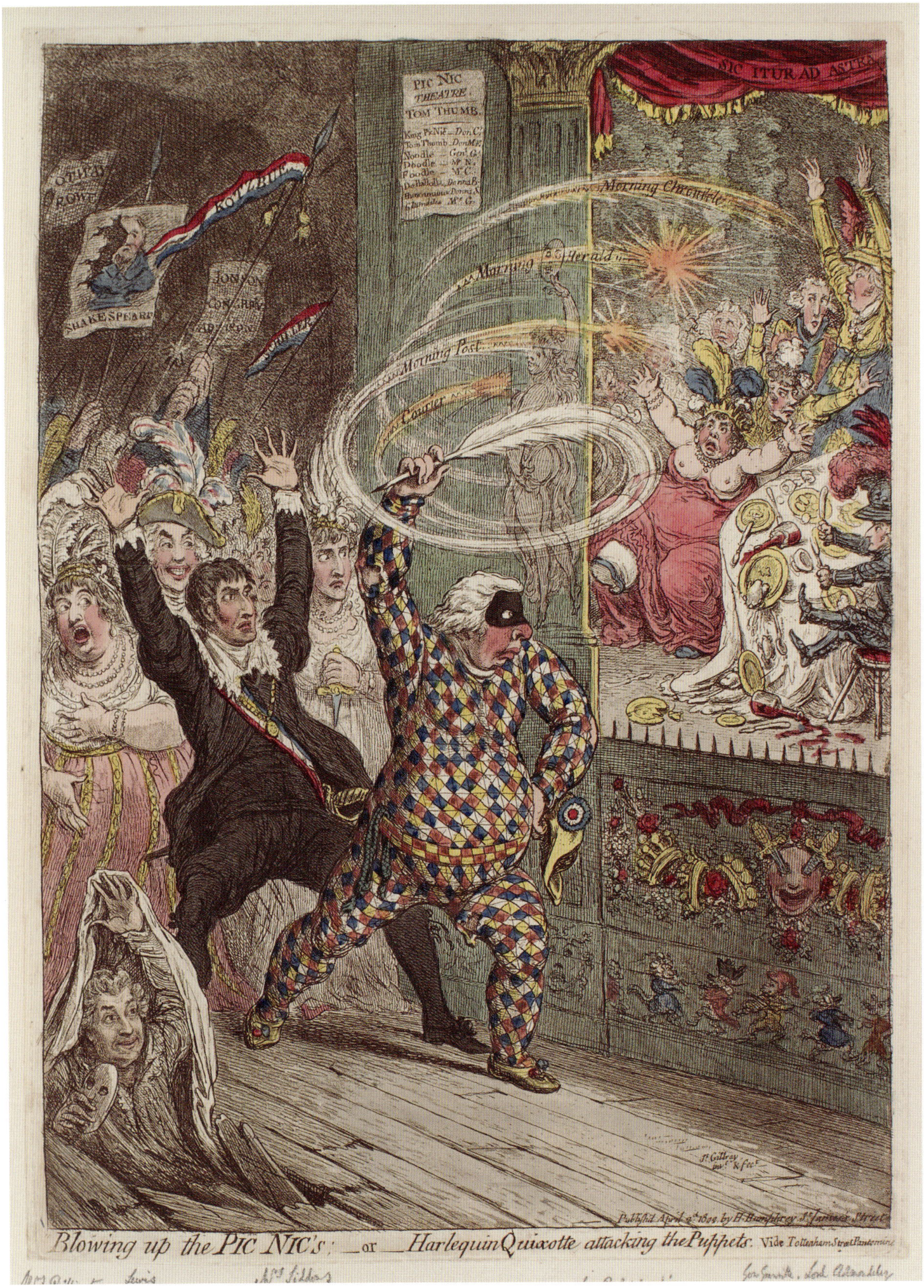

Fig.88

Blowing up the Pic Nic's – or –

Harlequin Quixotte attacking the Puppets

James Gillray, 1802

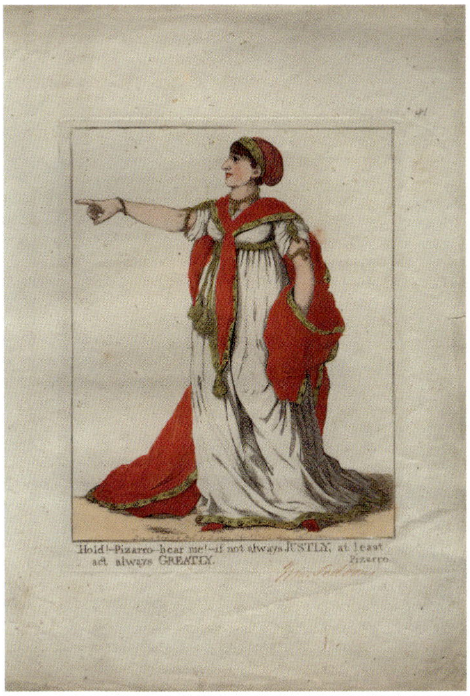

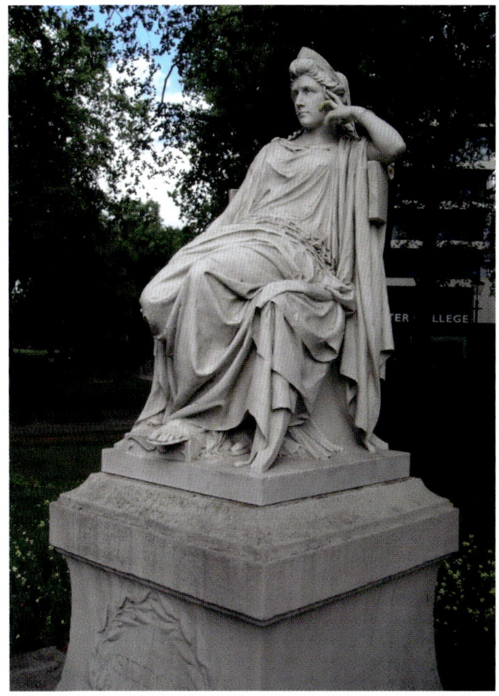

Celebrity and Portraiture: Then and Now

Despite the obvious historical differences, parallels are often drawn between the growing commercial culture of consumption of the eighteenth century and that of our own times. According to Stella Tillyard, 'celebrity appears to have been made in the eighteenth century and in particular eighteenth-century London, with its dozens of newspapers and print shops, its crowds and coffee houses, theatres, exhibitions, spectacles, pleasure gardens and teeming pavements.'[12] By 1770 London could boast sixty weekly newspapers, a seemingly insatiable market for biographies of the famous, combined with (as we saw in the Introduction) the increased dissemination of prints and copies of painted portraits. This public appetite for representations of a recognisable 'face', mixed with scurrilous gossip facilitated by weak personal libel laws, contributed to the fantasy of 'public intimacy' – an imagined access to private lives that provides the oxygen of celebrity culture.

As this book has demonstrated, this culture often had a distinctively feminine face. Actresses and their representations were at the centre of a popular and voyeuristic obsession with feminine glamour and its intimate associations. In this respect the word 'celebrity' is often distinguished from that of 'fame', a recurring theme in eighteenth-century literature, often attributed to male figures who had achieved military glory or success in poetic, artistic or literary endeavours. Recent accounts of Sir Joshua Reynolds have shown that he desired and achieved fame 'above all else'. This was then seen as a genteel aspiration that would guarantee posthumous respect, especially for professional men.[13] Although the terms 'celebrated' and 'celebrity' were in circulation in the eighteenth century, the noun and its plural 'celebrities' have been much used in the twentieth and twenty-first centuries, and are now understood as hybrid terms that mean more

Fig.89 (above left)

'Hold! – Pizarro – hear me!' (Sarah Siddons)

Robert Dighton, 1799

Fig.90 (above right)

Sarah Siddons as the Tragic Muse

L.J. Chavalliaud, 1897

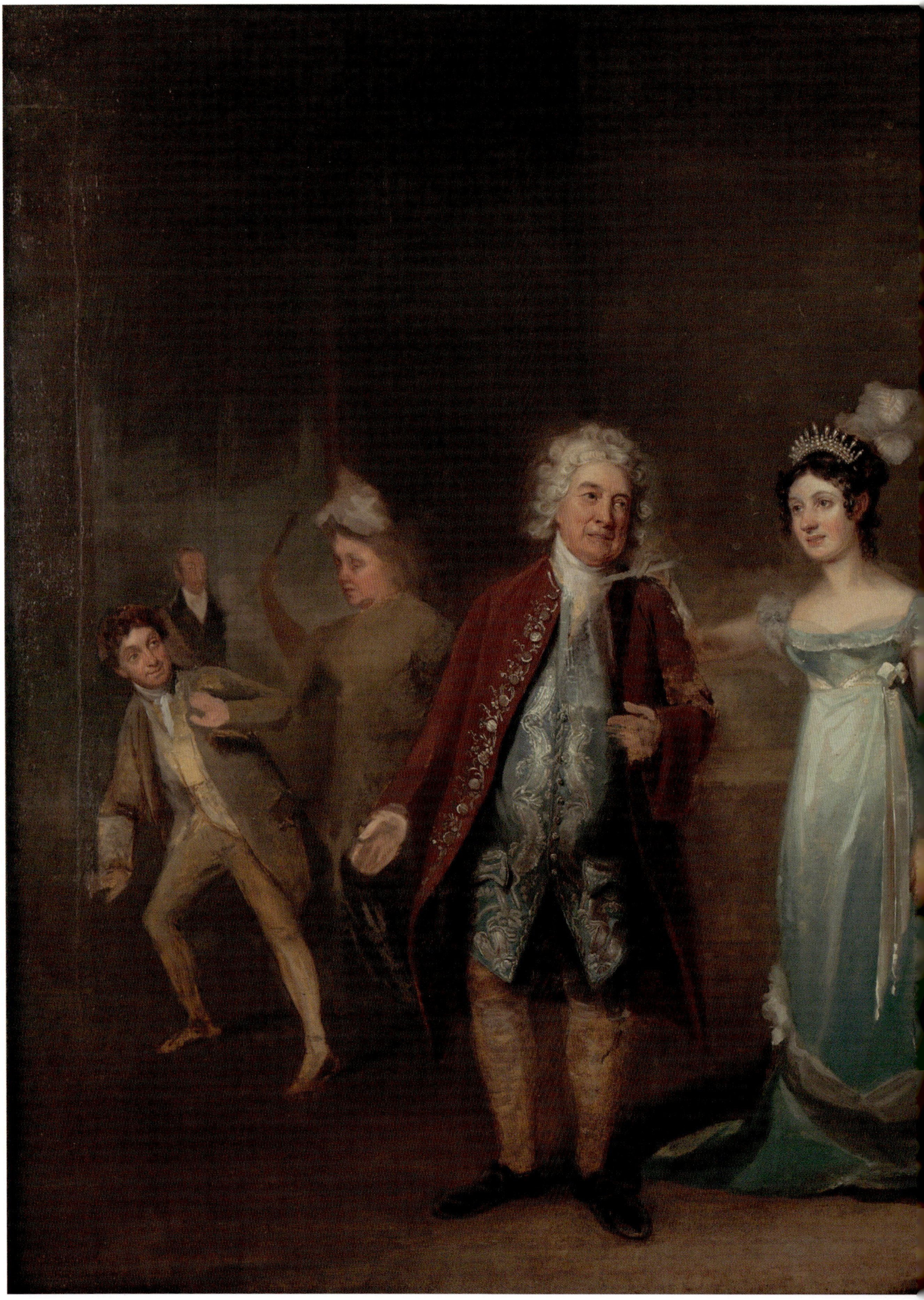

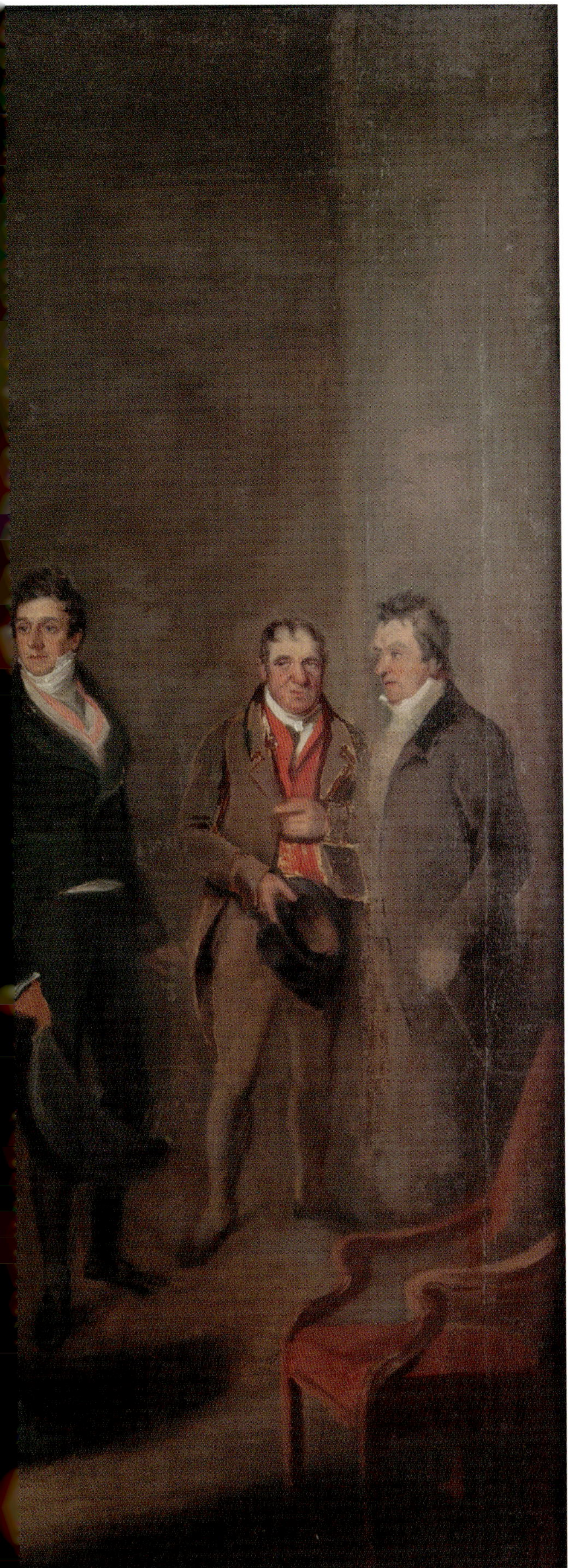

Fig.91

Richard Suett and Mrs Henry in *All the World's a Stage*

Samuel de Wilde, 1803

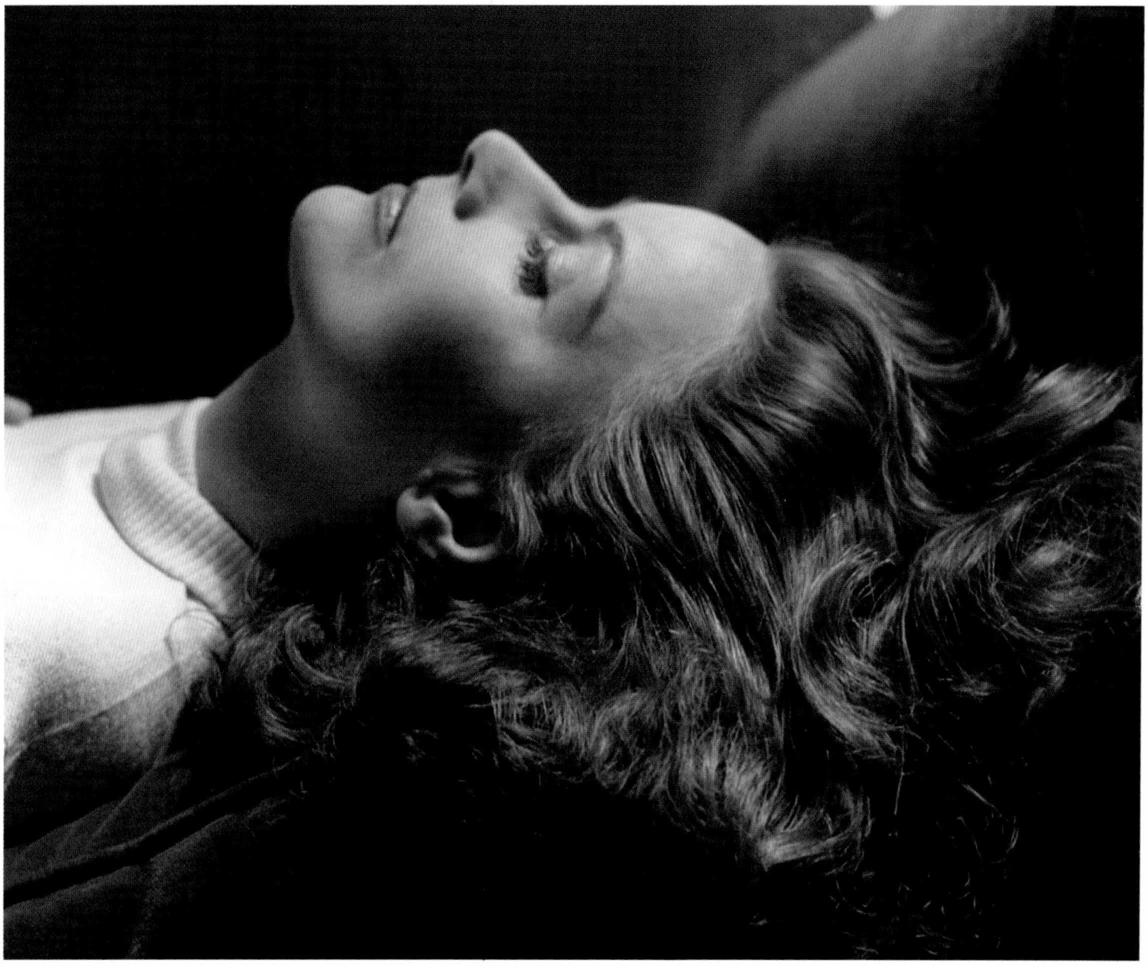

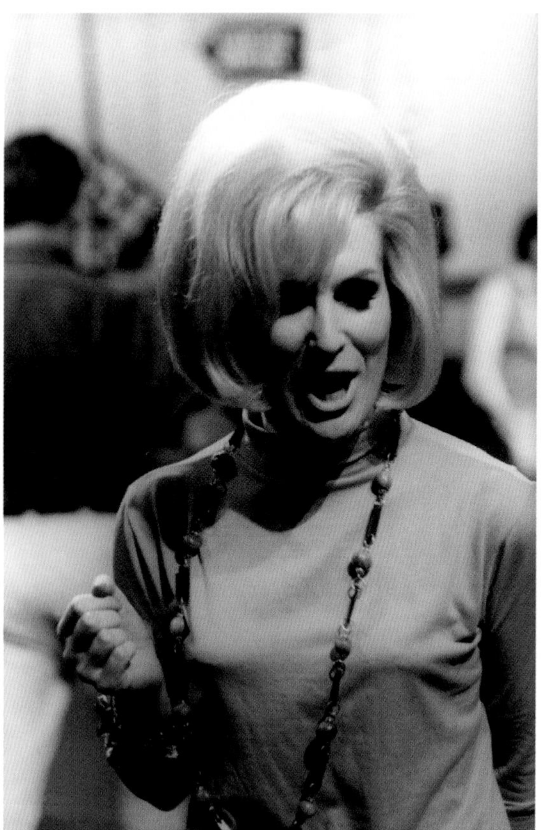

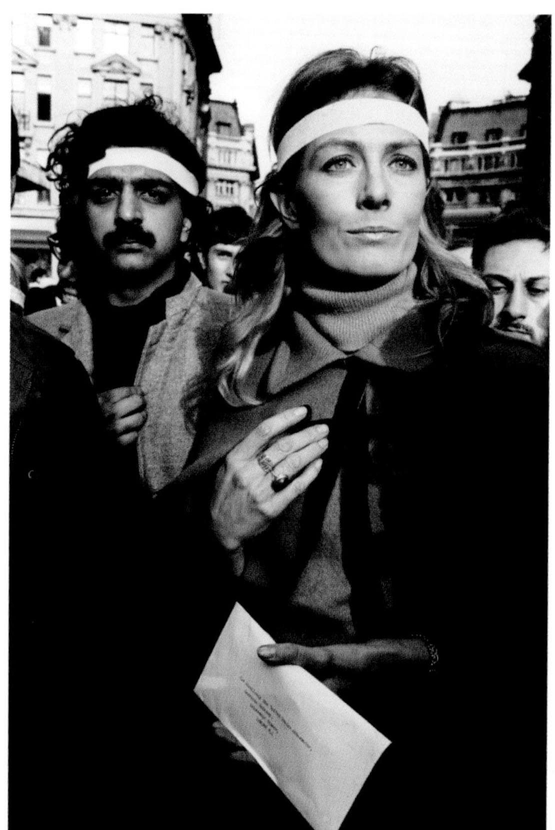

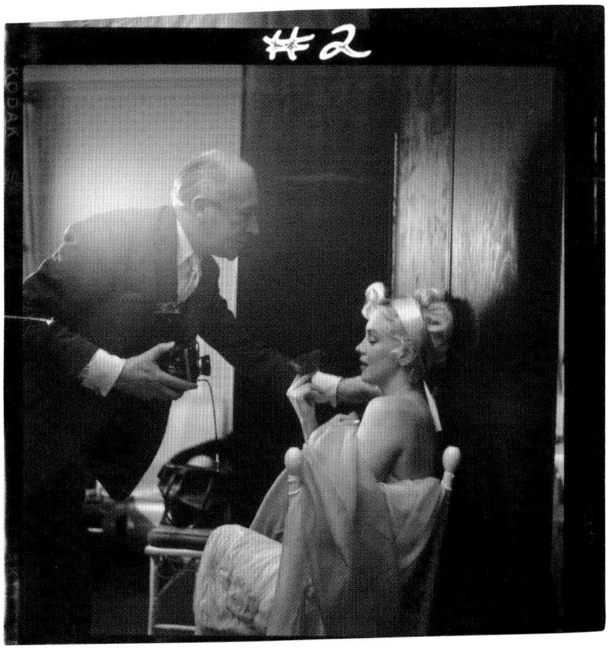

Fig.92 (opposite page, top)
Greta Garbo
Cecil Beaton, 1946

Fig.93 (opposite page, bottom left)
Dusty Springfield
Val Wilmer, 1964

Fig.94 (opposite page, bottom right)
Vanessa Redgrave with Tariq Ali
John Walmsley, 1968

Fig.95 (left)
Cecil Beaton photographing Marilyn Monroe
Ed Pfizenmaier, 1956

than simply being well known.[14] While 'celebrity', with its Latin root *celebrem*, can incorporate fame, it also denotes a cult of personality and a more fleeting or transient status that is at least partly dependent on the relationship with an audience. The source of celebrity power is the taste of the public, which is often fickle and may reflect changes in social, cultural and economic life.[15] The important role of the modern 'fan' who, through emulation, fan clubs or rogue activities (such as parody) can help to shape celebrity cults, has become a topical subject in recent studies of the media.[16]

Many of the attributes of both fame and celebrity that we have identified in our eighteenth-century cast of characters are those that we recognise today, despite the fact that our own visual culture is saturated with media representations and digital creations that would no doubt cause Reynolds to turn in his grave. Whatever the original talents or charismatic appeal of the actresses featured in this book, their public identities have been carefully manipulated. Then as now, celebrities were fabrications – fantasy figures constructed through representations in paint, print, gossip columns, biography, folklore and graphic imagery. Moreover, their success was also dependent on what we now call a strong 'fan base'. Many of the most captivating actresses featured in this book have entered into modern celebrity discourse and continued to absorb their fans. Joseph Roach has shown earlier the enduring obsession with the character and image of 'Nell'. The star qualities of Sarah Siddons have also been sustained and commodified for history in print form, as sculptures in porcelain and as commemorative statues (figs 10, 89, 90). Several private houses across Britain have been named after her, as has the 'Sarah Siddons Fan Club Theatre Company'[17] – not to mention the Metropolitan Railway locomotive *Sarah Siddons*, built in 1921 and still preserved in working order.

Ideas of 'stardom' are often associated with the development of the film industry in the first half of the twentieth century, especially of Hollywood and the powerful American studio system.[18] And the construction of the star's image has depended on the management of her famous roles, her visibility in the media, and the ubiquitous role of photography. This medium has provided modern celebrity culture with an enormously powerful means of staging and reframing the visual imagery of the actress and her star qualities, disseminated to a global audience. In the 1930s and 1940s a tradition of Hollywood 'glamour photography', closely allied with fashion photography, epitomised in the work of Horst P. Horst and continued in the portraits of George Hurrell and Cecil Beaton in the 1950s (fig.92), provided visual equivalents of the actress's supposedly 'divine' status, echoing at least some of the eighteenth-century portrait conventions we have explored in this book. Staged sets, lighting, soft-focus lenses, drapery and art historical props, dramatic poses and fashionable accessories were all deployed to create enthralling objects of worship.

This photographic style is exemplified in Horst's portraits of actresses from the 1940s and 1950s. The actress as a fashion icon and style leader is a pervasive stereotype that both historical portraits and more recent photographs have consistently reworked, producing images that suggest conspicuous consumption, extravagance, style and social aspirations. And the fashionableness of a famous actress or singer is often tied to cultural and national politics, as in many photographs of British performers from the 1960s, framed with visible signs of 'Swinging London' or British politics of the period (figs 93, 94). At the same time, some twentieth-century photographers have displayed an awareness of their own artistry in their celebrity portraits (figs 95, 97). Angus McBean's photographs from the 1940s and 1950s were often staged as surreal plays, as in his

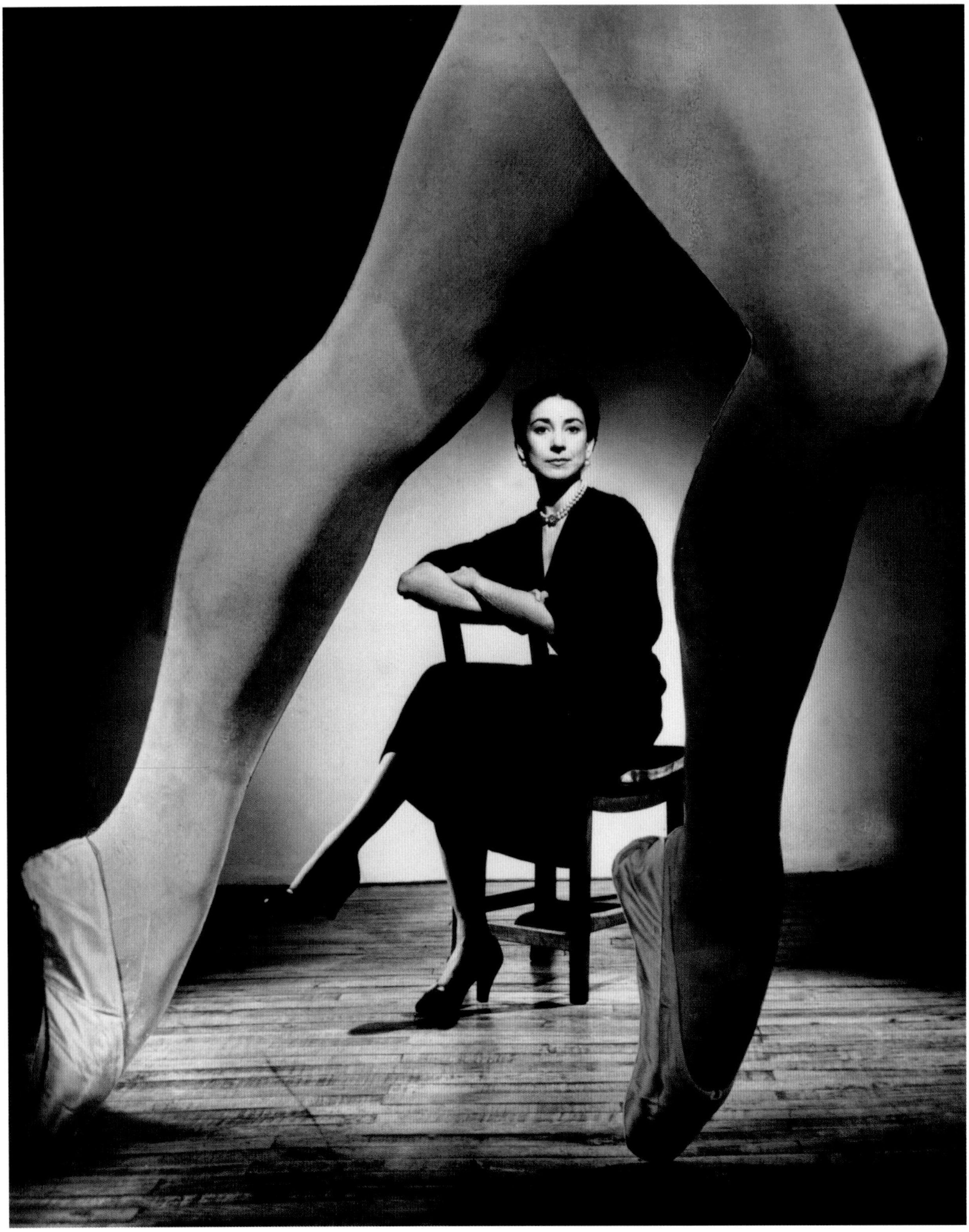

Fig.96

Margot Fonteyn

Angus McBean, 1951

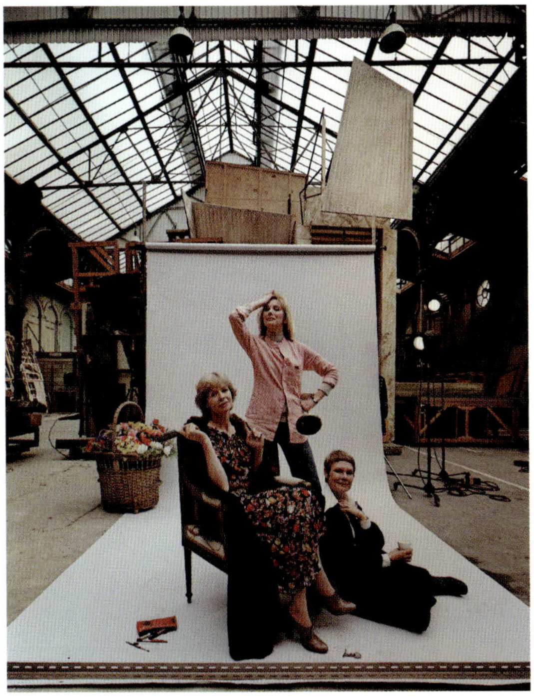

Fig.97 (left)

Actresses (Covent Garden)

(Susannah York, Susan Hampshire, Judi Dench)

Arnold Newman, 1978(?)

Fig.98 (following pages, left)

Fiona Shaw

Victoria Russell, 2002

Fig.99 (following pages, right)

Mary Wells in *The Merry Wives of Windsor*

William Hamilton, 1790s

1949 portrait of Vivien Leigh, or his haunting study of the dancer Margot Fonteyn, framed by an image of her dancing legs superimposed onto the photographic portrait (fig.96). The conspicuously theatrical nature of such works tells us that they are also plays within plays, involving the restaging of performances for and by the photographer.

Despite obvious historical differences, many twentieth-century representations of celebrity can be traced back to those eighteenth-century perceptions of women explored in this book. The conflation of public and private identities, the voyeuristic obsession with her sexual adventures, physical appearance and fashionableness, and a persistent ageism, along with a rags-to-riches life-story, have dominated the histories of many female stars, both eighteenth-century and modern. The eighteenth-century portrait provided a visual embodiment (and sometimes resolution) of some of the contradictions within these ideas of female celebrity. That important aesthetic role has not died with history. Despite the ubiquity of photography, some modern painted portraits have contributed to the elevation of their famous sitters as worthy of artistic representation on canvas, helping to guarantee their posthumous lives as occupants of a *national* portrait gallery.

It might also be argued that some recent painted portraits provide modern artistic licence to distort or render ugly (rather than glamorous), to subvert the associations of feminine celebrity. While Andy Warhol's 1967 offset lithograph of Elizabeth Taylor contributed to the Pop Art aesthetics of fame and glamour, some recent portraits of British actresses have broken established codes for signifying star status. Victoria Russell's painting of Fiona Shaw of 2002 (fig.98) echoes the epic full-length size of some ambitious eighteenth-century muse portraits of both tragic and comic subjects, such as William Hamilton's depiction of Mary Wells in *The Merry Wives of Windsor* (fig.99). But Shaw is depicted here partly in her underwear, conspicuously without make-up or fashionable accessories. She is presented as an unconventional, anti-celebrity actress, as a 'real' person beneath the roles. Yet the work is also clearly staged and posed with white drapery, and by virtue of its position in a public gallery it contributes to the affirmation of fame. Given Shaw's public image as a serious and independent-minded actress, does this portrait also challenge some gendered celebrity myths? The actress gazes to one side, refusing to engage the viewer's look and without trace of those familiar, beguiling, feminine roles.

Studies of modern celebrity culture have identified many feminine stereotypes perpetuated through famous roles, biographies and visual representations. These include not only the 'pin-up girl' (Marilyn Monroe), and the expensive and beautiful (Elizabeth Taylor), but also the independent rebel (Bette Davis, Jane Fonda, Katharine Hepburn).[19] Although inevitably tied mostly to Hollywood and media stereotypes, this final category does, perhaps, offer the possibility of some alternative, challenging parts for actresses – on stage, in film and in modern portraiture.

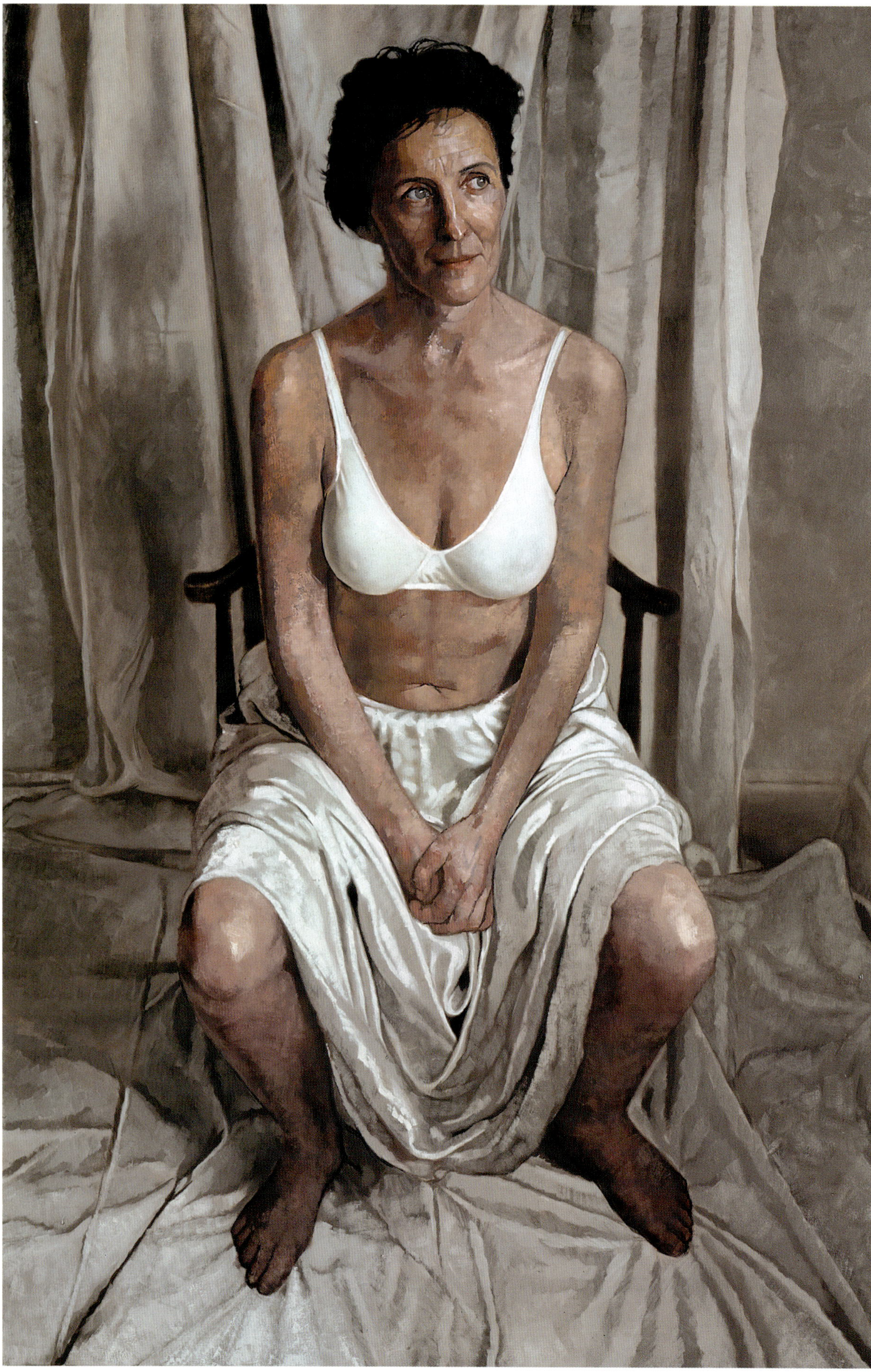

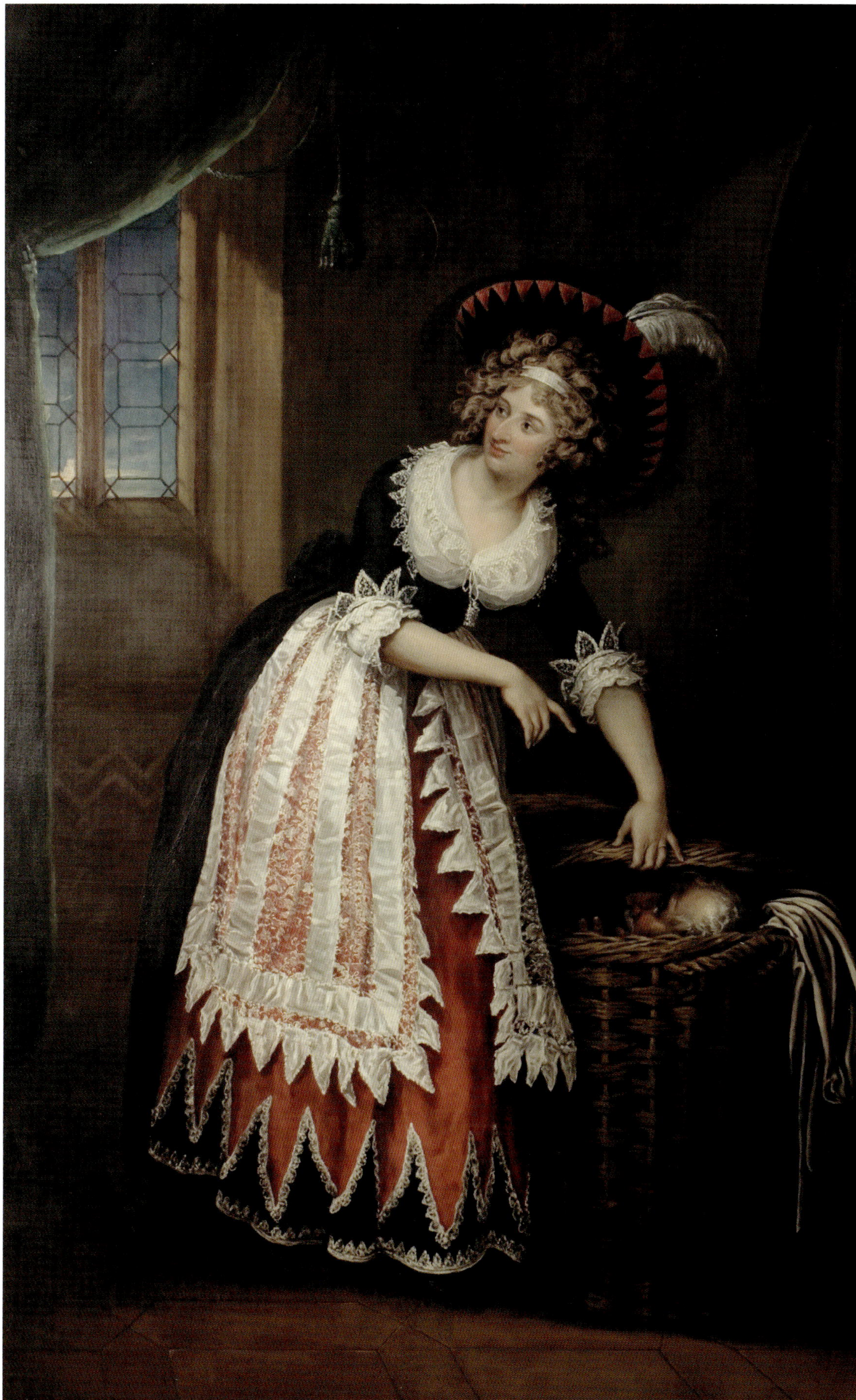

REFERENCES

Author's Acknowledgements
During the lengthy period of research and curatorial planning for this exhibition and book, I have been assisted by many generous and supportive friends and colleagues, both within and outside the National Portrait Gallery. I have learnt much from Lucy Peltz, the Gallery's Curator of Eighteenth-Century Portraits. Her curatorial and editorial skills have informed this exhibition and have improved my own ideas. I am much indebted to her knowledge and careful attention to detail. We have also been supported by an exceptional research assistant, Amanda Gubbins, who has diligently worked through archives and academic resources, and has made an invaluable contribution to the exhibition. I am also immensely grateful to Joseph Roach and Shearer West, whose excellent essays have enriched the content of this book.

I have sought advice and guidance from many other colleagues working in different areas of eighteenth-century studies. I am especially grateful to Berta Joncus for discussing our shared ideas on the relationship between music and the visual arts, and for directing me towards some useful publications. Christina Dennis, Judith Hawley, Donald Burrows, Michael Burden, Marcus Risdell, Brian Allen, Claire Hudson, Martin Postle, Gillian Dow and Marcia Pointon all provided helpful advice or answered queries, for which I am immensely grateful. I have also been encouraged by the enthusiasm and support for the project offered by Marina Warner and Sandy Nairne. And this list would not be complete without acknowledging the influential research of a late colleague of mine from the Open University, Elizabeth Howe, and the more recent work of literary scholar Felicity Nussbaum. Their pioneering research on seventeenth- and eighteenth-century actresses has inspired and informed this project.

I would also like to offer thanks to all those members of the National Portrait Gallery who have worked so hard to make this exhibition and book possible, and to show my gratitude for the painstaking commitment of my copy-editors, who have worked patiently and conscientiously through all stages of a complex production. And finally, I would like to show my gratitude to the Open University Arts Faculty Research Committee for its support of my work on both the exhibition and the book.

Editorial Note

The eighteenth-century use of 'Mrs' as a form of address has been omitted in the text of this publication, when referring to the actresses in question, to reflect twenty-first-century attitudes. Where actresses were known by a 'popular' name, this has been used. The media of all works illustrated are noted in the List of Works, pp.150–5.

Notes

Introduction: Painting Actresses' Lives

1 For example, obituaries of Natasha Richardson, who died in 2009, reveal a mixture of the two terms: *The Times* used 'actress', whereas the *Guardian* described her as 'daughter of actor Vanessa Redgrave' (both 19 March 2009).

2 Samuel Pepys, *The Diary of Samuel Pepys*, Robert Latham and William Matthews (eds), 11 vols (Berkeley and Los Angeles: University of California Press, 1983), 2 March 1667, vol. 8. The longer quotation is cited by Amy Scott-Douglass in her discussion of Aphra Behn's series of prologues and epilogues, *Covent Garden Drollery* (1672), which addresses the issue of all-female casting and perceptions of breeches roles: see 'Aphra Behn's *Covent Garden Drollery*: The First History of Women in Restoration Theatre' in Laura Engel (ed.), *The Public's Open to us All: Essays on Women and Performance in Eighteenth-Century England* (Newcastle upon Tyne: Cambridge Scholars, 2009), pp.98–127; cited on p.107.

3 By the 1790s both Covent Garden and Drury Lane theatres had undergone a series of renovations, and both had seating capacities of around 3,000.

4 I discuss some of these changes, and the roles of women as spectators of art and theatre, in my book *Spectacular Flirtations: Viewing the Actress in British Art and Theatre, 1768–1820* (London and New Haven: Yale University Press, 2007).

5 See Ellen C. Donkin, *Getting into the Act: Women Playwrights in London, 1776–1829* (London: Routledge, 1995); Misty G. Anderson, 'Women Playwrights' in Jane Moody and Daniel O'Quinn (eds), *The Cambridge Companion to British Theatre, 1730–1830* (Cambridge: Cambridge University Press, 2007), pp.145–58; Helen E.M. Brooks has also explored the activities of increasing numbers of actress-managers during the period in 'Women and Theatre Management in the Eighteenth Century' in Laura Engel (ed.), *The Public's Open to us All*, pp.73–95.

6 See Sandra Richards, *The Rise of the English Actress* (Basingstoke: Macmillan, 1993), p.30, and Elizabeth Eger, 'Spectacle, Intellect and Authority' in Maggie B. Gale and John Stokes (eds), *The Cambridge Companion to the Actress* (Cambridge: Cambridge University Press, 2007), pp.33–51.

7 A point also made forcefully by Laura J. Rosenthal in 'Entertaining Women: The Actress in Eighteenth-Century Theatre and Culture' in Moody and O'Quinn (eds), *The Cambridge Companion to British Theatre 1730–1830*, op. cit., p.159. James Van Horn Melton has also argued that 'Nowhere outside the salon did eighteenth-century women have more of a public presence than in the theatre', see *The Rise of the Public in Enlightenment Europe* (Cambridge: Cambridge University Press, 2001), p.174.

8 Felicity Nussbaum, *Rival Queens: Actresses, Performance, and the Eighteenth-Century British Theater* (Philadelphia: University of Pennsylvania Press, 2010), p.15.

9 See 'Star Systems' for a discussion of uses of the term 'celebrity'.

10 Chris Rojek, *Celebrity* (London: Reaktion, 2001).

11 Gale and Stokes (eds), *The Cambridge Companion to the Actress*, op. cit., p.12.

12 Richard Brinsley Sheridan, *The School for Scandal*, ed. Ann Blake (London: A & C Black, 2004), p.110.

13 Ibid, p.112.

14 Lisa Freeman has usefully explored the theatrical idea of 'character' and its relationship to subjectivity in eighteenth-century drama in her book *Character's Theater: Genre and Identity on the Eighteenth-Century English Stage* (Philadelphia: University of Pennsylvania Press, 2002).

15 I discuss this overlapping vocabulary, and the styling of theatrical tableaux in *Spectacular Flirtations* (op. cit.). See especially 'Introduction: Viewing the Actress' and chapter 2, 'Spectacular Appearances'.

16 Jim Davis has explored this relationship in his essay 'Spectatorship' in Moody and O'Quinn (eds), *The Cambridge Companion to the British Theatre 1730–1830*, p.60.

17 See Mark Hallett, *Hogarth* (London: Phaidon, 2000), p.48.

18 Kristina Straub, *Sexual Suspects: Eighteenth-Century Players and Sexual Ideology* (Oxford and Princeton: Princeton University Press, 1992).

19 A point made by Marcia Pointon in 'Portrait! Portrait!! Portrait!!!' in David Solkin (ed.), *Art on the Line: The Royal Academy Exhibitions at Somerset House, 1780–1836* (London and New Haven: Yale University Press for the Paul Mellon Centre for Studies in British Art and the Courtauld Institute Gallery, 2001), p.95.

20 Ibid.

21 *Gazeteer and New Daily Advertiser*, 30 April 1782. For a discussion of eighteenth-century uses of the term 'celebrated', see p.129.

22 Laetitia Matilda Hawkins, *Memoirs, Anecdotes, Facts and Opinions* (London: Longman, 1824), vol. 2, p.24.

23 I explore some of the problems of portraiture and the idea of 'double mediation' in *Spectacular Flirtations*, p.21.

24 Daniel Boorstin, in one of the earliest attempts to theorise modern celebrity, has described twentieth-century stars who become 'known for well-knownness'; see Daniel Boorstin, *The Image: A Guide to Pseudo-Events in America* (New York: Athenaeum, 1961), p.57.

25 As Cheryl Wanko has shown in her book *Roles of Authority: Thespian Biography and Celebrity in Eighteenth-Century Britain* (Lubbock: Texas Tech University Press, 2003), p.2.

26 These issues are explored in chapters 1, 2 and 5. See also discussions in Wanko, *Roles of Authority* (especially 'Introduction') and Mary Luckhurst and Jane Moody (eds), *Theatre and Celebrity in Britain* (New York: Palgrave Macmillan, 2005), p.3.

27 Anon., *The Life of Lavinia Beswick, Alias Fenton, Alias Polly Peachum* (London: A. Moore, 1728). These early biographies are discussed by Wanko, in *Roles of Authority*, chapters 2 and 3, who claims that *The Life of Lavinia Beswick* is the first 'actress-biography'.

28 Philip H. Highfill, Kalman A. Burnim and Edward A. Langhans, *A Biographical Dictionary of Actors, Actresses, Musicians, Dancers, Managers and Other Stage Personnel in London, 1660–1800*, 16 vols, 1973–93 (Carbondale: Southern Illinois University Press, 1978), vol. 6, p.221.

29 Straub, *Sexual Suspects*, op. cit., and Wanko, *Roles of Authority*, p.56ff.

30 *The Life of Lavinia Beswick*, p.14.

31 Wanko describes some of these conflicting interpretations in *Roles*

of Authority. She writes: '*The Life* implies that women pursue and enjoy such work, instead of being forced into it by economic necessity or even being drawn to it as a venue for performing talent' (p.76, and see also p.60).

32 Nussbaum has argued that this memoir suggested that her sexual behaviour was an unavoidable consequence of her profession, rather than a perverse desire, and that her celebrity worth might be assessed separately from her personal life. See Nussbaum, *Rival Queens*, p.100.

33 Charkes's *A Narrative* has been explored as evidence of the difficulties encountered by actresses who gained visibility in the male public sphere, but whose sexuality was deemed problematic in, for example, Wanko, *Roles of Authority* (see especially chapter 3) and Straub, *Sexual Suspects* (see especially chapter 7).

34 *A Narrative*, p.11. See E. Eger and L. Peltz, *Brilliant Women: 18th-Century Bluestockings* (London: National Portrait Gallery, 2008), for a discussion of the tradition of female apologies.

35 This illusion of secrecy, and the cultural and commercial value of 'public intimacy' for actresses, is discussed by Nussbaum in 'Actresses and the Economics of Celebrity, 1700–1800' in Luckhurst and Moody (eds), *Theatre and Celebrity*, p.150, and in her excellent book, *Rival Queens*.

Nell Gwyn and Covent Garden Goddesses

1 One of the most recent studies of the complex iconography of Nell Gwyn can be found in Catharine MacLeod and Julia Marciari Alexander (eds), *Painted Ladies: Women at the Court of Charles II* (London: National Portrait Gallery, and Yale Center for British Art, 2001).

2 David Piper, *Catalogue of the Seventeenth-Century Portraits in the National Portrait Gallery, 1625–1714* (Cambridge: Cambridge University Press, 1963), p.149.

3 Catharine MacLeod and Julia Marciari Alexander (eds), *Painted Ladies*, op. cit., p.50.

4 Claire Tomalin, *Samuel Pepys: The Unequalled Self* (New York: Knopf, 2002), p.49.

5 *Antony and Cleopatra*, II:ii.235–7.

6 *The Diary of Samuel Pepys*, Robert Latham and William Matthews (eds) (Berkeley and Los Angeles: University of California Press, 1970–83), vol. 8, p.503.

7 *Antony and Cleopatra*, II.ii.237–9.

8 Alison Conway, *The Protestant Whore: Courtesan Narrative and Religious Controversy in England, 1680–1750* (Toronto: University of Toronto Press, 2010), pp.3–4.

9 Janet Todd (ed.), *The Works of Aphra Behn*, 7 vols (Columbus: Ohio State University Press, 1992–6), vol. 6, pp.86–7.

10 Charles Beauclerk, *Nell Gwyn: A Biography* (London: Macmillan, 2005), p.3.

11 Ibid., p.307.

12 A representative list includes John Seymour, *Memoirs of the Life of Eleanor Gwinn* (London: Stamper, 1752); Peter Cunningham, *The Story of Nell Gwyn* (London: Bradbury & Evans, 1852); Cecil Chesterton, *Nell Gwyn* (London: Foulis, 1912); Lewis Melville, *Nell Gwyn: The Story of Her Life* (New York: Doran, 1924); Arthur Irwin Dasent, *Nell Gwynne, 1650–1687* (London: Macmillan, 1924); John Harold Wilson, *Nell Gwyn: Royal Mistress* (New York: Pellegrini and Cudahy, 1952); and Brendan Bevan, *Nell Gwyn* (London: Hale, 1969).

13 John Harold Wilson, *All the King's Ladies: Actresses of the Restoration* (Chicago: University of Chicago Press, 1958), pp.117–20, 146–9.

14 Most recently Gwyn appears as a character in Anthony Capella's *The Empress of Ice Cream* (London: Sphere, 2010) and Priya Parmar's *Exit the Actress* (London: Touchstone, 2011); her life on film began with the silent *Sweet Nell of Drury Lane* (1911) and continues through *Stage Beauty* (2004).

15 Elizabeth Howe, *The First English Actresses: Women and Drama, 1660–1700* (Cambridge: Cambridge University Press, 1992), p.34.

16 On fetishisation of Nell Gwyn's feet by her biographers, see Thomas A. King, '"As if (she) were made on purpose to put the whole world in good Humour": Reconstructing the First English Actresses', *The Drama Review: A Journal of Performance Studies*, 36(3), 1992, 95–6.

17 George Bernard Shaw, *Pygmalion: A Romance in Five Acts*, in *Selected Plays with Prefaces* (New York: Dodd and Mead, 1948–9), pp.281–2.

18 Philip H. Highfill Jr, Kalmin A. Burnim and Edward A. Langhans (eds), *A Biographical Dictionary of Actors, Actresses, Musicians, Dancers, Managers, and Other Stage Personnel in London, 1660–1800*, 16 vols (Carbondale: Southern Illinois University Press, 1973–93), vol. 6, p.463.

19 Charles Beauclerk, *Nell Gwyn*, op. cit., p.327.

20 *The Diary of Samuel Pepys*, op. cit., vol. 6, p.73.

21 *The Life of Mr. Thomas Betterton, The Late Eminent Tragedian* (London: Robert Gosling, 1710), p.10.

22 Walter Bagehot, *The English Constitution*, R.H.S. Crossman (ed.) (Ithaca, NY: Cornell University Press, 1966), p.248.

23 Elinor Glyn, *It* (New York: Macaulay, 1927), pp.5–7.

24 *The Diary of Samuel Pepys*, op. cit., vol. 9, pp.93–4.

25 Charles Dickens, *A Child's History of England* (London: Bradbury and Evans, 1854), vol. 3, p.259.

26 Mark Twain, *The Adventures of Huckleberry Finn* (New York: Harper Brothers, 1918), p.213.

27 Charles Dickens, *A Child's History of England*, op. cit., vol. 3, p.293.

Divas, Dancing and the Rage for Music

1 *The Craftsman*, 13 April 1728.

2 For an invaluable summary of the musical history, politics, gender and artistic associations of this genre, see *Ballad Operas Online*, http://www.odl.ox.ac.uk/balladoperas/stars.php. Here 'ballad opera' is defined as 'any British stage production from 1728 to 1760 that combines a comic or sentimental play with musical numbers that reused "common Tunes", i.e. airs whose broad circulation allowed them to be recalled by title only'.

3 Gay's work was among the first examples of this popular new genre of 'ballad opera'. See also Richard Traubner, *Operetta: A Theatrical History*, p.11. On the roles of women see *Ballad Operas Online*, 'Gender History', p.1.

4 For an excellent article on ballad operas, feminine stereotypes and the roles of Lavinia Fenton and Kitty Clive, see Berta Joncus, '"The Assemblage of Every Female Folly": Kitty Clive and the Ballad Opera', in Tiffany Potter (ed.), *Women of Fashion: Popular Culture in the Eighteenth Century and the Eighteenth Century in Popular Culture* (Toronto: University of Toronto Press, forthcoming, 2011). I am hugely indebted to Berta Joncus for steering me towards several useful publications, sharing her research with me, and for discussing our shared ideas on music and visual representation.

5 Bordoni made her London debut as Rossane in Handel's *Allesandro* on 5 May 1726, playing alongside Cuzzoni and 'Senesino'. Much has been made of her personal and professional rivalry with Cuzzoni, which allegedly turned into an on-stage fight at the King's Theatre in front of Caroline, Princess of Wales, during a

performance of *Astianatte* on 6 June 1727. See *Handel and the Divas*, exh. cat. Handel House Museum (London: 2008).

6 I discuss some eighteenth-century definitions of 'coquettes' and 'flirts' in *Spectacular Flirtations*, op. cit. See especially the Introduction and chapter 5, 'Murdered by Music'.

7 For a recent biography see Lisa Hilton, *Mistress Peachum's Pleasure: A Biography of Lavinia, Duchess of Bolton* (London: Weidenfeld and Nicolson, 2005).

8 Cited in *Ballad Operas Online*, 'Stars of Ballad Operas', p.1. The run of biographies included short accounts and puffs, and the more substantial *Life* described in the Introduction was probably the first actress-biography.

9 Nussbaum, *Rival Queens*, op. cit., p.16.

10 See Joncus, '"The Assemblage of Every Female Folly"', op. cit. *Ballad Operas Online* also explores some of these political issues, arguing that in prologues, epilogues and introductions, ballad operas helped to 'construct an imagined community of like-minded Britons ... By fusing English words with so-called British song, ballad opera playwrights claimed also to make manifest qualities which allegedly were inherent to the nation, such as rationality, wit and the desire for self-improvement.' See 'Political History', p.1.

11 The painting was previously attributed to Allan Ramsay but a prior attribution to Knapton now seems more likely. Alistair Smart's catalogue lists the attribution to Ramsay under 'Doubtful Attributions'. See Alistair Smart, *Allan Ramsay: A Complete Catalogue of his Paintings,* John Ingamells (ed.) (London and New Haven: Yale University Press and Paul Mellon Centre, 1999), p.209.

12 Aileen Ribeiro has explored this careful monitoring of the 'correct' arrangement of dress and accessories, and balance between richness and simplicity, in *Dress in Eighteenth Century Europe, 1715–1789* (London and New Haven: Yale University Press, 2002). See especially chapters 5 and 6.

13 According to Ribeiro, by the 1750s tiny wired caps, made of lace in the shape of a butterfly and influenced by French designs, were also the height of fashion. Ibid., pp.151–2.

14 Chris Rojek defines 'celebrity' as 'the attribution of glamorous or notorious status to an individual within the public sphere', in *Celebrity*, p.10. See also 'Star Systems', for a discussion of the meanings of this term.

15 Fenton sports some sort of cap in every known portrait, including Hogarth's later painting of the mature Duchess, now at Tate Britain (fig.48), in which she has abandoned the frivolous pastel colours and flowers of the earlier Knapton portrait, and now wears an understated round-eared cap, deemed more suitable for her later years.

16 There are six existing versions of this work. Hogarth shows the boxes on the stage for aristocratic patrons, and in several versions the Duke of Bolton sits enthralled as he faces Fenton at the front of the box on the right. See, for example, the version at Tate Britain.

17 The mask is partly painted in black, referencing perhaps the black Harlequin masks associated with masquerades and carnivals. On femininity and masquerades see Terry Castle, *Masquerade and Civilisation: The Carnivalesque in Eighteenth-Century English Culture and Fiction* (London: Methuen, 1986).

18 The 'Polly Row' and its effects on the celebrity status of Kitty Clive are discussed in Berta Joncus, '"In Wit Superior, as in Fighting": Kitty Clive and the Conquest of a Rival Queen', *Huntington Library Quarterly*, 74(1), 2011, pp.23–42.

19 Nussbaum has explored Clive's remarkable ability to market her image and her economic success into a 'marketable personhood that became a new sort of commercial property worthy of the high wages she commanded'. See *Rival Queens*, op. cit., p.152. See also Joncus, '"The Assemblage of Every Female Folly"', op. cit.

20 For an excellent exploration of the construction of Clive's star status, see Joncus, '"A Likeness where none was to be found": Imagining Kitty Clive (1711-1785)', *Music in Art*, 34(1–2), 2009, pp.89–106.

21 Joncus has suggested that each musical phase of Clive's life had a visual parallel. See Joncus, '"A Likeness where none was to be found", op. cit.

22 In the Introduction I cite Act IV of *The School for Scandal*, in which Sheridan seems to acknowledge the ubiquity of pastoral disguise for aristocratic women sitters. On the conventions of 'disguise' for eighteenth-century feminine portraiture see my essay 'Women in Disguise', op. cit.

23 See also William Jones, *Two Scenes from Colley Cibber's 'Damon and Phillida'*, 1740, oil on canvas, Tate Britain, which may be portraits of Clive (or possibly Charlotte Charke).

24 This portrait was presented to Clive's close friend Horace Walpole by her brother James Raftor, probably in the 1780s.

25 On the role of drapery in portraiture and visual culture see Gen Doy, *Drapery: Classicism and Barbarism in Visual Culture* (London: Tauris, 2002).

26 This coding is sustained in William Verelst's portrait of 1750 in the Garrick Club, London, in which she sits in front of a double harpsichord, wearing another, tastefully embroidered white satin robe with blue, poised to sing 'Sweet Bird' from Handel's *L'Allegro*.

27 For example, Garrick's famous Shakespeare Jubilee, a three-day festival held in Stratford-upon-Avon in 1769. Many of the country's best-known performers were invited to attend and join the procession of 'Shakespearean characters' who marched through the streets of Stratford. Thomas Arne was commissioned to compose several airs for the event. See Johanne M. Stochholm, *Garrick's Folly: The Shakespeare Jubilee of 1769 at Stratford and Drury Lane* (London: Methuen, 1964).

28 A summary of this law and the licence applications can be found in the London Metropolitan Archives, Information Leaflet Number 47, 'Sources for the History of London Theatres and Music Halls at London Metropolitan Archives'. See also John Brewer, *The Pleasures of the Imagination: English Culture in the Eighteenth Century* (London: HarperCollins, 1997), chapter 5, 'Performance for the Nation', p.384ff.

29 'Thoughts on the Present State and Moral Effect of the Drama', *Theatrical Inquisitor*, III (November, 1813), p.198. The anonymous author also blames this 'rage for music' and a perceived decline in the content of theatrical performance on the increasing size of theatres attracting a broader and less 'refined' audience. This sentiment was echoed in articles in theatrical journals from the last two decades of the eighteenth century.

30 Curtis Price, Judith Milhous and Robert D. Hume, *Italian Opera in Late Eighteenth-Century London: Vol 1 The King's Theatre, Haymarket 1778–1791* (Oxford: Clarendon Press, 1995), p.1. For useful information on the relationship of opera and drama in eighteenth-century London, see Ian Woodfield, *Opera and Drama in Eighteenth-Century London: The King's Theatre, Garrick and the Business of Performance* (Cambridge: Cambridge University Press, 2001).

31 For a discussion of the Pantheon as a popular 'zone of enchantment' patronised by women performers and spectators see Perry, *Spectacular Flirtations*, op. cit., p.140ff.

32 The *OED* gives 1883 as the date the term 'diva' was first used in the English language.

33 These castrati first sang in the church, and later on the opera stage in the seventeenth and eighteenth centuries.

34 Ibid., p.26. On Farinelli's star status see also Berta Joncus, 'One God, so many Farinellis: Mythologising the Star Castrato', *British Journal for Eighteenth Century Studies*, ed. Michael Burden, 28(3), 2005.

35 There are many references to the 'divine excess' of Siddons. See Perry, *Spectacular Flirtations*, op. cit., p.73ff. Baddeley's memoirs, written by her companion, Elizabeth Steele, often use the title 'the divine Baddeley' (ibid., p.148).

36 Publishers and film-makers have often appropriated these associations in their chosen titles. See for example, Ruth Brandon *Being Divine: A Biography of Sarah Bernhardt* (London: Mandarin, 1992) and Arthur Gold and Robert Fitzdale, *The Divine Sarah: A Life of Sarah Bernhard* (New York: Knopf, 1991). Corinne Griffith starred in *The Divine Lady*, a 1927 film directed by Frank Lloyd, and Greta Garbo as *The Divine Woman*, a lost silent film of 1928. A documentary video of 1990, *The Divine Greta Garbo*, reinforced the popular notion of Garbo as an idolised, unearthly 'divine'. See also 'Star Systems'.

37 Highfill, Burnim and Langhans, op. cit., vol. 2, p.122, and Martin Postle, *Joshua Reynolds: The Creation of Celebrity* (London: Tate Publishing, 2005), p.224.

38 A tasteful combination often depicted in feminine portraiture, as in the later portraits of Kitty Clive cited above and in note 25. See also Ribeiro, *Dress in Eighteenth-Century Europe*, op. cit., p.207.

39 The symbolic and rhetorical functions of the diva's mouth and throat, and their implications for traditional gender oppositions, are explored in Susan J. Leonardi and Rebecca A. Pope, *The Diva's Mouth: Body, Voice, Prima Donna Politics* (New Brunswick: Rutgers University Press, 1996).

40 Leonardi and Pope cite Judith Butler's reading of 'the threatening female mouth', alongside Freudian notions of the 'oral stage', to signal the sexual symbolism of the diva's mouth and its potential as a metaphor of female empowerment. Ibid., pp.18–21.

41 Some of these issues are explored by Richard Leppert in *Music and Image: Domesticity, Ideology and Socio-Cultural Formation in Eighteenth-Century England* (Cambridge: Cambridge University Press, 1988). See especially chapters 3 and 7, and also Perry, *Spectacular Flirtations*, op. cit., chapter 5. I am indebted to my colleague, the music historian Professor Donald Burrows, who has discussed with me the roles of women violin and oboe players, and their absence in pictorial representation. He has suggested to me that while within theatrical families there was the possibility of a profession as a female violinist, orchestras were all-male professions throughout the eighteenth century.

42 This famous role is discussed in Claire Tomalin, *Mrs Jordan's Profession: The Story of a Great Actress and a Future King* (London: Viking, 1994).

43 A contemporary diarist, cited in *Mrs Jordan: The Duchess of Drury Lane* (London: The Iveagh Bequest and English Heritage, 1995) p.62.

44 Dance history and choreography in Britain were poorly documented before the nineteenth century, presenting challenges for studies of eighteenth-century dance and its visual representations. Invaluable recent research has been done by Moira Goff on early eighteenth-century dancer-actresses including Hester Santlow, Margaret Bicknell and Elizabeth Younger. This work has shed light on rare portraits of British dancers, including John Ellys's portrait of Hester Booth which I discuss below. See Moira Goff, *The Incomparable Hester Santlow: A Dancer-Actress on the Georgian Stage* (Aldershot: Ashgate, 2007) and 'In Pursuit of the Dancer-Actress', in Lyn Matluck Brooks (ed.), *Women's Work: Making Dance in Europe Before 1800* (Wisconsin: The University of Wisconsin Press, 2007), pp.183–203.

45 Geoffrey Ashton identifies this image with Booth's performance as Harlequin Woman in John Thurmond's pantomime *The Escapes of Harlequin*, which she performed at Drury Lane between 1722 and 1725; see Geoffrey Ashton, *Catalogue of Paintings at the Theatre Museum, London,* James Fowler (ed.) (London: Victoria and Albert Museum, 1992), p.7. However, Goff argues that this was not her most successful role and that it is more likely to show her famous Harlequin solo, linking some of her steps with the choreographic notations of some French dancing Harlequins. See Goff, *The Incomparable Hester Santlow*, op. cit., p.75.

46 In fact a lesser-known copy of this portrait of Booth, attributed to Ellys, shows her skirt just above the ankles. This work is in a private collection, and the attribution to Ellys is insecure. It is also cited by Goff, ibid., p.76, n.33.

47 Goff has researched the choreography of the Harlequin dance, linking Booth's solo with the French dancing Harlequins, and suggesting she may have drawn on some of the motifs in notated dances. See Goff, ibid., p.75.

48 Dr John Doran, from *"Their Majesties' Servants": Annals of the English Stage from Thomas Betterton to Edmund Kean*, quoted in Goff, ibid., p.75, n.32.

49 Charles Le Brun's *Lectures on Expression*, first published in English in 1698, sought to codify expression of the 'passions' through the representation of facial expression. Along with the poses of classical sculpture, this was an influential source for eighteenth-century painters seeking to represent human emotions. Moreover, in theatrical portraits such codes had to be combined with the representation of established acting styles and techniques.

50 By 1793 he had succeeded Reynolds as portrait painter to the Prince of Wales.

51 See the review in *The Morning Herald*, 1 May 1786.

52 Reported in William Sharp, *Fair Women* (London: Sceley, 1894) p.59. William McKay and William Roberts, *John Hoppner, R.A.* (London: Colnaghi and Bell, 1909), p.121, suggest that the attribution to Hoppner is not certain, although the artist's reference to the portrait and admiration for the dancer cited in Sharp suggest that he was the artist. Moreover, the style of this facial portrait and the form of the diaphanous drapery have much in common with other female portraits by Hoppner, including *Mrs Jordan as the Comic Muse,* discussed above.

53 Highfill, Burnim and Langhans, op. cit., report that in 1795–6 her salary for a seven-month season at the King's Theatre was £1,000, a huge sum for that time (vol. 6, p.320).

54 After appearing with her sister Janet in a *pas de deux* in the ballet *Paul et Virginie*, one reviewer described her 'graceful figure and the naivety of her attitudes' (*The Morning Chronicle*, 13 January 1796).

55 *Gentleman's Magazine*, 1804, 74(I), p.87.

56 *The Morning Herald*, 20 April 1782. Also cited in Elizabeth Einberg, *Gainsborough's Giovanna Baccelli* (London: Tate Gallery, 1976), p.8.

57 Unless, of course, they were theatrical portraits in character, as opposed to representations of a married couple.

58 *St James's Chronicle*, 30 April 1782.

59 She is described as 'toe-poised' in *The Morning Herald*, 29 June 1785. The dance pose is similar to that depicted in James Roberts's portrait *Signora Baccelli in the Ballet (call'd) Les Amants Surpris* (engraved by J. Thornwaite and reproduced in *Bell's British Theatre 1791–1802*, 15 May 1781).

60 As quoted by her great-grandson, Lord Dufferin, in an annotated manuscript in the Dulwich Picture Gallery. See Perry, *Spectacular*

Flirtations, op. cit., p.150. For an account of her marriage to Sheridan and the debates it encouraged, see ibid., pp.147–58.

61 Bate Dudley, *The Morning Herald*, 30 March 1785.

62 Letter from Henry, 10th Earl of Pembroke to George Nassau, 3rd Earl of Cowper (Hertfordshire Record Office), quoted in Einberg, *Gainsborough's 'Giovanna Baccelli'*, op. cit., p.13.

Beauty, Ageing and the Body Politic

1 See Derek Lord, 'Age is no longer the barrier it was for ageing actresses', *Press and Journal*, 27 January 2010. See also Peter Martin, 'Should Hollywood Keep Ageing Actresses?', *Cinematical*, 25 March 2009.

2 This is argued by Alice Browne, *The Eighteenth-Century Feminist Mind* (Brighton: Harvester, 1987), p.23.

3 For the particular importance of the voice in eighteenth-century acting and criticism, see Maarten van Dijk, 'The Kembles and Vocal Technique', *Theatre Research International*, 8(1) (1983), pp.23–42, and Peter Holland, 'Hearing the Dead: The Sound of David Garrick', in Michael Cordner and Peter Holland (eds), *Players, Playwrights, Playhouses: Investigating Performance, 1660–1800* (Basingstoke: Palgrave, 2007), pp.248–70.

4 James Stewart, *Plocacosmos: or the Whole Art of Hair Dressing ...* (London: 1782), p.211.

5 Quoted in James Boaden, *Memoirs of Mrs Siddons; Interspersed with Anecdotes of Authors and Actors*, 2 vols (London: Henry Colburn, 1827), vol. 1, pp.287–9.

6 Sir Thomas Lawrence, *An Address to the Students of the Royal Academy* (London: W. Clowes, 1824).

7 William Hawkins, *Miscellanies in Prose and Verse. Containing Candid and Impartial Observations on the Principal Performers Belonging to the Two Theatres Royal* (London: 1775), p.52.

8 James Boaden, *The Life of Mrs Jordan; including original private correspondence, and numerous anecdotes of her contemporaries*, 2 vols (London: Edward Bull, 1831), vol. 1, p.46.

9 James Boaden, *Memoirs of Mrs Siddons*, op. cit., vol. 2, p.183.

10 For an excellent discussion of this painting and the ambiguities of class that surround it, see Perry, *Spectacular Flirtations*, op. cit., p.121.

11 Angela Rosenthal, '"She's Got the Look!": Eighteenth-Century Female Portrait Painters and the Psychology of a Potentially "Dangerous Employment"', in Joanna Woodall (ed.), *Portraiture: Facing the Subject* (Manchester: Manchester University Press, 1997), pp.147–66.

12 Perry, *Spectacular Flirtations*, op. cit., pp.123–5.

13 *The Morning Post*, 2 May 1785.

14 James Stewart, *Plocacosmos*, op. cit., p.238.

15 William Hawkins, *Miscellanies*, op. cit., p.26.

16 David M. Little and George M. Kahrl (eds), *The Letters of David Garrick*, 3 vols (London: Oxford University Press, 1963), 15 August 1775, vol. 3, pp.1026–7.

17 Katherine C. Balderston (ed.), *Thraliana: The Diary of Mrs. Hester Lynch Thrale 1776–1809*, 2 vols (Oxford: Clarendon Press, 1942), vol. 2, pp.876–7, 3 April 1794; James Boaden, *The Life of Mrs Jordan*, op. cit., vol. 2, p.61 and vol. 1, p.41.

18 Petronius Arbiter, *Memoirs of the Present Countess of Derby (late Miss Farren)* (London: Symonds, 1797?), p.17.

19 *The English Review; or, an Abstract of English and Foreign Literature* (London: John Murray, 1783–95), vol. 1, p.438.

20 George Somes Layard, *Sir Thomas Lawrence's Letter-Bag* (London: George Allen, 1906), p.15.

21 See Judith Fisher, 'Creating Another Identity: Aging Actresses in the Eighteenth Century', *Journal of Aging and Identity*, 4(2), 1999; pp.57–77, and Shearer West, 'Siddons, Celebrity and Regality: Portraiture and the Body of the Ageing Actress', in Mary Luckhurst and Jane Moody (eds), *Theatre and Celebrity in Britain, 1660–2000* (Basingstoke: Palgrave, 2005), pp.191–213.

22 Susannah R. Ottaway, *The Decline of Life: Old Age in Eighteenth-Century England* (Cambridge: Cambridge University Press, 2004), p.12.

23 C.A.G. Goede, *The Stranger in England; or, Travels in Great Britain*, 3 vols (London: J.G. Barnard, 1807), vol. 2, pp.210–11.

24 'Anthony Pasquin', *A Critical Guide to the Present Exhibition at the Royal Academy for 1797* (London: H.D. Symonds, 1797), p.13.

25 *The Morning Chronicle*, quoted in *An Apology for the Conduct of Mr. Charles Macklin, Comedian* (London: T. Axtell, 1773), pp.3–4, and William Cooke, *Memoirs of Charles Macklin, Comedian* (London: James Asperne, 1804), pp.284–5.

26 Eluned Brown (ed.), *The London Theatre 1811–1866: Selections from the Diary of Henry Crabb Robinson* (London: The Society for Theatre Research, 1966), pp.35, 36.

27 Charles Lamb, 'On Some of the Old Actors', in Thomas Hutchison (ed.), *The Works in Prose and Verse of Charles and Mary Lamb* (London: Oxford University Press, 1908), vol. 1, pp.636–48.

28 'Anthony Pasquin', *The Children of Thespis: A Poem* (Dublin: T. M'Donnell, 1787), p.19.

29 *The Advantages of Theatrical Entertainment Briefly Considered* (Glasgow: 1772), p.6.

30 Charles Churchill, *The Rosciad* (Dublin: 1761), pp.14–16.

31 Maria Ines Aliverti, *La naissance de l'acteur moderne : L'acteur et son portrait au XVIIIe siècle* (Paris: Gallimard, 1998), p.55.

32 Peter de Bolla has written perceptively of the shift to a visual turn in the eighteenth century that relied on a new 'language of the eye'. See Peter de Bolla, *The Education of the Eye: Painting, Landscape and Architecture in Eighteenth-Century Britain* (Stanford: Stanford University Press, 2003).

33 G.E. Lessing, 'Laocoön', from *Selected Prose Works*, Edward Bell (ed.) (London: George Bell, 1879), p.137.

34 Robert Baker, *Observations on the Pictures now in Exhibition at the Royal Academy Spring Gardens* (London: John Bell, 1771), p.20.

35 Little and Kahrl (eds), *Letters of Garrick*, op. cit., 8 Feb 1767, vol. 2, pp.556–7.

Star Systems: Then and Now

1 For an account of the Richmond House theatricals see Sybil Rosenfeld, *Temples of Thespis: Some Private Theatres and Theatricals in England and Wales, 1700–1820* (London: The Society for Theatre Research, 1978), pp.34–53. For an overview see also Gillian Russell, 'Private Theatricals' in *The Cambridge Companion to British Theatre, 1730–1830*, op. cit.

2 Among some of the most enthusiastic supporters of 'private theatricals' were Sir Watkins Williams Wynn at Wynnstay, and Horace Walpole, whose letters provide witty assessments of performances (see Perry, *Spectacular Flirtations*, p.170).

3 So-called 'Spouting Clubs' consisting mostly of young men of the middle and artisan classes were also springing up across the country in taverns and public spaces, further extending the class boundaries of private theatricals. See Russell, 'Private Theatricals', op. cit., pp.199–203.

4 Henry Fielding, *Tom Jones* (London: Penguin, 1966), pp.299–301. Fielding's comment is also cited in Richard Sennett's essay 'Man as Actor', in P. David Marshall, 'Introduction', *The Celebrity Culture Reader* (New York: Routledge, 2006), p.23.

5 Often traced back to lines from Shakespeare, including 'All the world's a stage/ And all the men and women merely players/ They have their exits and their entrances ...' in *As You Like It*, II.vii.

6 *The General Evening Post*, 7–10 April 1787. This review was cited in Christina Dennis's research paper 'Public Actress: Private Theatricals – Elizabeth Farren and the Richmond House Theatricals', presented at the conference 'What signifies a theatre? Private Theatricals 1780–1820', Chawton House, 11 December 2010. For an account of Farren's role in these theatricals see also Suzanne Bloxam, *Walpole's Queen of Comedy: Elizabeth Farren, Countess of Derby* (Ashford: Bloxam, 1988), pp.80–96.

7 David Marshall, *The Celebrity Culture Reader*, op. cit., p.4. Marshall argues that there has been a blurring of what constitutes celebrity and what constitutes news within modern media culture (p.5).

8 The eighteenth-century concept of the 'bluestocking' as a scholarly or intellectual woman is explored in Eger and Peltz, *Brilliant Women*, op. cit.

9 Letter, 14 July 1775, cited in *Byron's 'Corbeau Blanc': The Life and Letters of Lady Melbourne*, J.D. Gross (ed.) (Texas: Rice University Press, 1997), p.20.

10 Thomas Gisborne, *An Enquiry into the Duties of the Female Sex* (London: Cadell and Davies, 1797), pp.10–11.

11 From 1798 onwards the German journal *London und Paris* included a regular column on British caricature. See C. Banerji and D. Donald, *Gillray Observed: The Earliest Accounts of his Caricatures in London and Paris* (Cambridge: Cambridge University Press, 1999), p.136.

12 Stella Tillyard, '"Paths of Glory": Fame and the Public in Eighteenth-Century London' in Martin Postle (ed.), *Joshua Reynolds: The Creation of Celebrity* (London: Tate Publishing, 2005), p.61.

13 These issues are explored in relation to Reynolds's work in *Joshua Reynolds: The Creation of Celebrity*, op. cit. On Reynolds and 'fame' see Martin Postle, '"The Modern Apelles": Joshua Reynolds and the Creation of Celebrity', pp.17–33.

14 Stella Tillyard has suggested that although the term 'celebrity' was in circulation in the eighteenth century, the idea of 'a celebrity' distinguishes the modern concept. At the same time, she acknowledges that many of the attributes of celebrity that we identify today also preoccupied eighteenth-century audiences, op. cit. p.62.

15 For an analysis of the origins and connotations of the term 'celebrity', and its role in some recent social and media theory, see Chris Rojek, *Celebrity* (London: Reaktion, 2001), and Jessica Evans and David Hesmondhalgh, *Understanding Media: Inside Celebrity* (Maidenhead: Open University Press, 2005).

16 See, for example, Lisa A. Lewis, *The Adoring Audience: Culture and Popular Media* (London: Routledge, 1992); Henry Jenkins, *Textual Poachers: Television Fans and Participation* (London: Routledge, 1992); Matthew Hills, *Fan Cultures* (London: Routledge, 2002).

17 A modern theatre group specialising in idiosyncratic, historical performances and based in the Southampton region of England, which Siddons often visited. For details of this company see www.sarahsiddonsfanclub.org/index

18 Richard Dyer has explored modern notions of 'stardom' in his essay 'Stars as Images' in David Marshall (ed.), *The Celebrity Culture Reader*, op. cit., pp.152–76.

19 These stereotypes, and their sexual and theoretical implications in cinematic representation, are discussed in Dyer, 'Stars as Images', op. cit.

Select Bibliography

Anon., *The Life of Lavinia Beswick, Alias Fenton, Alias Polly Peachum* (London: A. Moore, 1728)

Geoffrey Ashton, *Catalogue of Paintings at the Theatre Museum, London*, James Fowler (ed.) (London: Victoria and Albert Museum, in association with The Society for Theatre Research, 1992)

Robyn Asleson (ed.), *Notorious Muse: The Actress in British Art and Culture, 1776–1812* (New Haven and London: Yale University Press and the Paul Mellon Centre for Studies in British Art, 2003)

Robyn Asleson (ed.), *A Passion for Performance: Sarah Siddons and her Portraitists* (Los Angeles: J. Paul Getty Museum, 1999)

Christiane Banerji and Diana Donald (trans. and eds), *Gillray Observed: The Earliest Account of his Caricatures in London und Paris* (Cambridge: Cambridge University Press, 1999)

Hannah Barker and Elaine Chalus, *Gender in Eighteenth-Century England: Roles, Representations and Responsibilities* (Harlow: Longman, 1997)

John Barrell (ed.), *Painting and the Politics of Culture: New Essays on British Art, 1700–1850* (Oxford: Oxford University Press, 1992)

Charles Beauclerk, *Nell Gwyn: A Biography* (London: Macmillan, 2005)

John Bell (ed.), *Bell's British Theatre, consisting of the most esteemed English Plays*, 34 vols (London: John Bell, 1780)

George Anne Bellamy, *An Apology for the Life of George Anne Bellamy*, 6 vols (London: John Bell, 1785)

Ann Bermingham and John Brewer (eds), *The Consumption of Culture, 1600–1800: Image, Object, Text* (London: Routledge, 1995)

Suzanne Bloxam, *Walpole's Queen of Comedy: Elizabeth Farren, Countess of Derby* (Ashford: Bloxam, 1988)

James Boaden, *Memoirs of Mrs. Siddons: Interspersed with Anecdotes of Authors and Actors*, 2 vols (London: Henry Colburn, 1827)

James Boaden, *The Life of Mrs. Jordan; including original private correspondence, and numerous anecdotes of her contemporaries*, 2 vols (London: Edward Bull, 1831)

Betsy Bolton, *Women, Nationalism and the Romantic Stage: Theatre and Politics in Britain, 1780–1800* (Cambridge: Cambridge University Press, 2001)

John Brewer, *The Pleasures of the Imagination: English Culture in the Eighteenth Century* (London: Harper Collins, 1997)

Paula Byrne, *Perdita: The Life of Mary Robinson* (London: Harper Collins, 2004)

Terry Castle, *Masquerade and Civilisation: The Carnivalesque in Eighteenth-Century English Culture and Fiction* (London: Methuen, 1986)

Charlotte Charke, *A Narrative of the Life of Mrs Charlotte Charke (Youngest Daughter of Colley Cibber, Esq), Written by Herself* (London: W. Reeve, A. Dodd and E. Cook, 1755)

Alan Chedzoy, *Sheridan's Nightingale: The Story of Elizabeth Linley* (London: Allison and Busby, 1997)

Linda Colley, *Britons: Forging the Nation, 1707–1837* (London: Pimlico, 1994)

Alison Conway, *The Protestant Whore: Courtesan Narrative and Religious Controversy in England, 1680–1750* (Toronto: University of Toronto Press, 2010)

Michael Cordner and Peter Holland (eds), *Players, Playwrights, Playhouses: Investigating Performance, 1660–1800* (Basingstoke: Palgrave Macmillan, 2007)

Ian A.C. Dejardin (ed.), *Mrs Jordan: The Duchess of Drury Lane* (London: The Iveagh Bequest and English Heritage, 1995)

Gabriella Dideriksen with Judith Milhous and Robert D. Hume, *Italian Opera in Late Eighteenth-Century London*, vol. 2, 'The Pantheon Opera and its Aftermath, 1789–1795' (Oxford: Clarendon Press, 2001)

Diana Donald, *The Age of Caricature: Satirical Prints in the Reign of George III* (London and New Haven: Paul Mellon Centre for Studies in British Art and Yale University Press, 1996)

Ellen C. Donkin, *Getting into the Act: Women Playwrights in London, 1776–1829* (London: Routledge, 1995)

Elizabeth Eger, 'Spectacle, Intellect and Authority: The Actress in the Eighteenth Century' in Maggie B. Gale and John Stokes (eds), *The Cambridge Companion to the Actress* (Cambridge: Cambridge University Press, 2007), pp.33–51

Elizabeth Eger and Lucy Peltz, *Brilliant Women: 18th-Century Bluestockings* (London: National Portrait Gallery, 2008)

Elizabeth Einberg, *Gainsborough's 'Giovanna Baccelli'* (London: Tate Gallery Publications, 1976)

Laura Engel (ed.), *The Public's Open to us All: Essays on Women and Performance in Eighteenth-Century England* (Newcastle upon Tyne: Cambridge Scholars, 2009)

Judith Fisher, 'Creating another identity: Aging Actresses in the Eighteenth Century', *Journal of Aging and Identity*, 4(2), 1999, pp.57–77

Robert Fiske, *English Theatre Music in the Eighteenth Century*, 2nd edition (Oxford: Oxford University Press, 1986)

Amanda Foreman, *Georgiana, Duchess of Devonshire* (London: HarperCollins, 1998)

Lisa Freeman, *Character's Theater: Genre and Identity on the Eighteenth-Century English Stage* (Philadelphia: University of Pennsylvania Press, 2002)

Maggie B. Gale and John Stokes (eds), *The Cambridge Companion to the Actress* (Cambridge: Cambridge University Press, 2007)

Richard Godfrey (ed.), *James Gillray: The Art of Caricature* (London: Tate Publishing, 2001)

Moira Goff, *The Incomparable Hester Santlow: A Dancer-Actress on the Georgian Stage* (Aldershot: Ashgate, 2007)

Moira Goff, 'In Pursuit of the Dancer-Actress', in Lyn Matluck Brooks (ed.), *Women's Work: Making Dance in Europe before 1800* (Wisconsin: University of Wisconsin Press, 2007), pp.183–203

Harriet Guest, *Small Change: Women, Learning, Patriotism, 1750–1810* (Chicago and London: University of Chicago Press, 2000)

Mark Hallett, *Hogarth* (London: Phaidon, 2000)

Handel and the Divas, exhib. cat., Handel House Museum (London: 2008)

John Harris, *Harris's List of Covent-Garden Ladies, or the Man of Pleasure's Kalender for the Year 1788 [&1789–93]. Containing the Histories and some Curious Anecdotes of the Most Celebrated ladies now in Town, or in Keeping, and also many of their Keepers*, 4 vols (London: H. Ranger, 1788–93)

Philip H. Highfill and Kalman A. Burnim and Edward A. Langhans, *A Biographical Dictionary of Actors, Actresses, Musicians, Dancers, Managers and Other Stage Personnel in London 1660–1800*, 16 vols (Carbondale: Southern Illinois University Press, 1973–93)

Lisa Hilton, *Mistress Peachum's Pleasure: A Biography of Lavinia Fenton* (London: Weidenfeld and Nicolson, 2005)

Elizabeth Howe, *The First English Actresses: Women and Drama, 1660–1700* (Cambridge: Cambridge University Press, 1992)

Derek Hughes (ed.), *Eighteenth-Century Women Playwrights*, 6 vols (London: Pickering and Chatto, 2001)

Elizabeth Inchbald, *The British Theatre: or, A Collection of Plays, Which are Acted at the Theatres Royal, Drury Lane, Covent Garden, and Haymarket; Printed Under the Authority of the Managers from the Prompt Books, with Biographical and Critical Remarks by Mrs Inchbald*, 25 vols (London: Longman, Hurst, Rees and Orme, 1808)

John Ingamells, *Mid-Georgian Portraits, 1760–1790* (London: National Portrait Gallery, 2004)

John Ingamells, *Mrs Robinson and her Portraits* (London: Wallace Collection Monographs, 1978)

Berta Joncus, '"A Likeness where none was to be found": Imagining Kitty Clive (1711–1785)', *Music in Art*, 34(1–2), 2009, pp.89–106

Berta Joncus, '"The Assemblage of Every Female Folly": Kitty Clive (1711–1785) and the Ballad Opera' in Tiffany Potter (ed.), *Women of Fashion: Popular Culture in the Eighteenth Century and the Eighteenth Century in Popular Culture* (Toronto: University of Toronto Press, forthcoming, 2011)

Berta Joncus, '"In Wit Superior, as in Fighting": Kitty Clive and the Conquest of a Rival Queen', *Huntington Library Quarterly*, 74(1), 2011, pp.23–42

William Van Lennep, Emmett L. Avery, Arthur H. Scouten, George Winchester Stone Jr. and Charles Breecher Hogan (eds), *The London Stage 1660–1800: A Calendar of Plays, Entertainments and Afterpieces*, 11 vols (Carbondale: Southern Illinois Press, 1960–8)

William Van Lennep (ed.), *The Reminiscences of Sarah Kemble Siddons, 1773–1785* (Cambridge, Mass: Widener Library, 1942)

Susan J. Leonardi and Rebecca A. Pope, *The Diva's Mouth: Body, Voice, Prima Donna Politics* (New Brunswick: Rutgers University Press, 1996)

Richard Leppert, in *Music and Image: Domesticity, Ideology and Socio-Cultural Formation in Eighteenth-Century England* (Cambridge: Cambridge University Press, 1988)

Mary Luckhurst and Jane Moody (eds), *Theatre and Celebrity in Britain, 1660–2000* (Basingstoke and New York: Palgrave Macmillan, 2005)

Iain Mackintosh, *The Georgian Playhouse: Actors, Artists, Audiences and Architecture 1730–1830* , exhib. cat. (London: Hayward Gallery, 1975)

Catherine MacLeod and Julia Marciari Alexander (eds), *Painted Ladies: Women at the Court of Charles II*, exhib. cat. (London: National Portrait Gallery and Yale Center for British Art, 2001)

David Mannings, *Sir Joshua Reynolds: A Complete Catalogue of his Paintings*, 2 vols (London and New Haven: Paul Mellon Centre for Studies in British Art and Yale University Press, 2000)

P. David Marshall (ed.), *The Celebrity Culture Reader* (London: Routledge, 2006)

William McKay and William Roberts, *John Hoppner, R.A.* (London: Colnaghi and Bell, 1909)

Jane Moody and Daniel O'Quinn (eds), *The Cambridge Companion to British Theatre, 1730–1830* (Cambridge: Cambridge University Press, 2007)

Felicity Nussbaum, *Rival Queens: Actresses, Performance, and the Eighteenth-Century British Theater* (Philadelphia: University of Pennsylvania Press, 2010)

Felicity Nussbaum and Laura Brown (eds), *The New Eighteenth Century: Theory, Politics, English Literature* (New York: Methuen, 1987)

Miles Ogborn, *Spaces of Modernity: London's Geographies, 1680–1780* (London and New York: Guilford Press, 1998)

Susannah R. Ottaway, *The Decline of Life: Old Age in Eighteenth-Century England* (Cambridge: Cambridge University Press, 2004)

Nicholas Penny (ed.), *Reynolds* (London: Royal Academy of Arts, published in association with Weidenfeld and Nicolson, 1986)

Samuel Pepys, *The Diary of Samuel Pepys*, Robert Latham and William Matthews (eds), 11 vols (Berkeley and Los Angeles: University of California Press, 1970–83)

Gill Perry, *Spectacular Flirtations: Viewing the Actress in British Art, 1768–1820* (London and New Haven: Yale University Press, 2007)

Gill Perry and Michael Rossington (eds), *Femininity and Masculinity in Eighteenth-Century Art and Culture* (Manchester: Manchester University Press, 1994)

Marcia Pointon, *Hanging the Head: Portraiture and Social Formation in Eighteenth-Century England* (London and New Haven: Paul Mellon Centre for Studies in British Art and Yale University Press, 1993)

Marcia Pointon, 'Portrait! Portrait!! Portrait!!!' in *Art on the Line: The Royal Academy Exhibitions at Somerset House, 1780–1836*, David Solkin (ed.), exhib. cat. (London and New Haven: Yale University Press for the Paul Mellon Centre for Studies in British Art and the Courtauld Institute Gallery, 2001), pp.93–110

Martin Postle (ed.), *Joshua Reynolds: The Creation of Celebrity* (London: Tate Publishing, 2005)

Martin Postle, *Sir Joshua Reynolds: The Subject Pictures* (Cambridge: Cambridge University Press, 1995)

Kirsten Pullen, *Actresses and Whores: On Stage and in Society* (Cambridge: Cambridge University Press, 2005)

Aileen Ribeiro, *Dress in Eighteenth-Century Europe, 1715–1789* (London and New Haven: Yale University Press, 2002)

Sandra Richards, *The Rise of the English Actress* (Basingstoke: Palgrave Macmillan, 1993)

Joseph Roach, *It* (Michigan: Michigan University Press, 2007)

Joseph Roach, *The Player's Passion: Studies in the Science of Acting* (Michigan: Michigan University Press, 1993; reprinted 2001, 2002)

Mary Robinson, *Memoirs of the late Mrs Robinson, written by herself, completed and edited by her daughter Maria and published in 1801* (republished London: Cobden-Sanderson, 1930)

Chris Rojek, *Celebrity* (London: Reaktion, 2001)

Sybil Rosenfeld, *Temples of Thespis: Some Private Theatres and Theatricals in England and Wales, 1700–1820* (London: The Society for Theatre Research, 1978)

Angela Rosenthal, '"She's Got the Look!": Eighteenth-Century Female Portrait Painters and the Psychology of a Potentially "Dangerous Employment"' in Joanna Woodall (ed.), *Portraiture: Facing the Subject* (Manchester: Manchester University Press, 1997), pp.147–66

Michael Rosenthal, *The Art of Thomas Gainsborough: "A Little Business for the Eye"* (London and New Haven: Yale University Press, 1999)

Michael Rosenthal and Martin Myrone (eds), *Gainsborough*, exhib. cat. (London: Tate Publishing, 2002)

Hallie Rubenhold, *The Covent Garden Ladies: Pimp General Jack and the Extraordinary Story of Harris's List* (Stroud: Tempus, 2006)

Gillian Russell, 'Private Theatricals' in Jane Moody and Daniel O'Quinn (eds) *The Cambridge Companion to British Theatre 1730–1830* (Cambridge: Cambridge University Press, 2007), pp.191–203

John Seymour, *Memoirs of the Life of Eleanor Gwinn* (London: F. Stamper, 1752)

Desmond Shawe-Taylor, *Dramatic Art: Theatrical Paintings from the Garrick Club*, exhib. cat. (London: Dulwich Picture Gallery, 1997)

Desmond Shawe-Taylor, *The Georgians: Eighteenth-Century Portraiture and Society* (London: Barrie and Jenkins, 1990)

David Solkin (ed.), *Art on the Line: The Royal Academy Exhibitions at Somerset House, 1780–1836* (London and New Haven: Yale University Press for the Paul Mellon Centre for Studies in British Art and the Courtauld Institute Gallery, 2001)

Elizabeth Steele, *The Memoirs of Mrs Sophia Baddeley late of Drury Lane*, 6 vols (London: 1787)

Kristina Straub, *Sexual Suspects: Eighteenth-Century Players and Sexual Ideology* (Oxford and Princeton: Princeton University Press, 1992)

Stella Tillyard, '"Paths of Glory": Fame and the Public in Eighteenth-Century London', in Martin Postle (ed.), *Joshua Reynolds: The Creation of Celebrity* (London: Tate Publishing, 2005), pp.61–9

Claire Tomalin, *Mrs Jordan's Profession: The Story of a Great Actress and a Future King* (London: Viking, 1994)

Amanda Vickery, *The Gentleman's Daughter: Women's Lives in Georgian England* (London and New Haven: Yale University Press, 1998)

Cheryl Wanko, *Roles of Authority: Thespian Biography and Celebrity in Britain* (Lubbock: Texas Tech University Press, 2003)

Giles Waterfield, *A Nest of Nightingales: Thomas Gainsborough and the Linley Sisters*, exhib. cat. (London: Dulwich Picture Gallery, 1988)

Shearer West, *The Image of the Actor: Verbal and Visual Representation in the Age of Garrick and Kemble* (London: Pinter, 1991)

Shearer West, 'Siddons, Celebrity and Regality: Portraiture and the Body of the Ageing Actress', in Mary Luckhurst and Jane Moody (eds), *Theatre and Celebrity in Britain, 1660–2000* (Basingstoke: Palgrave Macmillan, 2005), pp.191–213

John Harold Wilson, *All the King's Ladies: Actresses of the Restoration* (Chicago: University of Chicago Press, 1958)

Ian Woodfield, *Opera and Drama in Eighteenth-Century London: The King's Theatre, Garrick and the Business of Performance* (Cambridge: Cambridge University Press, 2001)

List of Works
An asterisk denotes a work in the exhibition, held at the National Portrait Gallery, London

Introduction: Painting Actresses' Lives

1* **An Actress at her Toilet, or Miss Brazen just Breecht**
Unknown artist, after John Collet, 1779
Hand-coloured mezzotint, 501 x 315mm
The Trustees of the British Museum
© The Trustees of the British Museum

2* **The Whore's Last Shift**
James Gillray, 1779
Hand-coloured engraving, 353 x 249mm
The Trustees of the British Museum
© The Trustees of the British Museum

3* **The Male Carriage or New Evening Dilly**
Richard Newton, 1798
Etching and aquatint with watercolour, 260 x 220mm
Andrew Edmunds, London

4* **Harris's List of Covent-Garden Ladies or Man of Pleasure's Kalender for the Year 1793**
John Harris, 1793
180 x 115mm, closed
The British Library Board
© The British Library Board

5* **Frances Abington, Thomas King, John Palmer and William Smith in *The School for Scandal***
James Roberts, 1777
Oil on canvas, 1000 x 1260mm
The Garrick Club
© The Art Archive/The Garrick Club

6* **Playbill for Richard Brinsley Sheridan's *The School for Scandal***
9 May 1777
600 x 450mm
The Board of Trustees of the Victoria and Albert Museum, London
© V&A Images/Victoria and Albert Museum, London

7 **Frances Abington as Thalia**
James Watson, after Sir Joshua Reynolds, published 1769
Mezzotint
National Portrait Gallery, London (NPG D7153)
© National Portrait Gallery, London

8 **A Map of the Parish of St Paul's, Covent Garden**
From John Stow's Survey of London, 1755
Hand-coloured plan, 178 x 305mm
The British Library Board
© The British Library Board

9* **Tiles showing Mary Ann Yates, Mary Bulkley, Ann Barry, Susannah Cibber**
Transfer-printed earthenware tiles, each 125 x 125mm
The Garrick Club
© The Art Archive/The Garrick Club

10* **Sarah Siddons as Lady Macbeth**
*c.*1840
Staffordshire pottery figurine, 200 x 95 x 75mm
The Garrick Club
© The Art Archive/The Garrick Club

11* **Catherine ('Kitty') Clive as Mrs Riot or The Fine Lady in *Lethe***
Charles Mosely, after a watercolour by Thomas Worlidge, 1750
Soft paste porcelain figure, 313 x 173 x 137mm
Fitzwilliam Museum, Cambridge
© Fitzwilliam Museum, Cambridge

12* **David Garrick as Ranger and Hannah Pritchard as Clarinda in *The Suspicious Husband***
Francis Hayman, 1752
Oil on canvas, 804 x 930mm
Museum of London
Image © Museum of London

13* **Strolling Actresses Dressing in a Barn**
William Hogarth, 1738
Engraving, 468 x 590mm
The Trustees of the British Museum
© The Trustees of the British Museum

14* **Frances Abington as the Widow Bellmour in *The Way to Keep Him***
Johan Joseph Zoffany, 1768
Oil on canvas, 990 x 1130mm
Petworth House, The Egremont Collection (acquired in lieu of tax by H.M. Treasury in 1957 and subsequently transferred to the National Trust)
Image © NTPL/Derrick E. Witty

15* **William Smith as Hamlet and Elizabeth Hopkins as Gertrude in *Hamlet***
James Roberts, 1777/8
Oil on canvas, 1270 x 1010mm
The Garrick Club
© The Art Archive/The Garrick Club

16* **Mary Ann Yates as Medea**
William Dickinson, after Robert Edge Pine, published 1771
Mezzotint, 618 x 484mm plate size
The Trustees of the British Museum
© The Trustees of the British Museum

17 **Mary Robinson – Perdita**
Sir Joshua Reynolds, 1782
Oil on canvas, 737 x 635mm
Waddesdon, The Rothschild Collection (National Trust)
Image: A.C. Cooper © National Trust, Waddesdon Manor

18 **Isabella Mattocks as Catherine in *Catherine and Petruchio***
Gainsborough Dupont, 1794
Oil on canvas, 737 x 610mm
The Garrick Club
© The Garrick Club

19* ***A Narrative of the Life of Mrs Charlotte Charke***
Charlotte Charke, 1755
165 x 113mm, closed
The Garrick Club Library
© The Garrick Club Library

20* ***Faithful Memoirs of the Life, Amours and Performances ... of Mrs Anne Oldfield***
Anne Oldfield, 1731
195 x 120mm
The Garrick Club Library
© The Garrick Club Library

21* **George Anne Bellamy**
Francis Lindo, mid-1750s
Oil on canvas, 692 x 540mm
The Garrick Club
© The Art Archive/The Garrick Club

22* **Memoirs of the Late Mrs Robinson**
Mary Robinson, published 1801
165 x 105mm
Chawton House Library, Hampshire

The Actresses: A Selection of Biographies

23* **Eleanor ('Nell') Gwyn**
Simon Verelst, *c.*1680
Oil on canvas, 737 x 632mm
National Portrait Gallery, London (NPG 2496)
© National Portrait Gallery, London

24* **Hester Booth**
John Ellys, *c.*1722–5
Oil on canvas, 1220 x 890mm
The Board of Trustees of the Victoria and Albert Museum, London
© V&A Images/Victoria and Albert Museum, London

25* **Lavinia Fenton**
Possibly by George Knapton, *c.*1739
Oil on canvas, 740 x 620mm
Private Collection

26* **Catherine ('Kitty') Clive** (pre-conservation)
Jeremiah Davison, 1735
Oil on canvas, 1251 x 1003mm
The Marquess of Bath, Longleat House, Warminster, Wiltshire
Reproduced by permission of the Marquess of Bath, Longleat House, Warminster, Wiltshire

27 **Margaret ('Peg') Woffington**
John Faber Jr, after John Giles Eccard, 1745
Mezzotint, 325 x 230mm paper size
National Portrait Gallery, London (NPG D4872)
© National Portrait Gallery, London

28* **Frances Abington as Miss Prue in *Love for Love***
Sir Joshua Reynolds, 1771
Oil on canvas, 768 x 638mm
Yale Center for British Art/Paul Mellon Collection

29* **Elizabeth Inchbald**
Attrib. John Hoppner, *c.*1789–95
Oil on canvas, 750 x 620mm
Private Collection

30* **Giovanna Baccelli**
Thomas Gainsborough, exhib. 1782
Oil on canvas, 2267 x 1486mm
Tate: Purchased with assistance from the Friends of the Tate Gallery, 1975
© Tate, London 2011

31 **Elizabeth Ann Sheridan**
Henry Meyer, after Ozias Humphry, 1816
Stipple engraving
National Portrait Gallery, London (NPG D5972)
© National Portrait Gallery, London

32* **Sarah Siddons**
Sir Thomas Lawrence, 1804
Oil on canvas, 2540 x 1480mm
Tate: Presented by Mrs C. Fitzhugh 1843
© Tate, London 2011

33* **Mary Robinson – Perdita**
John Hoppner, 1782
Oil on canvas, 794 x 660mm
Chawton House Library, Hampshire

34 **Elizabeth Farren, later Countess of Derby**
John Downman, 1787
Chalk, 203 x 171mm
Given by Mrs D.E. Knollys, 1934
National Portrait Gallery, London (NPG 2652)
© National Portrait Gallery, London

35* **Dorothy Jordan**
John Russell, 1801
Pastel, 760 x 610mm
Fenton House, The Goff/Fitz-Clarence Collection (The National Trust)
Image: © NTPL/Derrick E. Witty

36* **Elizabeth Billington**
John Hoppner, *c.*1801
Oil on canvas, 1275 x 1012mm
Peter Moores Foundation

Nell Gwyn and Covent Garden Goddesses

23* **Eleanor ('Nell') Gwyn**
Simon Verelst, *c.*1680
Oil on canvas, 737 x 632mm
National Portrait Gallery, London (NPG 2496)
© National Portrait Gallery, London

37* **Eleanor ('Nell') Gwyn** (pre-conservation)
Simon Verelst, *c.*1680–5
Oil on canvas, 935 x 740mm
Private Collection

38 **Samuel Pepys**
John Hayls, 1666
Oil on canvas, 756 x 629mm
National Portrait Gallery, London (NPG 211)
© National Portrait Gallery, London

39 **Eleanor ('Nell') Gwyn**
Gerard Valck, after Sir Peter Lely, *c.*1673
Engraving, 348 x 264mm paper size
National Portrait Gallery, London (NPG D10959)
© National Portrait Gallery, London

40* **Madame Ellen Groinn and her troo sons, Charles, Earl of Beaufort and James, Lord Beauclaire**
Unknown artist, after Henry Gascar, 1677–80
Engraving, 356 x 454mm
The Trustees of the British Museum
© The Trustees of the British Museum

41 **'The Indian Queen' (Anne Bracegirdle)**
William Vincent, *c.*1685–95
Mezzotint, 194 x 145mm plate size
Given by Sir Herbert Henry Raphael, 1st Bt, 1916
National Portrait Gallery, London (NPG D19498)
© National Portrait Gallery, London

42 **King Charles II**
John Michael Wright, *c.*1660–5
Oil on canvas, 1264 x 1010mm
National Portrait Gallery, London (NPG 531)
© National Portrait Gallery, London

43* **Mary ('Moll') Davis**
Sir Peter Lely, *c.*1674
Oil on canvas, 1245 x 1016mm
Trustees of the Weston Park Foundation
© The Trustees of the Weston Park Foundation UK / The Bridgeman Art Library

44 **'Nell Gwynne' (Effie Gray James)**
Rupert Potter, 1882–8
Albumen print, 211 x 163mm overall
Given by Jack Edward Ladeveze, 1993
National Portrait Gallery, London (NPG x131241)
© National Portrait Gallery, London

45 **Possibly Eleanor ('Nell') Gwyn**
Studio of Sir Peter Lely, *c.*1675
Oil on canvas, 1270 x 1016mm
National Portrait Gallery, London (NPG 3976)
© National Portrait Gallery, London

46 **James Beauclerk; Charles Beauclerk, 1st Duke of St Albans; Eleanor ('Nell') Gwyn**
Richard Tompson, after Sir Peter Lely, before 1693
Mezzotint, 362 x 292mm plate size
National Portrait Gallery, London (NPG D35093)
© National Portrait Gallery, London

Divas, Dancing and the Rage for Music

24* **Hester Booth**
John Ellys, *c.*1722–5
Oil on canvas, 1220 x 890mm
The Board of Trustees of the Victoria and Albert Museum, London
© V&A Images/Victoria and Albert Museum, London

25* **Lavinia Fenton**
Possibly by George Knapton, *c.*1739
Oil on canvas, 740 x 620mm
Private Collection

30* **Giovanna Baccelli**
Thomas Gainsborough, exhib. 1782
Oil on canvas, 2267 x 1486mm
Tate: Purchased with assistance from the Friends of the Tate Gallery, 1975
© Tate, London 2011

35* **Dorothy Jordan**
John Russell, 1801
Pastel on paper, 760 x 610mm
Fenton House, The Goff/Fitz-Clarence Collection (The National Trust)
Image: © NTPL/Derrick E. Witty

36* **Elizabeth Billington**
John Hoppner, *c.*1801
Oil on canvas, 1275 x 1012mm
Peter Moores Foundation

47* **Margaret ('Peg') Woffington**
John Lewis, 1753
Oil on canvas, 760 x 633mm
National Portrait Gallery, London (NPG 5729)
© National Portrait Gallery, London

48 **Lavinia Fenton, later Duchess of Bolton**
William Hogarth, *c.*1740–50
Oil on canvas, 737 x 584mm
© Tate, London 2011

49 **Lavinia Fenton, later Duchess of Bolton**
John Faber Jr, after John Ellys, 1728
Mezzotint, 350 x 254mm paper size
National Portrait Gallery, London (NPG D31934)
© National Portrait Gallery, London

50 **Gaetano Berenstadt; Francesca Cuzzoni; Francesco Bernardini ('Senesino') (detail)**
Unknown artist, 18th century
Etching, 102 x 140mm plate size, 130 x 148mm paper size
Bequeathed by Frederick Leverton Harris, 1927
National Portrait Gallery, London (NPG D13888)
© National Portrait Gallery, London

51 **Susannah Cibber**
Thomas Hudson, *c.*1749
Oil on canvas, 762 x 629mm
National Portrait Gallery, London (NPG 4526)
© National Portrait Gallery, London

52* ***The Beggar's Opera***
William Hogarth, 1726–8
Oil on canvas, 457 x 533mm
Birmingham Museums & Art Gallery
Purchased with a capital grant from the City of Birmingham, 1985
© Birmingham Museums & Art Gallery

53 **Catherine ('Kitty') Clive as Phillida in *Damon and Phillida***
John Faber Jr, after Peter van Bleeck, 1734
Mezzotint, 265 x 205mm paper size
Given by Henry Witte Martin, 1861
National Portrait Gallery, London (NPG D11272)
© National Portrait Gallery, London

54 **Catherine ('Kitty') Clive**
Alexander van Aken, after Jeremiah Davison, 1735
Mezzotint, 286 x 207mm paper size
National Portrait Gallery, London (NPG D1479)
© National Portrait Gallery, London

55 **Sophia Baddeley**
Robert Laurie, after Johan Joseph Zoffany, 1772
Mezzotint, 371 x 281mm paper size
National Portrait Gallery, London (NPG D7460)
© National Portrait Gallery, London

56 **Carlo Broschi ('Farinelli')**
Alexander van Aken, after Charles Lucy, 1735
Mezzotint, 352 x 260mm paper size
Given by the daughter of compiler William Fleming MD,
Mary Elizabeth Stopford, 1931
National Portrait Gallery, London (NPG D825)
© National Portrait Gallery, London

57 **Elizabeth Billington**
James Ward, after Sir Joshua Reynolds, published 1803
Mezzotint, 664 x 430mm paper size
National Portrait Gallery, London (NPG D31783)
© National Portrait Gallery, London

58* **Elizabeth Bannister**
John Russell, 1799
Pastel, 616 x 464mm
Bequeathed by the sitter's great-granddaughter,
Grace Hilda Bannister, 1916
National Portrait Gallery, London (NPG 1770)
© National Portrait Gallery, London

59 **Elizabeth Billington ('A Bravura Air')**
James Gillray, 1801
Hand-coloured etching and stipple engraving,
355 x 252mm plate size
National Portrait Gallery, London (NPG D12775)
© National Portrait Gallery, London

60* **Anna Maria Crouch**
George Romney, 1787
Oil on canvas, 1270 x 1016mm
The Iveagh Bequest, Kenwood (English Heritage)
© English Heritage Photo Library

61 **Anna Maria Crouch**
Edward Harding, after James Barry, late 18th century
Hand-coloured stipple engraving,
323 x 196mm paper size
National Portrait Gallery, London (NPG D13716)
© National Portrait Gallery, London

62* **Marie Sallé Dancing**
Nicolas de Larmessin, after Nicolas Lancret, *c.*1730–32
Engraving, 406 x 534mm
Private Collection

63 **Ars-Musica**
James Gillray, 1800
Hand-coloured etching and aquatint, 260 x 364mm plate size
National Portrait Gallery, London (NPG D12726)
© National Portrait Gallery, London

64 **'Modern grace, – or – the Operatical Finale to the Ballet of Alonzo e Caro' (Rose Didelot; Charles Louis Didelot; Mme Parisot)**
James Gillray, 1796
Hand-coloured etching, 261 x 363mm plate size
National Portrait Gallery, London (NPG D12571)
© National Portrait Gallery, London

65* **Dorothy Jordan as the Comic Muse**
John Hoppner, 1786
Oil on canvas, 2388 x 1461mm
The Royal Collection
The Royal Collection © 2011, Her Majesty Queen Elizabeth II

66 **Mlle Hilligsberg**
John Hoppner, *c.*1781
Oil on panel, 2400 x 1473mm
The Art Gallery of New South Wales
Photo © Christies Images/
The Bridgeman Art Library

67* **David and Eva-Maria Garrick**
Sir Joshua Reynolds, 1772–3
Oil on canvas, 1403 x 1699mm
National Portrait Gallery, London (NPG 5375)
© National Portrait Gallery, London

68 **David Garrick and his Wife, Eva-Maria**
William Hogarth, 1757
Oil on canvas, 1326 x 1042mm
The Royal Collection © 2005, Her Majesty Queen Elizabeth II

69 **Mary Robinson – Perdita**
Thomas Gainsborough, 1781
Oil on canvas 2337 x 1530mm
© Wallace Collection, London

70* **Elizabeth Linley (Elizabeth Ann Sheridan)**
Thomas Gainsborough, *c.*1785–7
Oil on canvas, 2200 x 1540mm
National Gallery of Art, Washington D.C.
Andrew W. Mellon Collection
Image courtesy National Gallery of Art, Washington D.C.

Beauty, Ageing and the Body Politic

28* **Frances Abington as Miss Prue in *Love for Love***
Sir Joshua Reynolds, 1771
Oil on canvas, 768 x 638mm
Yale Center for British Art/Paul Mellon Collection

32* **Sarah Siddons**
Sir Thomas Lawrence, 1804
Oil on canvas, 2540 x 1480mm
Tate: Presented by Mrs C. Fitzhugh, 1843
© Tate, London 2011

71* **Dorothy Jordan as Hypolita in *She Would and She Would Not***
John Hoppner, exhib. 1791
Oil on canvas, 749 x 620mm
Tate: Bequeathed by Sir Edward Stern 1933
© Tate, London 2011

72 **Sarah Siddons with the Emblems of Tragedy**
Sir William Beechey, 1793
Oil on canvas, 2456 x 1537mm
Given by Dr D.M. McDonald, 1977
National Portrait Gallery, London (NPG 5159)
© National Portrait Gallery, London

73* **Sarah Siddons as the Tragic Muse**
Studio of Sir Joshua Reynolds, 1784
Oil on canvas, 2380 x 1460mm
Cobbe Collection, Hatchlands Park

74* **Miss Rose in the Character of Tom Thumb**
Edward Fisher, after John Berridge, 1770
Mezzotint, 400 x 290mm
The Trustees of the British Museum
© The Trustees of the British Museum

75* **Dorothy Jordan as Rosalind in *As You Like It***
Sir William Beechey, 1787
Oil on canvas, 762 x 634mm
Private Collection

76* **Frances Abington as Lady Bab Lardoon in *The Maid of Oaks***
Thomas Hickey, 1775
Oil on canvas, 882 x 520mm
The Garrick Club
© The Art Archive/The Garrick Club

77 **Frances Abington as Scrub in *The Beaux' Stratagem***
After James Sayers, 1786
Etching, 183 x 126mm plate size
National Portrait Gallery, London (NPG D9580)
© National Portrait Gallery, London

78* **David Garrick in *The Provok'd Wife***
Johan Joseph Zoffany, 1763
Oil on canvas, 740 x 616mm
The Holburne Museum, Bath

79* **Henry Angelo as Mrs Cole in *The Minor***
Samuel de Wilde, *c.*1792
Oil on canvas, 365 x 280mm
The Garrick Club
© The Art Archive/The Garrick Club

80 **Dorothy Jordan as Lucy in *The Virgin Unmask'd***
Unknown artist, published 1787
Engraving, 125 x 84mm paper size
National Portrait Gallery, London (NPG D4418)
© National Portrait Gallery, London

81 **Sarah Siddons, said to be Mrs Haller in *The Stranger***
Sir Thomas Lawrence, *c.*1796–8
Oil on canvas, 762 x 635mm
© Tate, London 2011

82 **Fanny Kemble and her Aunt, Sarah Siddons**
Henry Perronet Briggs, *c.*1830–1
Oil on canvas, 1435 x 1133mm
Gift of Frances Anne Kemble, 1863
Boston Athenaeum

83 **Elizabeth Farren, later Countess of Derby**
Sir Thomas Lawrence, 1790
Oil on canvas, 2388 x 1461mm
Bequest of Edward S. Harkness, 1940. Acc.n.: 50.135.5 © 2011
Metropolitan Museum of Art, New York
Image © The Metropolitan Museum of Art/Art Resource/
Scala, Florence

Star Systems: Then and Now

84* **The Three Witches from *Macbeth* (Elizabeth, Viscountess Melbourne; Georgiana, Duchess of Devonshire; Anne Seymour Damer)**
Daniel Gardner, 1775
Gouache and chalk, 940 x 781mm
Accepted in lieu of tax by H.M. Government and allocated to the National Portrait Gallery, 2011
National Portrait Gallery, London (NPG 6903)
© National Portrait Gallery, London

85* **Elizabeth Farren as Thalia**
Anne Seymour Damer, *c.*1788
Marble, 597mm high
Given by Rupert Gunnis, 1965
National Portrait Gallery, London (NPG 4469)
© National Portrait Gallery, London

86 **Anne Seymour Damer**
Richard Cosway, 1785
Watercolour on ivory, 60 x 48mm
National Portrait Gallery, London (NPG 5236)
© National Portrait Gallery, London

87* **Dilettanti-theatricals: – or – a Peep at the Green Room**
James Gillray, 1803
Hand-coloured etching and aquatint, 320 x 496mm
National Portrait Gallery, London (NPG D13099)
© National Portrait Gallery, London

88 **Blowing up the Pic Nic's – or – Harlequin Quixotte attacking the Puppets**
James Gillray, 1802
Hand-coloured etching and aquatint, 350 x 260mm paper size
National Portrait Gallery, London (NPG D12786)
© National Portrait Gallery, London

89 **'Hold! – Pizarro – hear me!' (Sarah Siddons)**
Robert Dighton, 1799
Hand-coloured etching, 228 x 175mm plate size
Given by Henry Witte Martin, 1861
National Portrait Gallery, London (NPG D10687)
© National Portrait Gallery, London

90 **Sarah Siddons as the Tragic Muse**
L.J. Chavalliaud, 1897
White marble on Portland stone pedestal
Paddington Green, London

91 **Richard Suett and Mrs Henry in *All the World's a Stage***
Samuel de Wilde, 1803
Oil on canvas, 810 x 930mm
Theatre Royal Bath Collection
Theatre Royal, Bath

92 **Greta Garbo**
Cecil Beaton, 1946
Bromide print, 242 x 293mm
Given by executors of the Estate of Eileen Hose, 1991
National Portrait Gallery, London (NPG x40128)
© The Cecil Beaton Studio Archive at Sotheby's

93 **Dusty Springfield**
Val Wilmer, 1964
Bromide fibre print, 346 x 232mm
National Portrait Gallery, London (NPG x125340)
© Val Wilmer

94 **Vanessa Redgrave with Tariq Ali**
John Walmsley, 1968
Bromide print, 451 x 350mm
National Portrait Gallery, London (NPG x6394)
© John Walmsley

95 **Cecil Beaton photographing Marilyn Monroe**
Ed Pfizenmaier, 1956
Contact print, 2¼in square
Given by executors of the Estate of Eileen Hose, 1991
National Portrait Gallery, London (NPG x40278)
© Ed Pfizenmaier

96 **Margot Fonteyn**
Angus McBean, 1951
Bromide print, 244 x 198mm
Houghton Library, Harvard University (NPG P894)
© The President and Fellows of Harvard College

97 **Actresses (Covent Garden) (Susannah York, Susan Hampshire, Judi Dench)**
Arnold Newman, 1978(?)
Colour dye transfer print, 483 x 419mm
Given by *The Sunday Times*, 1980
National Portrait Gallery, London (NPG P150[44])
© Arnold Newman/Getty Images

98 **Fiona Shaw**
Victoria Russell, 2002
Oil on canvas, 1828 x 1220mm
Commissioned as part of the First Prize, BP Portrait Award, 2000, 2002
National Portrait Gallery, London (NPG 6609)
© National Portrait Gallery, London

99* **Mary Wells in *The Merry Wives of Windsor***
William Hamilton, 1790s
Oil on canvas, 2390 x 1488mm
Royal Shakespeare Company
RSC Collection

Index

Note: page numbers in *italics* refer to captions.

Published in Great Britain by National Portrait Gallery Publications, National Portrait Gallery, St Martin's Place, London WC2H 0HE

Published to accompany the exhibition *The First Actresses: Nell Gwyn to Sarah Siddons* at the National Portrait Gallery, London from 20 October 2011 to 8 January 2012.

This exhibition has been made possible with the assistance of the Government Indemnity Scheme provided by the Department for Culture, Media and Sport and administered by the Museums, Libraries and Archives Council.

For a complete catalogue of current publications please write to the National Portrait Gallery at the address above, or visit our website at www.npg.org.uk/publications

ISBN 978 185514 411 8

A catalogue record for this book is available from the British Library.

10 9 8 7 6 5 4 3 2 1

Head of Publications: Celia Joicey
Managing Editor: Christopher Tinker
Editor: Robert Davies
Design: Andrew Ross
Production Manager: Ruth Müller-Wirth
Printed and bound in China.

Endpapers, frontispiece: Eighteenth-century playbills, courtesy of The Garrick Club, London

FSC
www.fsc.org
MIX
Paper from responsible sources
FSC® C021256

Julia by Mrs. BA

Victoria by Mrs

I S A B

By Mrs. WO

To which will be added a

ORPHEUS an

Intermixed with a *Pantom*

C A

The *Metamorpho*

Boxes 5 s. Pit 3 s. First

⁎†⁎ As any Obstruction in the Mo
greatly prejudice the Performance
Persons will be displeased at their b